FIELDS OF PLAY

Fields of Play

AN ETHNOGRAPHY OF CHILDREN'S SPORTS

NOEL DYCK

UNIVERSITY OF TORONTO PRESS

Teaching Culture: UTP Ethnographies for the Classroom

LIBRARY AND ARCHIVES CANADA CATALOGUING IN PUBLICATION

Dyck, Noel

    Fields of play : an ethnography of children's sports / Noel Dyck.

(Teaching culture)
Includes bibliographical references and index.
Issued also in electronic format.
ISBN 978-1-4426-0079-9

    1. Sports for children—Social aspects—Canada. 2. Community life—Canada. 3. Ethnology—Canada. I. Title. II. Series: Teaching culture

GV709.2.D93 2012   796.0830971   C2012-905267-1

We welcome comments and suggestions regarding any aspect of our publications—please feel free to contact us at news@utphighereducation.com or visit our Internet site at www.utppublishing.com.

North America
5201 Dufferin Street
North York, Ontario, Canada, M3H 5T8

2250 Military Road
Tonawanda, New York, USA, 14150

ORDERS PHONE: 1–800–565–9523
ORDERS FAX: 1–800–221–9985
ORDERS E-MAIL: utpbooks@utpress.utoronto.ca

UK, Ireland, and continental Europe
NBN International
Estover Road, Plymouth, PL6 7PY, UK
ORDERS PHONE: 44 (0) 1752 202301
ORDERS FAX: 44 (0) 1752 202333
ORDERS E-MAIL: enquiries@nbninternational.com

This book is printed on paper containing 100% post-consumer fibre.

The University of Toronto Press acknowledges the financial support for its publishing activities of the Government of Canada through the Canada Book Fund.

Cover & Typesetting: Em Dash Design

Printed in Canada

RECYCLED
Paper made from recycled material
FSC
www.fsc.org   FSC® C103567

For Sarah, Zoë, and Aiden

CONTENTS

ACKNOWLEDGEMENTS

THE IMPETUS FOR WRITING this book came from a set of diverging passions that I have had the good fortune to share with a cast of family members, friends, sports people of all ages, students, and colleagues over many years. I am, first and foremost, indebted to all those who agreed to speak to me during the course of the various research projects that underpin this study. I also wish to thank all those with whom I have personally partaken of sport—whether by playing, coaching, organizing, talking, and/or watching—through activities and competitions of varied types from Saskatoon to England and British Columbia to Montreal. Special thanks are owing to my brothers—Ian, Philip, and Roger; my children—Sarah, Zoë, and Aiden; coaching partners—Bruce Holmgren, Barri Pearson, and the late Percy Perry; "foreign correspondents"—the late Eduardo P. Archetti, John Haskins, and Philip Moore; colleagues and students at Simon Fraser University, as well as the Department of Sociology and Anthropology at Concordia University, Montreal, where I was provided space and collegiality to complete the writing of this book; Anne Brackenbury at the University of Toronto Press; and Vered Amit, my partner in life and scholarship, without whom this book would not have been completed.

Chapter One

ENCOUNTERING THE
FIELDS OF PLAY

THE JOURNEY TOWARDS THIS book began inadvertently on a Sunday afternoon, a year before my eldest child's birth.[1] Strolling through a park, not far from the university where I had just taken up a teaching position, I happened upon a girls' soccer game. Community sports leagues in my childhood years had catered overwhelmingly to boys, so there was a certain fascination in watching a small, ponytailed winger adeptly cross the ball in from near the corner flag for her striker to blast into their opponent's net. This image remained firmly planted in my mind during the next few years and, in due course, my daughter was enrolled in soccer, becoming a part of that veritable hive of bees that in those early seasons buzzed around the ball on its irregular journeys back and forth across the field.

Despite a familiarity with the professional version of this sport acquired during several years of doctoral studies in northern England, as well as my own past as a child and youth athlete, I was surprised by several aspects of children's sports in my new place of residence. During my childhood years in a prairie city, most parents attended our scheduled community sports games only occasionally, if at all. Dutiful and supportive parents were those who were willing and able to underwrite the cost of enrolment fees and some level of expenditure on sports equipment. Having done this, they largely left it to their children to get on with it and make their own way to and from local sports venues. Transporting groups of players to "away" games usually depended upon the team coach and manager fitting as many boys as they could into their cars. One father who frequently attended our hockey games—to shout instructions to his son and dispute a fair proportion of referees' decisions—was viewed as a bit of an oddball in the neighbourhood. In contrast, as a new "soccer dad" in the suburbs of Vancouver, I discovered that typically at least one parent and often both would try to attend every one of their children's games or proffer an explanation of the circumstances that prevented them from doing so. The "odd parent out" here was the father or mother who consistently did not accompany their progeny to matches and did not provide a "good" reason for "neglecting" to do so.

In the early years of this new way of life that combined developing an academic career, maintaining a home, and rearing children, I would dutifully arm myself with unread books or student papers before setting off to spend my share of time in providing transportation and waiting while my children attended music lessons, swimming classes, and soccer games. Attempts to optimize use of waiting time by catching up on reading or dabbling in other tasks were, however, rarely satisfying, let alone productive. Eventually I resolved to separate the demands of work and home and to pass the hours spent watching children's soccer matches or attending athletics competitions amiably and paternally. I began to look forward to these weekly outings and to casual conversations with other parents encountered there as a welcome "time out" from the rigours of departmental meetings and the routine of researching and writing about relations between Aboriginal peoples and governments.[2] In the absence of other volunteers, I even helped out as a coach in soccer and athletics.

This congenial division of paternal and professional labours began to unravel during a children's track meet held on a summer weekend.[3] During such meets, medals or ribbons are typically awarded to first-, second-, and third-place winners in each age- and gender-differentiated event. The presentation of awards occurs routinely and continuously throughout a meet, and winners tend either to stuff medals and ribbons into carrying cases or to hand them over to parents or friends for safekeeping before trundling off to their next athletic event. What caught my attention that particular afternoon was a man of approximately my age who, like many other parents and coaches, was dressed for the hot weather in a pair of shorts, sandals, and a sports shirt. What seemed remarkable, however, was that he also wore two gold medals around his neck and an enormous smile on his face. I was struck with a powerful impression that here was the father of a successful athlete who was acting almost as though he had won the medals himself.[4]

In the following days I related this incident to several people, including a mother with whom I shared a waiting room while our daughters took their weekly piano lessons. Recounting the story of the man with the medals around his neck, I reached my verdict-cum-punch line: "It was almost as though he had won the medals himself!" After politely chuckling at my story, she paused for a moment, and then observed thoughtfully, "Well, in a way he had."

With that comment she deftly connected an incident that had initially seemed humorous, if somewhat odd, to an ongoing discourse on parenting that I had been sharing, without consciously recognizing it, with her and other parents during the previous months. What I had tended to view as friendly "small talk" that made the time pass congenially was revealed to be a discourse centrally concerned with the aspirations, sacrifices, and values of parenting. Her quietly stated contention suddenly jolted me into registering how boys' and girls' games and achievements might actually be treated by some not as matters that children should be largely left to get on with as they wish, but rather as the objects and products of adults' "work." With this, my carefully nurtured partition between a career as an academic and time spent attending and helping with community sports activities for children began to crumble. From that point on my curiosity as an anthropologist was increasingly drawn to the complex ways in which children's sports in Canada revolve around various modes of work that are engaged in by parents and coaches as well as the boys and girls who venture onto the fields, rinks, and other venues of community sports.

I started to take note of reports about community sports that appeared in local newspapers and to listen more carefully to parents', coaches', and athletes' talk, albeit in ways that followed no particular plan beyond that of better understanding a field of personal interest and involvement. In due course this shifting posture led me to inflict my stories and tentative analyses upon those university colleagues who exhibited even the slightest interest in sports or child rearing. Finally, after a protracted period of struggling with doubts about the merits of proceeding any further, I decided to undertake formal research in this field and to transform what had been a mostly enjoyable personal and domestic pastime into the focus of professional inquiry. I had been drawn by stages into conducting anthropological research at playing fields and other locales of community sports that had previously been more or less comfortable and taken-for-granted parts of my life.

IMAGES OF CHILD AND YOUTH SPORTS

My decision to commence research on the social construction of child and youth sports initially sparked roughly equal measures of incomprehension and disinterest within my own discipline as well as the broader academic community. By and large, anthropologists and their colleagues in sister disciplines have tended to view sport as a topic not really deserving of serious scholarly inquiry.[5] Nor was the extent of my perceived deviation mitigated much, if at all, by the fact that I was looking into children's sports. Most academics seem only too happy to classify these as "child's play," a term that can be applied to anything that, according to the *Oxford English Dictionary*, "involves very little trouble, or is of very little importance."

Beyond university corridors, discussions that do address children's sports and the issues these raise are liable to provoke more spirited and partisan engagement. In part this reflects the stylized and oscillating coverage that child and youth sports receive in newspaper and television reports. On the one hand, positive media recognition of the accomplishments of particularly successful young athletes and teams tends to be fulsome, if not downright gushing, in its volume and sentiments. From this perspective, sports are cast as entirely natural and appropriate activities for children and youth that not only furnish them with healthy leisure but also prepare them for their future lives as adults. Weekly community newspapers along with big city dailies delight in showering attention upon local elite youth athletes who, in recognition of their athletic prowess, have been or are likely to be offered an athletic scholarship by one or more American universities.[6]

No less tightly grasped in the proverbial other hand is a litany of reservations and laments about child and youth sports. The stereotypical villain in many of these is the oft-mentioned "vicarious parent" who is taken to be pursuing his/her own dreams of achieving sporting acclaim through the athletic accomplishments of a daughter or son. In this rhetorical incarnation, a parent who surrenders to the temptation of basking in the reflected success of his/her child's achievements falls prey to committing all manner of grievous social transgressions that will sooner or later bubble up to "spoil the fun" and compromise the "simplicity" that "ought" to epitomize children's sports.[7] From time to time heated disputes between parents and coaches or sport organizations may lead to conflict and occasionally even to legal actions that are likely to evoke criticism from judges and news reporters about the ways in which adults can descend to chasing after their own selfish interests rather than respecting those of children. Egregious cases involving those few parents and coaches who spectacularly lose control of their emotions and strike a referee, one another, or a child athlete receive serious coverage by the Canadian news media.[8] No matter how statistically infrequent and atypical such outbursts may be, each reoccurrence triggers a collective outcry for parents to "step up and do the right thing" or, alternatively, to "step back and let the kids play." Hues of black and white are preferred for debating these matters, along with appeals for "simple common sense" to prevail to protect the loftier ideals attached to children's sports.[9]

What these familiar representations of children's sports have in common is an inclination to define these as important activities *for* children that, nonetheless, must be appropriately arranged *by* adults. Children and youths are implicitly envisioned here as entities to be organized and acted upon by adults. What it is that good and conscientious mothers, fathers, coaches, and sport officials ought to be doing—or not doing—is assumed for the most part to be obvious. Nevertheless, the line between what is labelled as meritorious and what as inappropriate in the field of children's sports is by no means always self-evident, let alone an agreed upon matter. To move beyond the limitations of the conveniently dichotomized interpretive schema employed in media accounts of children's sport, it is necessary to look into the actual and varied experiences of those who have for longer or shorter periods, with greater or lesser enthusiasm, been more or less intimately involved in the diverse roles, relationships, and activities that constitute children's sports.

This approach is not, of course, especially well suited to churning out unqualified and incontrovertible verdicts on children's sports. The social roles enacted within these activities—including those of young athletes, coaches, officials, and parents—constitute decidedly different entry and vantage points for participating in and making sense of the assorted activities and arrangements that can be gathered under the heading of children's sports. Paying attention to all of this offers valuable means for coming to terms with disparate personal experiences, related from particular points of view, that when drawn together serve to reveal the complexity of children's sports in perceptive and ironic ways. If one accepts the likelihood that the truth about this or any other field is likely to be plural, contested, and more nuanced than a slogan to be appliquéd on a ball cap or T-shirt, then this approach offers a realistic starting point.

STUDYING CHILDREN'S SPORTS

Although initially kindled by personal involvement in community sports as a parent of two daughters and a son, my continuing investigation of children's sports has generated several overlapping projects over a period of almost twenty years. Along the way it has also been leavened by my experience as a coach in girls and women's soccer and as a coach and technical official in track and field. One of the preliminary tasks undertaken when I opted to conduct formal research within this field was a survey of community sports clubs and associations for children and youth in an area comprising three suburban cities in the Lower Mainland of British Columbia (Dyck and Wildi 1993). The survey not only provided a valuable overview of the extent of community sports participation and investment in this area (about which more will be said in the next chapter), but also served as a public announcement that I was, in fact, conducting a larger, independent investigation of children's sports. To ensure that those who had previously encountered me primarily or solely as a parent or coach would be made aware that I was conducting an anthropological study of children's sports, I arranged with a local community newspaper to publish an article on my research that included my photograph and a request that anyone who was interested in being interviewed for the project could contact me through my university. Having thereby "outed" myself as a practising anthropologist, I began to interview a range of child and youth athletes, coaches, officials, and parents about their respective involvements in and views about community sports for children and youth. In due course the findings were reported in academic publications.[10]

In subsequent years I mounted other related research projects that have, respectively, involved looking into the ways in which participation in amateur sport serves to facilitate or frustrate the social and interpersonal incorporation of immigrants into Canadian society; examining the ways in which the awarding of athletic scholarships to young Canadians by American universities and colleges impacts individual athletes, their families, and the organization of child and youth sports in their home communities; and, most recently, assessing some of the impacts of hosting the 2010 Olympics in Vancouver upon child and youth sports activities in this urban region.

Merely to list in summary manner the various research projects upon which this book is based would be to overlook vital developments that have occurred within the broader discipline of anthropology during the past two decades. These have been pivotal in shaping my continuing study of children's sports. The recent rejuvenation of the anthropology of childhood has transformed it into a thriving area of study within which major analytical and ethnographic advances are being registered.[11] The critical rethinking of developmental notions of socialization that had long depicted children as being relatively passive, if not always biddable, figures who need to be guided along the journey from infancy to adulthood (e.g., Stephens 1995; Thorne 1993; Prout and James 1990; Fog Olwig and Gulløv 2003) has been overtaken by a politics of childhood perspective that approaches boys and girls as actors who possess and endeavour to exercise agency in their own right, if not always in the conditions that they might choose.

A newer field of anthropological inquiry that has also materialized is rapidly coming to grips with sport in all of its dimensions and manifestations both within and beyond the Western world. Working with ethnographic, interpretive, and comparative precepts and practices that are characteristic of social and cultural anthropology as a discipline, practitioners in this emerging field are tackling the ways in which sport intertwines embodied sporting practices with systems of governance and symbolic meaning. What is more, sport activities often revolve around issues of performance, identity, gender, and transnational movement. Works by Archetti (1997a, 1999), Brownell (1995, 2008), Carter (2008), Klein (1991, 1993, 1997, 2006), MacAloon (1981), and others[12] illustrate how anthropological inquiries grounded in particular places and practices that are, nonetheless, comparative in analytical orientation can speak in compelling ways to larger theoretical and substantive issues.

Research that conjoins the study of childhood and sport (e.g., Anderson 2008; Grasmuck 2005) has been especially instructive for my undertaking.[13] Most important, this body of work has underlined the importance of taking on the challenge of addressing a set of overlapping concerns without reducing either children and childhood or sports activities and performances to backdrops or vehicles for the pursuit of more singularly focused investigations.[14]

SOME PROPERTIES OF ANTHROPOLOGICAL ACCOUNTS

Anthropologists go about the business of examining social practices and ways of being in the world in a somewhat different manner than scholars in most other disciplines. As a result, those not familiar with the processes by which anthropologists conduct their inquiries and report their theoretical and substantive findings sometimes express impatience with published anthropological accounts for, in effect, not doing what these were intentionally designed *not* to do. Conversely, the thrust and import of the types of questions and phenomena that anthropologists *do* select for examination may be unwittingly disregarded or misunderstood by practitioners of other disciplines who don't recognize or fully appreciate some underlying dissimilarities in how they and anthropologists engage with theory in their investigations.[15] My reason for raising these matters here is to direct the reader's attention from the outset to what any given anthropological account does and does not aim to accomplish.

In several social science disciplines a chasm has opened up between theory and empirical investigation. Over time this has given rise to an intellectual division of labour that often privileges those who concern themselves primarily with theory. Yet this tends to relocate social theory into a zone of abstract contemplation within which those drawn to theory devote themselves to annotating and parsing in minute detail the nuances and conceivable implications of key texts by celebrated theorists. The greater the value placed upon so-called pure theory within systems of academic prestige, the greater the inclination of the enthusiasts of one or another leading theorist to treat him/her as a veritable oracle whose writings might be consulted for prophetic advice or marshalled as an authoritative guide to further thinking and writing about any number of topics. Those concerned primarily with social theory may also exempt themselves from having to demonstrate in any sustained manner the practical utility and durability of their preferred ways of interpreting the world. That task is delegated to those further down the intellectual hierarchy who are charged with the responsibility of using the social theory that others create to investigate actual social issues and questions. To work beyond the precepts of one or another recognized theoretical approach would be to risk being labelled an "atheoretical" empiricist who merely collects and assembles social facts about one or another topic.

Within anthropology the collection of data and the work of theorizing tend to be inextricably attached to one another. When anthropologists propose more general ways of thinking, investigating, and writing about social phenomena, they expect their colleagues to demand more than a few anecdotes or hypothetical cases to illustrate the validity and utility of their analytical insights. Even the most mundane report of anthropological findings must anticipate two interconnected lines of questioning from anthropological readers: First, why are you telling us about this topic? What is the more general analytic importance of the matters that you have investigated and the substantive findings and analytical conclusions that you are now reporting on? Second, where is the evidence that supports your analysis? How valid are the observations and conclusions that you present?

Between these two axes of interrogation that anthropologists apply when reading each other's work it is not only possible, but, indeed, essential to proceed in a manner that should *always* be both theoretically mindful and substantively grounded. Unlike studies that select a set of theoretical categories and positions from the outset and then proceed to collect data—in the form of statistics, texts, or interviews—that can be fitted into this conceptual framework, anthropologists approach their work with a different set of objectives and procedures. Anthropological research involves interacting, observing, and talking with people to gain detailed accounts of their personal experiences of social life, their shared and individual ways of relating these, and their understandings of the manner in which their lives are shaped by various agencies and factors. This method of inquiry does not typically seek to obtain statistically representative findings of the type that survey research, when properly conducted, is capable of producing. Instead, it aims both to obtain detailed understandings of the workings of social processes as well as to examine critically the starting assumptions, questions, and analytical categories that the anthropologist brings with her/him into the research project.

Hence, rather than simply testing the validity of a hypothesis or collecting information that supports one or another theoretical interpretation of how social life is organized, an anthropological investigation intentionally remains open to taking notice of a far broader range of considerations. Within more conventional forms of social science, matters and concerns that were not anticipated at the outset of a research inquiry cannot readily be made part of questionnaires, survey forms, structured interview schedules, or preferred interpretive schema once the collection of data has commenced. In contrast, a more flexibly structured approach to research permits anthropological inquiries to be adjusted and readjusted in quite significant ways as the investigation proceeds to take account of emerging findings.

Far from signalling an incomplete or faulty research design, this is an allowed-for outcome that plays upon one of the fundamental strengths of this approach: a built-in capacity to reassess and recalibrate at every stage of a research project the investigator's understanding of what is being looked at, why, and by what means. Research of this type is not designed and, thus, should not be expected to provide statistically representative findings about a given topic. That is, of course, a legitimate and valuable task for social science, but it is not the only one that merits commendation. Anthropology's contributions are purposefully exploratory in nature, searching out new forms of social relationships and practices and reassessing known ones, not least to expand our understanding of how social life can most effectively be examined in differing contexts.

The ethnographic research method of participant/observation that originally developed within anthropology and that continues to be used by anthropologists is, however, no longer unique to this discipline. Qualitative and ethnographic approaches to research have become popular in recent years across many of the social sciences. A more distinctive facet of anthropological inquiry is the manner in which its practitioners strive to study highly particular situations and arrangements by means of a comparative perspective. Thus, to observe that the organizational form and purposes of community sports for children and youth in Vancouver differ in some key respects from those found in, for instance, Copenhagen (Anderson 2008) is to raise questions about how and why these differences exist and what other social factors might be at work in shaping these outcomes. In effect, anthropologists are attuned to looking for similarities and differences in the ways in which social life is organized in different places and situations. Our attention zooms in on what can be learned from differences within these similarities, not to mention similarities within what might otherwise be presumed to be markedly different settings and circumstances. Above all, anthropologists remain skeptical about the wisdom of wielding universal and categorical definitions of human arrangements as if these comprise unquestionable means for investigating and understanding social and cultural phenomena. Accordingly, when Canadian adults explain their involvement in child and youth sports in terms of the commonplace phrase that "we do it for the kids," an anthropologist is more likely to wonder about the varying reasons why and contexts within which individuals might resort to making this claim than to conclude that since it is so frequently heard that it likely signifies an indisputable and unambiguous value for Canadians.

MAKING SENSE OF SPORT

Sports of many types, including those played by children and youths, are familiar features of everyday life in Canada. How, then, can we make sense of them as social and cultural phenomena? A first step is to recognize that sports are hardly simple and transparent activities and enthusiasms. They are, instead, fundamentally multi-dimensional in nature, so various approaches serve to illuminate one or another dimension of sport. One might begin by examining the acquisition of disciplined forms of movement highlighted in given sports, or the rules and purposes of games and competitions, or the organizational structures of clubs and leagues that arrange and manage sports events. Alternatively, we might wish to grasp the meanings attributed to sport by looking into the personal experiences of athletes, coaches, organizers, and other sport enthusiasts, as well as those of individuals whose previous encounters with sports now incline them to keep it at arm's-length. Attention might also be focused on the proclaimed benefits of or perceived problems with sport, matters periodically attended to in media accounts. We might further explore sport as a temporally demarcated social space that captivates and convenes not just athletes, organizers, and fans but also the varied desires and concerns they bring with them to sports events. Envisioned thus, sport might be mapped as a sort of social territory or field within which individuals pursue pleasures and strive to shape their own aspirations, commitments, and lives, as well as those of others who seek to share these spaces with them. Sport might even be regarded as a zone of social endeavour within which diverse activities, relationships, and identities are constructed, reconstructed, and consumed. Or sport could be regarded as a vantage point from which to observe movements and feats that not only figure centrally in games and competitions but also reflect other aspects of contemporary life.

Another way of proceeding would be to assemble an inventory of distinctive characteristics or properties of a given sport. Blanchard's definition of a sport as "a game-like activity having rules, a competitive element, and requiring some form of physical exertion" (1995, 31–2) furnishes a basic point of departure for such an exercise. An implicit corollary of this definition is that even though a sport is supposed to be situated somewhat apart from quotidian social life, it becomes for many people an abiding and sometimes pre-eminent part of their daily existence. The capacities and techniques that athletes so often pull out all the stops to acquire can also serve as objects of rapt attention and endless discussion by spectators and other athletes alike, transforming physical movements into modes of performance designed to be watched and appreciated. Renowned for its power to generate fun, excitement, and other intrinsic pleasures, sport may also be harnessed to extrinsic purposes of many sorts, thereby drawing attention to how this is accomplished.

Far from being a singular or constant form of activity or practice, what is deemed as constituting a sport often remains a matter for discussion and negotiation. The actual venues within which various sports may be performed range from fields, paved tracks, rinks, pools, steep mountainsides, and specially equipped gymnasia or courts within buildings of varying size. What is required in the way of facilities to stage a game or sporting contest runs the gamut from temporary, informally used, and roughly demarcated spaces to expensive, purpose-built, and exclusive ones. By the same token, under the banner of sport can be found athletic games and contests that may be played with little or no fanfare or expense but which can also be reconfigured to absorb substantial investments of money, time, and other resources.

In the case of community sports in Canada, transgenerational relationships are a hallmark of activities designed and controlled by adult coaches and officials but played by child and youth athletes. Community sports also tend to be underpinned by concerns with child rearing that preoccupy parents as well as public agencies, governments, and businesses. At one level community sports are overwhelmingly volunteer, unpaid, and amateur activities that require cooperation and goodwill on the part of coaches, organizers, parents, and athletes. Yet in recent years an ostensibly auxiliary but manifestly powerful set of sport advocacy and governance agencies has been erected above the local level, and these entities do furnish livelihoods for a growing number of sport experts and planners. At both of these levels individual adults as well as institutions often explain the measures that they propose by claiming that they wish to act simply on behalf of the kids, thereby staking out a claim of selfless benevolence.

The task of synthesizing the workings of this complicated amalgam of activities, arrangements, objectives, and rationales for community sports clearly involves rather more than just keeping tabs on given sport competitions, organizational structures, or journalistic coverage. Participation in community sports is being progressively intensified with respect to the amounts of time and levels of commitment demanded of many individual athletes and adults. Ironically, just when the levels of money and support invested in sport by some parents and communities are mushrooming as never before, the proportion of children taking part in community sports has started to decline.[16]

Taking all of these factors into account, which analytical approaches can assist us to make better sense of the dynamics of community sports? One way of proceeding would be to pay close attention to the experiences and views of those who are involved in community sports, a strategy often used in newspaper articles reporting on community sports. Another would be to study the structures of sport activities and organizations and to focus primarily on the various functions that these are seen as fulfilling. From this perspective, a sport practised in any given setting could be deemed significant and interesting insofar as it could accomplish certain functional outcomes, such as providing healthy exercise, creating sociability, rallying national audiences, socializing children, and so on. Depicted thus, a sport becomes a curiously taken-for-granted but dependable instrument for facilitating one or another set of desirable social outcomes. This scenario, of course, blithely presumes some degree of agreement and consensus among different types of participants in a sport, even when they may differ fundamentally from one another in terms of age, class, gender, or ethnicity, not to mention the vital distinction between individuals and institutions that present themselves as "stakeholders." Nevertheless, how exactly is some workable form of agreement about what a community sport should seek to accomplish and how it should be played actually arrived at?

Fundamental differences in the preferences and experiences of various participants in community sports are not, in fact, all that difficult to find. Consensus and cooperation are by no means always easily achieved or maintained. Sports are labile, emotional undertakings that can trigger misunderstandings and conflicts that can rapidly imperil the existence of a team, club, or league. Hence, the need for an analytical approach that pays attention to the complicated but illuminating matter of how sports are organized, played, and consumed in varying ways.

APPROACHING COMMUNITY SPORTS AS A SOCIAL FIELD

Field theory provides an analytic approach well suited to explain the dynamics of different realms of social endeavour, including that of community sports. Lewin's early definition of a social field as "a totality of co-existing facts that are conceived of as mutually dependent" (1951, 240) astutely captured the manner in which aggregations of individuals, groups, and institutions that might not often or ever be in close contact can, nonetheless, affect one another. Field theorists seek to elucidate emerging regularities in the actions of participants in or components of a realm by taking account of their relative positioning within an intuitively recognized sector of common interest. While a participant's positioning in a given activity sector determines the potential field effects experienced by that person, group, or institution, these effects or forces impinge "from the inside" rather than from external compulsion (Martin 2003, 1). A field begins to align "when units interact in such a way that they develop a mutual influence" (Martin 2003, 26) that reaches beyond pre-existing institutional channels or preferences.

Bourdieu (1984) observed that self-contained social fields such as sport or art each possess their own themes and problems. In consequence, every field "possesses a coherence based on a working consensus as to the nature of the game, and people take predictable sides due to the more general structuring of social space" (Martin 2003, 23). This coherence remains a dynamic and changing one, for every field is "the site of a more or less overt struggle over the definition of the legitimate principles of the division of the field" (Bourdieu 1985, 734). Thus, what is "at stake in a chess, tennis, or sumo tournament is not simply which individual will be the winner, but what *kind* of chess, tennis, or sumo (and hence what *kinds* of players) will dominate the field in the future" (Martin 2003, 23). Within crowded social fields, participants or units diversify and move to occupy different locations within this space: "more structure arises with the presence of similar organizations of the same kind, which must be taken into account by each organization when planning its strategy. Now action takes on the characteristic of a game in the technical sense" (Martin 2003, 27).

The application of field theory to the study of community sports permits analysis of varied but mutually significant and interdependent elements and activities within this commonly recognized realm of shared interest. Yet doing this entails something more than simply declaring the actuality of a social field of indeterminate dimensions and attributing certain forces or effects to it. To the extent that a social field is inherently perceivable but not directly measurable, its operational existence must be demonstrated through its observable effects. Thus, the identification of a social field must remain a tentative matter that requires continuing empirical verification of how the forces or effects detected within such a sector shape some aspects of the behaviours of participants located at different points in it. Of course, not all human behaviour or action that occurs "in the field" can be attributed to a field effect (Martin 2003, 33). The onus placed on the analyst within this approach is not to indicate at the outset all that might transpire within a given social field, let alone predict likely outcomes. It is instead to conduct empirical inquiries that interrogate and explicate the activities, interests, and perspectives of various participants in a field and discern whether and how their respective modes of engagement might influence those of others in this shared space.

In practical terms this necessitates looking into how fields give rise to sets of roles specific to them. Although the sharing of role expectations across a field potentially constitutes one of its effects, the potential for a discrepancy between such expectations and the choices made by a given person or organization inevitably remains. Notwithstanding this possibility, what is needed is "descriptions of the patterned motivations of persons who are distributed (or who have distributed themselves) in some field" (Martin 2003, 37). Since the motivations of varied participants in a field might coincide in some respects and diverge in others, a good way of understanding "a field's ability to provide goals while being a site of conflict seems to be along the lines of considering the field as a 'game' with rules" (Martin 2003, 31). But in the case of a social field, the struggles that ensue are both over and within the rules: "thus, the 'game' is not some sort of overarching formal framework that in some obscure way *forces* persons to do this or that" (Martin 2003, 31).

Approaching community sports as a social field involves taking account of the respective positioning of and influences exerted by the diverse persons, groups, and institutions that participate in and constitute the myriad activities of this burgeoning sector. Given the range and extent of organized athletic activities for children and youths operated by community groups in different localities and provinces, it is, not surprisingly, a large and complex field. It features participation by girls and boys of various ages as well as parents, coaches, sports organization personnel, and government officials. A generally recognized repertoire of roles circumscribes many aspects of individuals' behaviour within this overall field. A central task for this book, then, will be to examine the motivations and experiences associated with each of the main types of roles identifiable in this field and to ask how each of these is also shaped and affected by the roles played by other types of participants. The cumulative objective is to determine how different roles and interests collide and coalesce within this voluntary field of endeavour.

WHAT THIS BOOK IS AND ISN'T ABOUT

This book examines how, why, and with what outcomes various key actors—including child and youth athletes, coaches, technical officials, and parents—participate in community sports for children and youth in Canada.

It is not intended to serve as either a muckraking exposé of the alleged problems and excesses of child and youth sports or a partisan celebration of the oft-proclaimed benefits and virtues of these activities, although it does scrutinize each of these stances and asks how they might be connected to one another. The book is, instead, more modestly presented as an anthropological study that seeks to elucidate the complexities and consequences of the ways in which Canadians arrange their involvement in this far from monolithic sector of everyday life.

The analysis developed here is based upon an ethnographic approach to the ways in which childhood and sports may in effect be fused to one another within the venues of community sports. The book does not aim to provide a comprehensive overview of all sports played in all regions of Canada. Nor does it purport to provide a statistically representative rendering of sport in Canada generally. Instead, it looks into particular instances and differing forms of involvement in several community sports settings that the reader is invited to relate to her/his own experience and understanding of community sports. Teams and sport organizations can vary enormously in terms of where they are located, the sports they offer and the levels of intensity at which they seek to compete. Readers will recognize which of the practices and problems reported here resemble those found within the community sports scenes they know best and which may be less familiar to them.

I harbour no illusions about this book providing anything like an authoritative version about or the last word on children's sports in Canada, let alone in other Western industrial countries. There are simply too many differences within and between the myriad activities that make up community sports for children in Canada to expect that one study could easily take account of all of these. By the same token, no single sport should be regarded as the pre-eminent one against which all others ought to be measured and assessed. For those involved in swimming, track and field, speed skating, soccer, tennis, curling, and so many other sporting pursuits, hockey is just another sport. To organize a study of children's sports upon the basis of what is the most popular child and youth sport in terms of its levels of participation (i.e., soccer) or reputedly the most culturally significant would, for my purposes, be beside the point. My interest is in what we can learn about the ways in which childhood, families, parenting, and communities are touched by and reflected within the many different community sports activities and arrangements that cater to children and youth in Canadian communities.

What similarities and differences exist, and what might a more nuanced appreciation of these bring to light?

While the book examines the experiences and insights of particular girls and boys, men and women, immigrants and those born in Canada, it does not seek to reduce or simply slot these individuals' experiences into one-dimensional categories of social class, race, or gender. Instead, the focus will be on the ways in which the entanglement in community sports of *actual* children and adults—as opposed to so-called average or typical children and adults, sons and mothers, and so on—intersect with and illuminate broader social, economic, and cultural influences that mould individual, family, and community undertakings within this field.

This study deals with community sports activities that operate outside of and apart from intermural, extramural, and curricular physical education sport programs in schools. School sport programs are no more or less valuable, significant, or controversial in their own right than are their community sports counterparts. They do not, however, for the most part permit or require parent participation and support in the same ways that community sports programs do. The same also applies to sport programs or individualized coaching and training services for young athletes—including, for instance, summer sport camps or "schools"—that oblige parents to pay coaches or trainers to hone their sons' and daughters' athletic skills and capacities. The role of parents in these settings is largely reduced to that of recompensing a professional to provide a service. This is unlike most community sports organizations where parents and other volunteers combine their efforts to operate leagues, teams, and competitions for children.[17]

However pleasurable and rewarding being involved in community sports in one capacity or another may be, the efforts that young athletes, coaches, technical officials, and parents invest into these activities also constitute forms of predominantly unpaid work. These are commonly considered to be voluntary activities: any child or adult who is determined either to avoid entering into or to terminate their participation in these activities presumably may do so. But this characterization ignores the ongoing application of social inducements and pressure upon individual children and adults to join and remain supporters of a given team, club, or sport—not to mention the energy that goes into fielding and responding to these pitches.

As a noun, work entails any activity involving mental or physical effort done to achieve a purpose or result.[18] Although often applied more narrowly to instances where such activity provides a means of earned income or employment, regardless of whether it is paid or unpaid, work can also designate the place where it is performed, the period of time spent doing it, and the task or tasks to be undertaken: in short, what it is that a person has to do, be it wage labour or moral deeds that are identified as "good works." When used to identify what has been made or done, we speak of a literary or musical work, a usage well suited to accommodate the outstanding performances of virtuoso athletes as well as the accomplishments that may be claimed by adult organizers and parents in the realm of children's sports.

As a verb, "work" pertains not only to being engaged in physical, mental, or social activity or to being employed in a specified occupation or field but also to the manner in which a system may be made or caused to operate properly and effectively. "To work," in this sense, is to bring about, to produce as a result, or to contrive a given outcome. Closely joined to this is the meaning of "working on" or "upon" something—or, in the case of a social system, *someone*—to facilitate a given purpose. Traditionally employed to speak of the manner in which human agents have acted purposively upon things—as, for instance, in working a material such as clay into a desired shape or consistency or working a ship against the wind—the emphasis is placed on the activity of causing something to move gradually or with difficulty into another position, characteristically through the application of pressure. As we shall see, this sense of "working" within children's sports draws our attention to the ways in which participants strive to achieve often-varying purposes.

The line of questioning pursued in this book has grown out of personal insights, continuing ethnographic research, and a critical reading of literatures on sport, childhood, and social and cultural organization more generally. Among other things, the book asks what attracts child and youth athletes, parents, volunteer coaches, and sport officials to become involved in community sports, to continue to take part in these activities for longer or shorter periods, and to leave these in due course or to quit abruptly? What are the differing ways in which sports can be played and child and youth sports organizations and activities designed and operated? How and in what ways are community sports constructed and understood by kids, parents, coaches, officials, and other parties that hold an interest in these activities, including governments, businesses, educational institutions, and professional sports leagues? How are the operations of primarily volunteer-based community sports organizations sustained, given the significant demands of time, money, and facilities that these consume? How do the various parties involved in children's sports manage to turn activities that are commonly referred to in terms of "fun" and "games" into "work," and, conversely, strive to transform "work" into "play"? What are the sources of disappointment and of satisfaction in ongoing attempts to reconcile ideals and actualities in children's sports? How and between whom do disputes and conflicts tend to occur within community sports, and how might these be resolved or at least partially contained, even if only temporarily? These are certainly not the only questions that might be asked about children's sports in Canada, but they are important ones that have too often been neglected.

An assortment of concepts and analytic approaches will be enlisted to serve alongside "work" in the chapters that lie ahead. Conceptualizations of the "child," "childhood," "parents," "parenting," and "families" have been attended to in intriguing ways in recent years, and some of the insights and concerns gleaned from these discussions will be presented in subsequent chapters. Notions of "community," "sport," "competition," and "winning" will also figure within the interpretation of episodes that speak to various aspects of the construction of community sports. Miller's (2001) cogently stated and eminently sensible approach to "discourse," which he anchors within the dynamics of everyday social relationships, offers a discriminating means for delving into the ways that participants in activities such as children's sports both produce and consume discourses. Rapport's (2000) identification of narratives as stories we tell ourselves about ourselves also treats "saying" as a form of "doing" in a performance-based analytical approach that exposes the binary opposition that is too often presumed to separate the two. Finally, the workings of social class, morality, and discipline, viewed in conjunction with community sports, will also be considered in the pages to come.

THE STRUCTURE OF THE BOOK

The underlying aim of the book, as outlined above, is to examine how and why community sports for children and youth in Canada take the forms that they do. The second chapter considers the scope, rationales, and organizational attributes of community sports for children and youth. It makes use of published statistical findings to outline some aspects of the broader social landscape within which community sports exist in Canada. This chapter also probes the ways that discourses emanating from various sources can play an essential part in socially constructing these activities, including the utilization of children's sports as a means for invoking different forms of community. The third chapter turns to the involvement of parents in children's sports and asks why and how some parents may be drawn to registering their sons and daughters in these activities. It looks into how the resulting forms of involvement for children and parents may be converted into quasi-domesticated mechanisms for addressing parental child-rearing responsibilities and for enacting versions of family through engagement in community sports.

Chapter 4 investigates the participation of coaches, technical officials, and other sport leaders in organizing and directing particular teams, clubs, and leagues as well as sometimes becoming prominent "builders" of the larger structures and infrastructures of community sports. The tensions generated within both recreational and elite levels of sport competition are discussed in terms of the pressures placed upon coaches to produce winning teams and athletes. The fifth chapter surveys the experiences, sport careers, and childhoods of child and youth athletes in their own words. Of particular interest here are the insights of girls and boys concerning how sport can become a focal part of not only their lives but also those of parents and other family members. Young athletes' readings of what motivates parents and coaches potentially offer them a means to exert a greater measure of agency in shaping their own lives both on and off the fields of play.

Chapter 6 focuses on some of the more potent and problematic properties of children's sports, including the forms of jealousy that are triggered in a realm that continually exposes intimate aspects of private lives within highly public settings. Attention is given here to the oft-encountered claim that adults who are involved in community sports are merely "doing it for the kids." In fact, the ways in which young athletes, as well as parents, coaches, and sport officials are obliged to reconcile their differing interests in community sports stands as one of the distinctive features of this overall field. The seventh chapter looks into the manner in which sporting dreams of various types flourish within community sports, particularly dreams linked to the pursuit of athletic scholarships offered by American colleges and universities. The pursuit of these scholarships involves not only individual athletes but also parents and coaches whose involvement in community sports may be recognized and validated by the winning of such awards by young Canadians. Taking account of the actual experiences of young men and women who have "gone south" to take up these awards serves to situate this type of sporting dream beyond the discourses that celebrate such possibilities. Finally, the concluding chapter presents an extended ethnographic account of a community sports event that serves to draw together and extend the analytical concerns developed in this book.

The overall objective for the book, then, is to identify and interrogate the social, physical, and organizational complexities brought together and highlighted within community sports. It discusses the types of pleasures and desired outcomes that attract different types of participants to community sports, the means by which they seek to attain these, and the ways in which individuals' hopes and expectations may be satisfied, frustrated, or met by both. The book considers the views of not only the promoters and critics of community sports, but also those of parents, coaches, and child and youth athletes whose involvement in sport is too often taken for granted and depicted in clichéd and stereotypical terms. Kids, it is argued here, need to be treated as complex and essential figures in their own right if we really wish to comprehend the nuanced and varied nature of their involvements in and experiences of playing sport. Why, indeed, do some of them continue to play community sports long after many others have stopped doing so, while yet others never get a chance to join in or strenuously work to avoid community sports from the outset? The book traces the ways in which community sports fit with other parts of participants' lives, raising the matter of whether these invariably represent a welcomed "time out" from the routine demands of everyday life or may ironically sometimes become just another demanding chore. To what extent might community sports simply reflect contemporary Canadian society? Conversely, in what ways might community sports offer a social space within which participants of various ages may seek to reshape or intensify aspects of their lives and social circumstances in ways that better suit them?

NOTES

1 An account of the events of that afternoon also appears in Dyck (2010a).

2 My work in this field (Dyck 1985, 1991, 1997) has focused especially on systems and practices of coercive tutelage that have so often characterized relations between government departments and other agencies serving as tutors and Aboriginal peoples as the involuntary clients of such tutelage.

3 An account of the events described here also appears in Dyck (2000a). I have also written about the ways in which my memories of childhood sport activities and involvements have shaped my investigations in this field (Dyck 2010a).

4   This impression remained, even though I noted that he didn't have any pockets into which he might have put the medals. Since that time I have occasionally noticed other parents wearing their children's medals at athletics meetings.

5   See Dyck (2000d, 13–15) for a discussion of why anthropologists have traditionally, but not invariably, eschewed the study of sport. I would, however, note that this inclination to treat sports as matters that do not readily warrant intellectual examination is by no means limited to anthropology.

6   See, for instance, an article by Dan Stinson (2004) in the *Vancouver Sun* that reports how a local middle-distance and steeplechase runner had realized "a childhood dream" and accepted a "full ride" track and field scholarship from the University of Oregon.

7   Although the existence of the "vicarious parent" is treated as an inescapable fact within children's sports, I have never heard any adult identify him/herself as being one. It remains an identity that is applied to others.

8   See an article by Rob Andrusevich (2003) entitled "Hockey dad charged with assaulting daughter at game."

9   One example of this way of defining and then seeking to resolve the problems that parents are believed to pose within children's sports was provided by a compulsory program for parents implemented by the Hockey Calgary minor hockey program in the autumn of 2010. This hour-long, online program, the first of its kind in Canada, must be completed by at least one of a child's parents before the child is allowed to play in this league. Press coverage of the program identified its subject matter as dealing with "respecting referees, parents living vicariously through their kids, and parents physically or verbally abusing opposing players or even their own" (Maki 2010). How effective this program proves to be in eliminating inappropriate behaviour on the part of a minority of parents remains to be seen. It certainly reinforces the notion of sport parents in general being persons who ought to be considered and dealt with as though they are potentially problematic individuals.

10 See Dyck (1995, 2000a, 2000e, 2002, and 2003).

11 The American Anthropological Association's Children and Childhood interest group is one of the fastest growing and most active of the sections and interest groups that make up this professional body.

12 This list should also include the contributors to Dyck (2000b), Dyck and Archetti (2003), Eastman, Ralph, and Brown (2008), MacClancy (1996), as well as books by Alter (1992), Armstrong (1998), Azoy (1982), Blanchard (1995), Brownell (1995), and Howe (2004).

13 Other anthropological accounts of child and youth sports include Lithman (2000), Weiss (2000), Anderson (2003), and Broch (2003). Grasmuck (2005), like Thorne

(1993), is a sociologist. Yet their approaches to children's sports and children's play are quite like those favoured by anthropologists.

14 See, for instance, Thompson (1999) and Messner (2009).

15 Drawing the reader's attention to salient differences that characterize diverging disciplinary approaches should not, however, be interpreted as constituting a call to arms or a declaration of the intellectual superiority of one approach over others.

16 This development will be considered in greater detail in Chapter 2.

17 There are, in fact, community sports that provide some level of remuneration for coaches, as in swimming and tennis, and for technical officials, as in soccer and hockey. The line between community sports organizations that rely wholly or primarily upon volunteers, even if they pay for some services to support their activities, and businesses—such as a hockey school—that exist to sell a service can be drawn in many different ways that defy easy definition. Nonetheless, the distinction is an important one.

18 The second edition of the *Oxford English Dictionary* (1989) is the original source of the various meanings of "work" and "working" considered here.

Chapter Two

"WHAT KIDS REALLY NEED": THE SYSTEMATIZING OF SPORT IN CANADA

MINUTES BEFORE THE FIRST game of a new soccer season, Shauna,[1] a "rookie" member of the six- and seven-year-old girls' team that I was coaching, ran up to warn me that "We can't play yet, we can't play yet!" When asked why the match couldn't begin, she pointed across the field to the other team: "Those girls don't have the same jerseys [as us—so] we can't play yet!" Shauna had anticipated that she and her teammates would play the game *with* those other girls once all of them were suitably garbed in the same uniforms. In fact, the team's pre-season practices had thrust Shauna and her new teammates into a series of drills and scrimmages that they had performed and taken part in together, so her preliminary reckoning of what soccer involved was not without basis. Nevertheless, with the opening whistle she was obliged to accept not merely contrasting uniforms but also the oppositional structure and competitive ethos of a game that in at least some respects entailed something other than what she had expected.

When parents first register a son or daughter in a local sport activity, they too happen upon existing arrangements and organizational practices that tend to be construed as a condition of their children's participation. Individual coaches and volunteer officials introduce newcomers to the ways that things are supposed to be done within a given team or club, thereby conjoining the practices and key personalities that parents and children must learn to live with, work around, or walk away from. Coaches and local sport officials do not, however, account for all of the parties or priorities that shape the operations of local sport organizations. In addition to child and youth athletes and their parents, there exist other "partners" and "stakeholders" who, though seldom encountered in person at the venues of local sports, nonetheless seek to steer community sports in certain directions and to harness these to a range of additional purposes.

The entities engaged in these higher levels of sport advocacy, planning and coordination include provincial and national sport organizations; governments at municipal, provincial, and federal levels; sport advocacy bodies; and corporate and business groups, all of which pursue their respective institutional interests in and through community sports. The forms of action that ensue at these levels of an emerging sports industry tend to be more opaque and less immediately absorbing than the on-field exploits of child and youth athletes, but their impact on shaping child and youth sports in Canada should not be overlooked. While their dealings with *actual* community sports organizations are seldom as supportive or non-instrumental as their rhetoric might imply, nonetheless, governments[2] and other self-defined institutional stakeholders have made themselves active "players" in the larger field of Canadian amateur sports. Their priorities include, among other things, a concerted drive to systematize sport and employ it as a compliant vehicle for policymaking and service delivery in a range of sectors.

THE DIMENSIONS OF CHILD AND YOUTH SPORTS IN CANADA

What is the extent of sport participation in Canada and, in particular, participation in community sports? Although an obvious and essential question, the challenges involved in determining levels of sport participation underscore some of the complexities intrinsic to this field of embodied, social, and competitive activities. To begin with, there is the matter of how "children," "sport," and "participation" are to be defined and then counted or measured. The General Social Survey (GSS) on Canadians' time use, a periodic social survey conducted by Statistics Canada, envisions children as persons aged 5 to 14, leaving persons aged 15 years and older in what is sometimes implicitly referred to as the "adult" category. The National Longitudinal Survey of Children and Youth (NLSCY) Participation in Activities, however, collects data on persons aged 6 to 9 as well as from self-reporting persons aged 10 to 17 years of age

(Statistics Canada 2001). What "sport" constitutes for the purposes of these surveys has also differed over time in larger and smaller ways. The GSS on time use defines sport as "mainly team or organized activity such as hockey, baseball, golf, competitive swimming and soccer" (Clark 2008, 59). A large number of recreational physical activities such as non-competitive aerobics, bicycling for recreation or transportation, body-building or dance are excluded from this definition of sport. Yet in 2005 the previously omitted activities of cheerleading and skateboarding were reclassified as sports. In contrast, the NLSCY has sometimes tracked what it has defined as either "organized" or "unorganized" sports (Statistics Canada 2001, 2). More recently, it has collected data regarding "participation in sports with a coach or instructor" and "participation or instruction in other physical activities such as dance, gymnastics and martial arts with a coach or instructor" (Guèvremont et al. 2008, 66). Responses for both of these categories are subsequently combined under a single heading, namely that of "organized sports." As one interpreter of GSS findings has noted, respondents classified as "non participants" or as being "inactive" may in fact be very physically active in pursuits that were excluded from the survey's definition of sport (Ifedi 2008, 8). Nor does the GSS distinguish between sports played in community leagues and clubs and those played through school teams.

In general terms, sports participation in Canada is reported to have declined across all age categories in recent years. By 2005 there were some 7.3 million Canadians aged 15 years and older who were active participants in amateur sport, representing a participation rate of 28 per cent of that segment of the population, a rate that had declined sharply from 34 per cent in 1998 and 45 per cent in 1992 (Ifedi 2008). In 2005, 51 per cent of children aged 5 to 14 (2.0 million children) had regularly taken part in sports during the previous 12 months (Clark 2008, 54). Between 1992 and 2005, boys' participation rates slipped from 66 per cent to 56 per cent while those of girls changed somewhat less, dropping from 49 per cent to 44 per cent. In 2005, 51 per cent of "sport active" children were involved in more than one sport and on average attended sport activities 2.6 times per week during the sport's season. Sports participation for children and youths tends to peak in the early teenage years but remains the most likely choice for participation in extracurricular, out-of-school activities for children between 10 and 13, and particularly for boys (Statistics Canada 2001).

Surveys such as the GSS have also given attention to various social factors associated with sports participation (see Ifedi 2008). Among Canadians aged 15 years or older, more men than women take part in sport, although the gender gap is gradually narrowing. Educational attainment stands as a key indicator of active sports involvement: the higher the level of education, the more likely a person is to participate actively in sport. Income also has a major influence on sports participation and increases as household income grows. In 2005 members of families in the income range of $80,000 and over were twice as likely to participate in sport than those with household incomes of less than $30,000. Persons born in Canada participate in sports more than do immigrants, although recent immigrants tend to lag behind the Canadian-born rate of sports participation somewhat less than immigrants who arrived in Canada before 1990. At different times there have been varying findings concerning the regional dimension of sports participation in Canada. It appears that there are greater levels of participation in smaller towns and cities than in the cities of Vancouver, Toronto, and Montreal. While more than a hundred different sports are played in Canada, adult participation seems to be largely concentrated in about 20 of these, including golf, ice hockey, swimming, soccer, basketball, volleyball, skiing, and cycling.

A similar but not identical set of factors have been reported with respect to sports participation by those aged 5 to 14 (see Clark 2008). Household income and the education levels of parents strongly influence children's sports involvement. Participation is highest among boys and girls from high-income households and lowest for those in lower-income households. Children with a parent holding a graduate or first professional degree were more likely to play sports (60 per cent) than those whose parents have only a high school diploma (42 per cent), while children of parents who have not graduated from high school are even less likely to be sports participants (22 per cent). No less important for children is the impact of their parents' involvement or lack of involvement in sports: 24 per cent of children participated in sports if their parents were not involved in sports in any way; 69 per cent of children whose parents themselves play sports are active participants in child and youth sports; and sports participation is highest among children whose parents are involved in refereeing, coaching or in volunteer sports administration (82 per cent). Family structure can also affect sports participation, with the highest rates for children (53 per cent) occurring in "intact" families where both birth parents are present. Among two-parent families, children's participation rates are highest where the mother works part-time and the father works full-time (66 per cent), slightly lower when both parents work full-time (58 per cent), and lowest when the mother is not working (38 per cent). This finding, notes

Clark (2008, 56–7), "reinforces the argument that children's sports participation entails the use of many family resources, including both money and
time." The children of recent immigrants are also less likely to participate in
sports than those of Canadian-born parents, raising the possibility that the
challenge of achieving economic stability in their new country may impose
financial barriers for their children's participation in sports. Clark sums up
key aspects of their participation in these terms:

> Boys are more likely than girls to be sports participants, but this gender gap
> is narrowing. Those in their early teens are more likely to be in sports than
> younger children. Children from households with high incomes and those
> with highly educated parents are much more likely to be sports participants
> than those from low-income families or those whose parents have a high
> school diploma or less.
>
> Parents who are involved in sports activities themselves boost the sports
> participation rates of their children, even if they are only spectators of
> amateur sport. In two-parent families, children's sports participation rates
> are highest if both parents are involved in sports activities. (Clark 2008, 59)

While active participation in sport (i.e., that of athletes or competitors)
may have declined in Canada, volunteering in amateur and community sports
has in aggregate increased substantially (see Ifedi 2008). Between 1998 and
2005 the number of amateur coaches grew to more than 1.7 million, meaning that approximately 7 per cent of adults (i.e., aged 15 and older) were
involved in coaching. Although the number of volunteer referees, umpires,
and technical officials declined during the same period to a total of 800,000,
there was an 18 per cent increase in the number of Canadians active as sport
administrators or helpers. A 15 per cent rise during this period in the number
of women coaches has left them outnumbering their male counterparts by a
slight margin, marking a significant shift within a field that was previously
dominated by men. Women also accounted for almost half of more than 2
million volunteer sport administrators. Totaling up the figures cited above,
there were some 4.5 million Canadians involved in amateur sport as coaches,
technical officials, and volunteer sport administrators, compared to the
approximately 9.3 million child, youth, and adult athletes, yielding a ratio of
athletes to officials of just over 2 to 1. In addition to overall increases in sport
volunteering, the number of adults involved in amateur sport as spectators
nearly doubled in the 13 years after 1992, reaching a total of 9.2 million by

2005. A large proportion of those who watch amateur sports include parents who attend their children's community sports competitions.

Although these findings provide a useful overview of some dimensions of sport in Canada, it remains difficult to distinguish between levels of participation in community sports, school sports, and other forms of amateur sport. To obtain a clearer sense of the extent of community sports for children and youths it would be necessary to obtain detailed data from local sport organizations. One might expect this to be a reasonably straightforward undertaking, a matter of simply identifying community sports organizations, requesting pertinent data from them, and then analyzing and reporting the findings. At least that is what I expected to be the case when I first proposed undertaking such a study in a suburban area to the east of Vancouver, known locally as the Tri-Cities area (TCA),[3] during the 1992–93 season. Specifically, the study sought to identify the range of community sports activities and rates of participation within an area that was spoken of locally as "a good place to raise children." The study focused on athletes under the age of 19 who were active in organized community sports offered primarily within the study area (thereby excluding participation by area residents in sports such as downhill ski racing that were situated outside of the study area).

The survey form was sent to 45 community clubs and associations that together offered 20 different sports for children and youths. The total of 14,687 boys and girls registered in these community sports during the 1992–93 sport season was estimated to represent approximately 50 per cent of area residents aged 5 to 18.[4] The age distribution of young athletes showed that involvement in community sports begins at an early age and tapers off in the teenaged years: 9.4 per cent of the registered athletes were under 6 years of age; 6–10 year-olds accounted for 44.7 per cent of registrations; 11–15 year-olds accounted for 33.7 per cent of registrations; and 16–18 year-olds accounted for the remaining 9.3 per cent of registrations. On the basis of the information gathered, it was estimated that participation rates for athletes between 5 and 10 years of age were likely well in excess of 50 per cent of the total number of children in the study area while participation rates appeared to drop to around 20 per cent of those older than 15. Approximately 66 per cent of the athletes involved in community sports in the TCA during the 1992–93 season were boys and 34 per cent girls, with the gendered imbalance of community sports participation being reflected from the earliest age levels.

Levels of participation by adults as head coaches (832), assistant coaches (1,030), managers (412), club executive members (441), referees (397), and other sport "helpers" (352) were no less significant, totaling nearly 3,500, with male officials outnumbering their female counterparts by a ratio of almost 3 to 1. Also interesting was the finding that 563 youths under the age of 19 were also active in community sports as assistant coaches (120) and as referees (443). Except for small payments made to referees in some, but not all, sports, these adult and youth sports officials were volunteers who dedicated anywhere from 100 hours per season to community sports to upwards of two, three, or four times this amount. Employing a figure suggested by Statistics Canada at that time as an appropriate value for this type of volunteer effort on the part of community sports officials (i.e., $12.80 per hour), a conservative estimate of the dollar value of their efforts during this season would have surpassed $4 million, while a more complete accounting of the time actually contributed would likely have increased this amount significantly.

The community sport organizations that were asked to outline and enumerate their operations were generally most cooperative, permitting the study to attain a response rate of over 90 per cent.[5] Yet the inherent difficulty of fitting a range of complex and varying sport activities and club operations into a common set of categories and a standardized seasonal time-line comprised one of the limitations of this undertaking. In consequence, parents who helped out informally were, in the case of some clubs, counted as adult sport "helpers." Their counterparts in other clubs, however, were simply regarded as parents and, therefore, not included in the enumeration of club officials and coaches, notwithstanding the acknowledged importance of their efforts in fundraising and other tasks central to the operations of these clubs. Nor was it possible to determine how many actual children and youths—as distinguished from easily counted child and youth registrations—were involved in community sports since some boys and girls were involved in two or more community sports during the same year. Thus, the sum total of flesh and blood individuals playing community sports was lower than the total number of registrations within different sports, but how much lower was difficult to say. What the project did seem to confirm, however, was the local perception of these suburbs being a hotbed of kids' sport. This conclusion muted a dimension of local involvement in community sports that emerged more clearly in a study conducted eight years later within Coquitlam, one of the three cities in the Tri-Cities area. A $40,000 study funded by the municipality to identify the gender gap in the city's recreation services revealed that by then that gap had become "a hairline crack compared to the age chasm" (Trotter 2001). Data collected about the usage of municipal recreational facilities and playing fields revealed that three-quarters of child and youth participants were under the age of 13, with both girls and boys dropping out of sports and recreation programs rapidly from the age of 13.[6]

What became apparent from this attempt to survey community sports participation in the Tri-Cities area, above and beyond the particular findings presented above, was how complicated and demanding this task proved to be. For community sport organizations that depend overwhelmingly upon volunteers to mount their operations, collecting statistical information about their diverse activities in all of the detail and categories that might satisfy the curiosity and meet the demands of academics and other researchers is not, for good reason, necessarily a top priority. Local clubs and sport associations understand and record their operations in what are for them decidedly practical ways. What this means is that beyond the level of local sport organizations, precise and relatively complete information about community sports becomes increasingly more difficult to obtain. This does not, however, seem to constrain provincial and national sport organizations, governments at different levels, or sport advocacy and business and corporate groups from speaking about and for community sports with anything less than certainty.

STAKING CLAIMS ON SPORT IN CANADA

Community sports have come to represent a fundamental, if not always clearly delineated, reference point within successive official policy statements on sport in Canada. Periodically issued communiqués contribute to a growing corpus of government and organizational proclamations about sport that typically feature bold metaphors and resolute mission statements. Dramatic assertions of just how important sport is for Canada and for Canadians typically introduce announcements by government departments, agencies, organizations, advocacy groups, and corporate sponsors about the particular program initiatives, campaigns, or contributions that they will be making to build sport in Canada.

This was clearly exhibited in the report of the Canadian Task Force on Amateur Sport Policy that was commissioned in the wake of a formal inquiry—sparked by the Ben Johnson scandal at the 1988 Olympic Games in Seoul[7]—which investigated the extent of Canadian athletes' use of prohibited drugs.[8] The report, entitled "Sport: The Way Ahead" (Minister's Task Force on Federal Sport Policy 1992) addressed a variety of issues, including the place and purpose of sport in Canadian society, the values and ethics that shape its conduct, the roles and responsibilities of national sport governing bodies, and the government's future role in sport policy and programs. The task force made several intrepid claims. It presented sport as a solution for all manner of societal problems, challenges, and concerns. What was required, according to the report, was a fundamental reform of the sport system in Canada because of:

> ... the importance of sport in our society.... [A] majority of Canadians (90 per cent) agree that sport is just as much an element of Canadian culture as music, films or literature....
>
> Sport is pervasive. It is the topic of conversation around the water cooler at work. At times it dominates the airwaves and forms a major portion of our daily newspapers....
>
> Competitive sport is an expression of our nature, our search for fun and fair play and of our national character as we challenge the land, water, snow, ice and mountains of Canada....
>
> On an individual level, sport gives us the opportunity to test and develop ourselves—physically and personally—and to pursue and achieve excellence. At the community level, sport is a basis for social interaction, community building, developing intercultural relationships and local pride. At the national level, sport plays an important part in developing feelings of national unity and pride....
>
> Sport also helps Canadians face the reality of globalization by developing competitive skills and behaviours that are rapidly becoming essential to our economic survival. As well, on the economic side, sport is a multi-billion dollar industry providing jobs to thousands of Canadians....
>
> For all these reasons, the Task Force concludes that sport—from recreational sport through organized competitive sport to high performance sport—must be promoted and [made] accessible to all Canadians. (Minister's Task Force on Federal Sport Policy 1992, 9–11)

Concerning children's sports, the report of the task force claimed that:

> Traditionally, values and ethics have been instilled in children through parenting, church and formal education. Today, however, with the realities of single [parent] families, working parents and difficult economic times, the stresses placed on family life leave less time for values and ethics

development. The church's position as a teacher of ethics and morals has diminished. In schools, less time is devoted to sport and physical educa-tion and to building discipline, learning fair play and following rules. Educational budgets have decreased; class size and composition cause stress on teachers, leaving them with less energy for extracurricular sport activity. All these factors, the Task Force concludes, have combined to erode the moral development of Canadian youth at a time when this development is becoming more critical.

The Task Force says that sport is beginning to address this societal gap by accepting a leadership role in instilling values and ethics in Canadian youth. (Minister's Task Force on Federal Sport Policy 1992, 22)

This curious ordering of claims is reflected not only in this report but also in other pronouncements issued by a developing sport lobby or industry.[9] Sport is almost invariably mooted as being "good for kids" and touted as a "solution." Thereafter attention is given to identifying "problems" or "needs" of Canadian children and communities that could be suitably rectified by sport. Implicit in this formulation is the notion that the rearing of children in contemporary Canada will remain incomplete and faulty unless supple-mented by the beneficial effects of participation in organized sport. What is also implied is that traditional institutions for ensuring the appropriate socialization of children—families, schools, and the church—are, if left to their own devices, no longer capable of preventing the moral erosion of Canadian children and youth. A notion of child socialization, in terms of which responsible adults are seen as acting appropriately upon otherwise passive and dependent children, is wielded to support the claims of the sport industry and to sanction the extension of its involvement in the lives of a significant number of Canadian children and their families.

Ten years later, a newly drafted *The Canadian Sport Policy* (Federal-Provincial-Territorial Conference of Ministers Responsible for Sport and Recreation 2002) that claimed to present "a powerful vision for sport in Canada" underlined the extent to which the institutional staking of claims in and on Canadian sport had proceeded in the interim. Noting that the making of public policy was ultimately a government responsibility, federal officials responsible for sport, fitness, and recreation consulted over a two-year period with recognized "stakeholders" to consider ways of making the Canadian sport system more "effective and inclusive." Provincial and territo-rial governments had also been formally engaged in the process to finalize an overarching national sport policy and an implementation framework for collaborative action in sport during the coming decade.

Allowing that "sport is fun" (Federal-Provincial-Territorial Conference of Ministers Responsible for Sport and Recreation 2002, 5) and that it pervades the lives of Canadians, the policy went on to characterize it as an essential tool for "social and personal development, health and well-being, culture, education, economic development and prosperity, tourism and entertainment." Over and above the personal satisfaction and sense of physical and emotional well-being said to be furnished by sport participation, the policy compiled a list of its broader benefits:

... better marks at school, a decrease in cigarette smoking, reduced crime rates, and reduced use of illicit drugs ...

... [increased] resistance to such diseases as heart disease, cancer, diabetes, osteoporosis, arthritis, and obesity and to mental health disorders. An increased investment in sport means an increase in health quality and a decrease in health care costs....

Through sport we learn values and behaviours that we apply to all aspects of our society—hard work, discipline, the value of fun, teamwork, respect for others, and fair play....

Social capital is built by learning to organize meetings, negotiate for the use of shared facilities, and deal with expectations, triumphs and failures....

Sport generates substantial revenues, whether from professional sport or from hosting national or international events. Hosting sports can also have a vital long-term impact on local and regional economies. (6)

The objectives set by the Canadian Sport Policy encompassed several general aims, including addressing and reversing declining rates of sport participation among Canadians; eliminating barriers to sport participation; and improving school sport and physical activity as a means of making sport available to children who might otherwise not be able to afford to take part. A set of more specific goals pertinent to the development of high performance athletes and the upgrading of coaching development programs are identified as means for bolstering the international competitive success of Canadian athletes. Interestingly, although community sports represent one of the larger segments of organized sports in Canada, local sport organizations were not referred to directly in the 2002 Canadian Sport Policy.[10] The key elements of the "sport system," as outlined in this policy, operate above and beyond local-level community sport organizations and, indeed, are intended to discreetly lead and direct community sport and other forms of amateur sport. Included within these select ranks are national, provincial and territorial sport organizations, governments, and other "stakeholders in sport" who are envisaged as central players who will act to ensure that sport in Canada is made to serve the public interest. Local volunteers who may individually contribute many hundreds of hours to community sport clubs and associations each season merited scant mention in this document. Yet the games and activities that they sustain through their time and efforts have become not only the objects of concerted enhancement and governance but also the basis of professional livelihoods[11] for those who have parachuted themselves in to direct the emerging "sport system."

At a provincial level, this distinction between "partners" in the sport and physical activity "delivery system" and "participants" who use these "services" is illustrated in *BC's Policy on Sport and Physical Activity* (British Columbia, Sport Branch 2004). The partners, according to this policy statement, include different orders of government, the health, education, and social service sectors, and the private and non-profit sectors, all of which would

> contribute to and benefit from strong, effective, inclusive, innovative and enduring sport and physical activity systems.... This shared leadership approach includes harmonizing policy objectives with those of the Canadian Sport Policy and other strategic directions—here at home and abroad, so that British Columbia leads the way nationally and internationally. By setting and achieving global standards for quality of life, British Columbia will attract investment and other opportunities. (British Columbia, Sport Branch 2004, 4)

As for the "participants," much seems to depend upon their embodied engagement in these activities or, to put it a different way, their "use" of these "services":

> Full of Hope—our sport and physical activity system will provide hope for today's and future generations of British Columbians. It will provide a legacy of better health, positive role models, prosperity and opportunities for all citizens.... Quality of Life—British Columbians' quality of life (health, economy, social aspects) will be enriched by increased participation in sport and physical activity. This enhancement will contribute to reduced

health care costs, an improved economy and more positive social interaction amongst British Columbians. (5)

Within this policy statement, volunteers are identified as being part of the "strong and sustainable structures" that will deliver programs and services to British Columbians, albeit located at the bottom of this structural pyramid, beneath the level of governments, organizations, and sport leaders.

The values attributed to sport and physical activity within this policy announcement run well beyond the oft-cited hope that these might reduce provincial health expenditures. Sport, it is asserted, will:

- Provide significant economic benefits and will be considered in the same light as other industry sectors, such as agriculture, mining and tourism.
- Promote multiculturalism, social cohesion and encourage harmonious interaction by allowing citizens of all backgrounds to participate and intermingle with others from their community, province, country and around the world.
- Shape our sense of identity and uniqueness as British Columbians and Canadians, while celebrating our diversity.
- Encourage investment as in green spaces and community infrastructure.
- Can be used as an instrument to break the cycles of poverty, substance dependency, idleness, violence and anti-social behaviour. (British Columbia, Sport Branch 2004, 9)

What is especially instructive in this policy statement is the manner in which community sport is figuratively folded into a sport delivery system that will be "integrated, with clearly defined roles and responsibilities, to maximize efficiency and ensure harmonized policies, programs, and services for participants" (British Columbia, Sport Branch 2004, 11). Furthermore, the policy calls for effective, value added approaches:

The dynamic and complex nature of sport and physical activity requires innovative and strategic partnerships. Media, corporations, international and intergovernmental relations, industry and public sectors (e.g., tourism, education, health, social services and environmental) and global technology ... all need to be used to their potential. These partners will have appreciation for sport and physical activity as an investment rather than an expense. (British Columbia, Sport Branch 2004, 14)

The most recent updating of sport policy in Canada has involved discussions and consultations leading up to the anticipated adoption of a renewed Canadian sport policy in 2012. The draft form of the "Canadian Sport Policy 2.0"[12] does, in part, shift the stance adopted in Sport Policy 1.0 (Federal-Provincial-Territorial Conference of Ministers Responsible for Sport and Recreation 2002) by formally acknowledging the existence of community sport, which is now characterized as a "vibrant field of sport that is practised in communities" (2). What is less clear, however, is whether the central "sport system" that is of prime concern in this document might not in practical terms still be envisioned as standing apart from or, perhaps, over and above community sports. On the one hand, CSP 2.0 notes that its predecessor document "was effectively a government policy centred on competitive sport and traditional sport sector stakeholders" (CSP 2.0, 16). The focus of CSP 2.0 is intended to be broader, connecting with a broader range of partners, including those "in both sport and related sectors—at the community, provincial/territorial, and national levels" (CSP 2.0, 16). On the other hand, when this draft policy statement specifies the roles and responsibilities of "all government, institutions and organizations that hold a stake in sport," the community sports sector is notably absent from this listing. While "communities" are mentioned along with "individuals" and "society" as entities that might be positively impacted in sport, community sports organizations are again left off the list of significant stakeholders.[13]

In effect, amateur sport in Canada—of which, community sports for children and youth represents one of the larger segments—has become an entrepreneurial zone for politicians, bureaucrats, sport advocates, and corporate and media groups. They, in tandem with a new class of sport professionals, are busily engaged in spinning a cornucopia of claims concerning the benefits of sport that come close to transfiguring it into a modern-day equivalent of the mythical "horn of plenty," a mysterious mechanism that provides whatever might be desired. Unobtrusively attached to these claims is the proviso that these new agencies, partnerships, and sport professionals ought to be empowered and funded to oversee and direct what has only relatively recently been "rebranded" as an overarching "sport delivery system." Yet a substantial part of this newly declared system actually consists of community sport organizations created and maintained over many decades by local groups of parents and other volunteers gathering and relying upon local resources, an arrangement that is unlikely to end anytime soon.

SOME FEATURES OF COMMUNITY SPORTS

Besides having been discursively conscripted into this recently proclaimed sport delivery system, what are some of the general features of community sports? From the perspective of children and parents who are joining one or another community sports club, what is most immediately encountered is a series of practice sessions, scheduled games, fundraising activities, and other more or less time-consuming undertakings and occasions that make up a season of sport. What also have to be met are the cash costs of participation, including registration fees, the purchase or rental of individual sports equipment, and the cost of transport to and from practices and competitions, some of which may involve out-of-town travel and incur charges for hotel accommodation and restaurant meals. The extent of these costs can vary substantially from one sport or one club to another. Some families are in a position to subsidize a son's or daughter's participation in a given community sport more fulsomely than the parents of some of his/her teammates. Social class distinctions may sometimes be glossed over or intentionally undercommunicated in community sports, yet salient differences in tastes, priorities, what can be afforded, and who might be excluded remain significant factors that shape these activities.

Yet at some point what all of these athletes and parents will stumble across are the logistical limitations that tend to crop up in most community sports activities precisely because these depend so thoroughly upon volunteers. For instance, figure skating requires capable and experienced judges to grade performances and render decisions that are fundamental to competitions. Nevertheless, there is sometimes such a volume of young competitors—and, hence, such an overwhelming demand for judges and technical officials—that parents and others, who may never have claimed to have an extensive background in or knowledge of the sport, might be pressed into service as judges. While club officials understandably wish to fill an empty judge's slot with the best available candidate who happens to be in attendance at the time of a competition, nonetheless, the cumulative consequence of doing so may serve to erode the confidence and patience of competitors and parents. An organizational commitment to the notion that the "show must go on" may, therefore, collide head-on with athletes' and parents' pursuit of competitive excellence. The stress and frustration that can ensue when expectations of skilled judging are perceived as having been seriously compromised, if not outright dashed, can in turn generate dissension and protests that make participation in these activities at least temporarily a fraught experience for all concerned. Sport is not always fair, but then, as this popular saying claims, neither is life. Yet, in the words of an experienced volunteer coach and administrator in track and field, "try telling that to parents who feel that their kid is being shortchanged."

Another ironic aspect of community sport is the manner in which organized athletic activities for boys and girls differ so fundamentally from deeply rooted images of and notions about what children's sports ideally ought to entail. In Canada a nostalgic and oft-invoked national representation of both sport and childhood is that of "pond" or "river" hockey.[14] In this scenario children are envisioned as clearing snow from naturally occurring ice surfaces and entering into spontaneous games that incorporate any number of players. Scores, if kept at all, tend towards ties, for the initiation and continuation of this type of fluid, informal contest depends solely upon the inclination of players to brave the cold and to keep the "game on." In this romanticized rendering of "pick-up" hockey as the quintessential Canadian pastime, skaters glide freely, enthusiastically, and creatively into a zone of playful exuberance and delight that stands well apart from and in marked contrast to the workaday world of adults and the tutelary realm of the schoolroom. Pond hockey cannot be readily envisaged without at least an implicit sketching in of attendant qualities of freedom, fun, and innocence.[15] Thus, adults *as* adults rarely figure in public imaginings of this confluence of sport, childhood, and nature that resurface rhetorically and intermittently from one sport setting to another.[16]

Yet beneath the canopy of these romanticized ideals of sport and childhood exists a vast complex of formally structured community sports activities, organizations, and leagues that are unambiguously shaped and operated *by* adults *for* children and youths in Canada. In contrast to pond hockey, community sports organizations are substantially defined and driven in terms of the dutiful commitment and meritorious tasks performed by parents and other adult participants. They do this, they explain, so that children may enjoy the diverse benefits of playing carefully structured sports on properly lined playing fields or in climate-controlled indoor ice rinks. Unlike school activities, community sports do not merely tolerate carefully limited forms of parental involvement on certain specified occasions. It would, in truth, be impossible to operate and maintain community sports without the ongoing support and cooperation of parents. Along with this reliance upon parent participation is an inclination on the part of more than a few mothers and fathers to employ children's sports as means for, among other things, building better children. Arriving at some consensus among parents about which uses might appropriately be connected to community sports and which ought to be avoided is not always easy to do. What exactly it is that children need or that parents or club officials ought to do can, of course, be viewed in differing ways, and it can become difficult to evade the impacts of the convictions and campaigns of others.

What community sports also constitute are recurring social engagements that bring boys and girls, parents, coaches, and others together again and again throughout a season. The hours spent each week with those who until recently might have been strangers but who might never exactly become friends effectively places everyone who takes part in community sports in any capacity inside the social equivalent of a goldfish bowl. Over a season, one's mannerisms, enthusiasms, and domestic relations can be observed and subjected to interpretation and commentary by others. To enter into community sport activities, even as a silent and intentionally inconspicuous spectator along the sidelines, is to open one's self and one's personal relationships to some measure of scrutiny. Mothers' and fathers' interactions and conversations with sons and daughters at sport competitions often involve matters that one or another of them might prefer to confine to the realms of family privacy. Yet, in community sports settings, people spend substantial amounts of time with consociates, individuals who are neither family members or intimate friends nor total strangers.[17] Consociate relationships arise through casual co-participation with others within one or another delimited field of happenings or activities (Sansom 1980, 138). Within community sports, parents who temporarily become consociates can, if predisposed to do so, begin to piece together details concerning one another that they as individuals might otherwise prefer to keep private or let slip only with those whom one is unlikely ever to meet again. Unlike forms of impersonal interaction on city sidewalks[18] or in elevators that can be navigated by use of more or less accepted conventions of public behaviour, the intense physical and social togetherness of community sports, not to mention their lack of anonymity, combine to fuel a privacy-invasive form of sociability that may take some getting used to.

The athletic competitions that lie at the heart of community sports serve to produce victories and losses, along with the occasional tie.[19] The relative emphasis placed upon winning versus that of simply participating in athletic events remains a matter of signal importance in community sports, with the proponents of participation and those of unadulterated competition endlessly clashing with one another. Initiatives that seek to resolve these arguments by institutionally separating recreational and elite levels of sport competition never seem to achieve quite what they are meant to. What this means is that the manner in which competition is and ought to be managed within a given team or club never entirely disappears as a matter for potential concern and contestation. This issue may never be fully and finally resolved, but community sports organizations do tend to experience greater or lesser rates of turnover in athletes, parents, coaches, and officials every season. The pyramidal age-structure of athletes in these activities means that parents and other adults who persist and become active within a team, club, or sport over many years are more likely to become prominent and powerful figures within these. This, in turn, sets up ongoing encounters between newcomers and old-timers that can prompt a revisiting and questioning of arrangements and priorities struck in previous seasons. Yet the coming and going of athletes and adults in community sports sometimes also offers leeway for experimentation by newcomers in situations where a team or club must either be reconstituted or disappear. In consequence, most community sports organizations are never quite as set in their ways or as precarious as they might initially appear to be.

Viewed from an ethnographic perspective, community sports consist of sets of distinctive practices that begin with the embodied ones that athletes strive to acquire in training sessions and display in competitions and that extend to include the modes of deportment that adults adopt while watching or coaching from along the sidelines of child and youth sports activities. The ways that various logistical aspects of community sports are organized—for instance, the scheduling of compulsory team training sessions during family vacation periods—also constitute social practices that can loom large in the lives of those engaged in these activities. In short, practices, in this sense and in these settings, are understood to constitute ways of doing the various types of actions that make up a day, a week, a season, or a career of involvement in community sport. The practices acquired and performed by individuals, including both embodied and social ones, are not necessarily unique to them, and may well have been copied in large part from those exhibited by others. Neither are these practices simply structurally determined routines that are unconsciously and unquestioningly carried out by individuals. Although practices found in community sports are often taken for granted by those who have become familiar with these, they can also be examined quite self-consciously and retained, modified, or replaced by ones that are reckoned to be more suitable.

An especially prominent form of practice within community sports is that of reporting, discussing, or debating what is actually happening in any given context, relationship, activity, or event in light of what ought to be occurring. A commonsensical distinction often drawn between talk and action, saying and doing, presumes that these are dichotomous and binary in nature.[20] But to consign conversations, explanations, declarations, confessions, and arguments to the realm of "non-action" and treat these as being without consequence is absurd. These should, instead, be regarded as forms and exchanges of discourse that are, in their own right, modes of practice and ways of doing. Discursive actions, no less than physical feats, represent critical parts of the essence and experience of community sports. Discourse is sometimes implicitly treated as the prerogative of powerful classes and agencies that determine arrangements, define meanings, and disseminate or dictate these to less powerful persons and populations.[21] According to this line of thinking, these outcomes ensue from the propagation or imposition of preferred models that serve to foreclose the independence of subordinate individuals and groups. By one means or another, subordinates are purportedly obliged or encouraged to adjust the ways in which they experience life so that it will match the normative frameworks they have been persuaded to adopt as their own. While governments, corporations, and other social forces most certainly do seek to influence how people perceive and engage with their worlds, it does not follow that individuals are for the most part restricted to being mere receivers of discourses.

In this book all those involved in community sports are regarded as both consumers and potential creators of discourses.[22] They are considered to be capable not only of hearing and talking about what, according to various sources, ought to occur within a given field of activity, but also of comparing these normative expectations or standards to what actually happens to them and those they accompany into this social realm. These ongoing comparisons of what is and of what should be engender a dialectic that highlights discrepancies between the two as well as possible measures that might be taken to resolve these. The upshot of adopting this analytical approach to discourse and applying it to the study of community sports is that it moves us beyond the limitations of a functionalist analysis. Accordingly, in subsequent chapters we will consider the ways in which, for instance, parents seek to understand how their support of their child's involvement in sport might benefit her/ him and, furthermore, what they might have to do to ensure that this takes place. Paying attention to these and other everyday matters will enable us to identify the ways in which community sports are socially constructed not just by organizers and sport leaders but also in varying ways by all who are involved in these.

It is not, then, merely a matter of identifying a dominant or hegemonic discourse that is viewed as determining de facto what sport means and what it will entail, but rather of taking account of the multiplicity of discourses that swirl around and through community sports. Which of these are persuasive, when, and for whom, cannot be determined simply by consulting policy statements or survey results. People involved in community sports activities are, in fact, hungry for discourses that might permit them to compare their own circumstances, relationships, and behaviour to models of how these ought to be organized and experienced. This gives rise to a field of social interaction wherein coaches, athletes, and parents attempt to select or improvise and then employ for their own purposes one or another normative model with which they seek to negotiate their respective actions as parents, coaches, and kids. In this respect, participants in community sports might be said to be using one another as mirrors, scrutinizing one another to obtain reflections of their own performances. While searching for similarities between their own ways of being and acting in community sports and those of others, they are also mindful of styles and assumptions that differ from their own. What they seek is some indication that they are getting at least some parts of this right, all the while wondering whether they might just be getting much or all of it terribly wrong. What is sought is not so much superiority over others as deeply desired reassurance that they are not going at this the wrong way. Discourses are, therefore, routinely and eagerly sought out, consumed, worked, and shared as essential parts of the varied experiences of participation in community sports. Hope springs eternal that one or another discourse might just serve to reveal more of what one might wish to learn about the best ways to involve oneself or one's family members in community sports.

Community sports generate an abundance of discourses and practices, all of which involve rather more than is envisioned within official models of sport delivery systems. Local sport bodies do not invariably share a standard organizational form or pursue a singular set of objectives shared from one sport, league, or club to another. What it is that "kids really need" from sport remains a matter for discussion and possible contestation between different participants and organizational entities. Looking into what is actually involved in the playing and staging of particular athletic competitions by actual athletes, coaches, and parental spectators therefore affords a more complicated account of the nature and significance of community sports than sport policy papers ever suggest.

NOTES

1 Pseudonyms are used throughout the book to preserve the confidentiality of individuals.

2 This is more the case with governments at provincial, territorial, and national levels than with municipal governments and school boards that have long provided community sport organizations with access to sport facilities as well as other forms of direct and indirect assistance.

3 The Tri-Cities area of the Lower Mainland of British Columbia includes the cities of Port Coquitlam, Coquitlam, and Port Moody, as well as the small villages of Anmore and Belcarra.

4 This figure was reached by starting with 1991 census data for those 19 years or younger in the area and then deducting all those who were older than 18 years of age and younger than 5.

5 Information concerning the aggregate number of children participating in the three clubs that did not reply to the study was, however, obtained from provincial sport organizations and included in the study findings.

6 According to a city parks and recreation official who commented upon the report findings, the 13 and older age group were a tough group to keep involved in these programs: "… unlike children whose parents make the decisions about … recreation, youths have a mind of their own" (Trotter 2001, n.p.).

7 Ben Johnson, the winner of the men's 100 metre sprint competition at the 1988 Olympic Games was disqualified from the competition and forced to return his gold medal when post-race testing revealed that he had used steroids, a banned substance, to achieve his victory.

8 An earlier discussion of this task force report appears in Dyck (2000e).

9 In addition to the government policy documents cited in this chapter, see Mulholland's *What Sport Can Do: The True Sport Report* (2008) published by the Canadian Centre for Ethics in Sport, and Bloom, Grant, and Watt's *Strengthening*

Canada: The Socio-Economic Benefits of Sport Participation in Canada (2005)
published by the Conference Board of Canada.

10 This telling omission has been repaired in part in the discussions and consultations
leading up to the anticipated adoption of a renewed Canadian Sport Policy (CSP)
in 2012. A commissioned report entitled "Towards a Renewed Canadian Sport
Policy Discussion Paper, October 28, 2011" prepared by the Sport Information
Resource Centre (accessed 1 December 2011 from http://sirc.ca/CSPRenewal/
documents/2011/Discussion_Paper.pdf) as the basis for discussion at the
Canadian Sport Policy national consultation meeting, summarized the results
of consultations on the subject of a renewed CSP carried out by each province,
territory, and the federal government during 2010 and 2011. In contrast to the
policy documents leading up to and emanating from the adoption of the 2002
CSP, this report acknowledges the existence of community sport as "a vibrant field
of sport practice self-sustaining at the community level" (18). The report goes on
to suggest that "a significant enhancement to the renewed [CSP] policy would
be its added focus on sport as it is practiced at the community level, recognizing
that 'core' and 'community' sport do not represent mutually exclusive fields of
activity" (19). What is also mooted is a need for a renewed CSP to serve as a
sort of "roadmap" that would provide "direction in a non-coercive manner" (19).
While the Intersol Group's "Canadian Sport Policy Renewal National Gathering:
Summary Report," prepared during a gathering in Toronto on November 9–11,
2011 (accessed 28 February 2012 from http://sirc.ca/CSPRenewal/documents/
Summary_National_Gathering.pdf) indicated that most of the participants at this
meeting endorsed the proposed "roadmap," there remained some participants who
felt that the map was restrictive and did not accurately reflect the ways in which
individuals are introduced to sport (13).

11 See Macintosh and Whitson (1990) and Thibault, Slack, and Hinings (1991) for
analyses of the impacts of paid professional positions in provincial and national
sport organizations in Canada. See Parent and Harvey (2009) for a model of
community-based partnerships in sport, and Doherty and Misener (2008) for
an assessment of the links between community sports organizations and external
stakeholders.

12 Sport Information Resource Centre, "Canadian Sport Policy 2.0 – Draft –
February 14, 2012" (CSP 2.0), accessed 28 February 2012 from http://sirc.ca/
CSPRenewal/documents/CSP20DRAFTEN.pdf

13 The key actors identified in CSP 2.0 as making up the sport sector are "athletes/
participants and coaches/leaders"; national sport organizations; provincial/
territorial sport organizations; and multisport organizations.

14 An earlier statement of the nature and significance of pond hockey appears in Dyck (2003, 55–6). A visual image of pond hockey and other winter sporting pursuits can be found on the current Canadian five-dollar bill.

15 In this, as in other respects, pond hockey (or "shinny," as it is also sometimes known) has much in common with the forms of unorganized football played on *potreros* in Buenos Aires (Archetti 1997b, 35) and the *peladas* (Leite Lopes 1997, 85) of Brazil. All three types of venues stand apart from the organized spaces and activities of everyday life.

16 Although players of the ages of 4 to 94 might conceivably engage in pond hockey, age and status demarcations between children and adults are not recognized. Within the bounds of this imagined game, a player is a player and there are no coaches or referees.

17 See Dyck (1995) for a more detailed discussion of consociate relations. Further attention will be given to consociate identities and relationships in the following chapter.

18 Jane Jacobs explored these dynamics of everyday life in intriguing ways in her classic study of urban life, *The Death and Life of Great American Cities* (1961).

19 Whether a given sport competition can end in a tie depends, of course, on the rules of that sport.

20 My grandfather's rendering of this distinction was, "Talk's cheap, but it takes money to buy good whisky," an odd choice of terms given that he was a "teetotaller."

21 There is an enormous and contentious literature in the social sciences on the nature and significance of discourse and discourse analysis, much of it deriving from the writings of Michel Foucault. A review of this literature is beyond the scope of this book. Nevertheless, my treatment of discourse reflects an anthropological approach to discourse outlined by Rapport and Overing (2000) as well as that articulated by Miller (2001).

22 In doing so I follow the approach outlined so compellingly by Daniel Miller, particularly in his study *The Dialectics of Shopping* (2001).

Chapter Three

BECOMING SPORT PARENTS

IN THE COURSE OF a Saturday morning in the spring spent selling hot dogs and soft drinks outside a suburban supermarket to raise funds for the local track and field club, Kelly and I chatted amiably about all manner of things. (We were both of us club "volunteers" that day.) After discussing the club's plans for the coming season, our children's activities outside of track, and how different their lives were from those that we had experienced as children, Kelly reflectively concluded, "Actually, our family only happens on weekends in the summer." Initially it struck me that her assessment seemed to skip over or, perhaps, take for granted the many other afterschool and weeknight commitments that, in addition to operating a small business together, Kelly and her husband shared in supporting their children's participation in various activities. From extracurricular school events to community sports and arts programs, one or the other of them—and frequently both—were there to provide rides, watch games, attend parents' meetings, and, as often as not, to help out as volunteer officials, results compilers, or hot dog venders. Yet by Kelly's reckoning, the summer weekends devoted to attending track meets in which their daughter and son competed were when all of them were "most together."

The implications of Kelly's comment come to mind when pondering the differing forms of and reasons for parents' participation in community sports. Among other things, her remark raises the prospect or hope that the conscientious performance of specific tasks or roles by parents may lead to highly valued results—for instance, weekend track meets when a "family happens" because all of its members are not only together but also are joined in a common, pleasurable undertaking. This is, however, by no means an automatic, certain, or typical outcome. Parents' aspirations and children's experiences in community sports depend upon and reflect many factors and considerations, including, not least, the decision of whether or not to enrol one's son or daughter in a community sport and to accept the involvements and obligations that come with it. Why, indeed, are some parents willing to become involved and invested in their children's sports activities? Since this sort of involvement was neither expected of parents nor generally the case in previous generations, why and how is it happening now? What prompts Canadian mothers and fathers to become "sport parents" and to shoulder the diverse demands and costs entailed in so doing?

To delve into these questions obliges us to look carefully into the choices made and steps taken by parents to provide their children with opportunities to participate in one sport or another. This requires more sustained and reflective scrutiny than can be found by resorting to stereotypes such as those of the "overinvolved" or "out-of-control" sport parent or their opposite number, the so-called good or normal parent. Depicting the fathers and mothers of young athletes simplistically as though they, or at least some segment of them, are either to be commended for the "self-evident" benefits or, conversely, held responsible for the "implacable" problems that have been variously attributed to child and youth sports is to resort to rhetorical images that lead inevitably to hackneyed and shopworn conclusions. Exploring the diverse ways that actual parents and children make their ways into and through various sectors of the larger field of community sports permits grounded and nuanced insights into the sources of both the popularity and complications of these activities. Nevertheless, before turning to these matters, it is necessary to take account of some general features of parenting and of families today.

PRACTICES OF PARENTING

To an extent that we rarely appreciate, declares Csikszentmihalyi (1993, 31), it is children that give meaning to adult life, for no community "could survive without the link to the future, which gives stability and purpose to the energies of its members." Employing a similar logic, James (1998, 143–4) concludes that a couple cannot readily transform a home into the locus for family life without children. What these along with so many other recent works on parenting speak to is a renewal of interest within the social sciences in the dynamics and significance of child rearing. Anthropologists have traditionally tended to focus on social and cultural factors that in particular times and places have given rise to sometimes overlapping, but just as often diverging, premises and practices of parenting. Thus, ethnographic studies such as Broch's (1990) examination of childhood among the Bonerate people of Indonesia, Briggs' (1998) analysis of the emotional education of a three-year-old Inuit girl in northern Canada, and Hecht's (1998) account of the arrangements that separate "nurtured" middle-class Brazilian children from that country's "nurturing" street children—who are expected to make significant contributions to the livelihoods of their families—serve to remind us that parenting is socially, not biologically, determined.

Within contemporary Western societies like Canada, childhood is by and large understood as a period of innocent dependency within which children are often denied responsibility for themselves and seen to possess only partial competence (James 2002, 147). Far from being a straightforward outcome of or response to a natural biological phase, childhood comprises varying sets of cultural arrangements for the early part of the life course that remain historically and politically contingent and subject to change (James and James 2004, 13). Children are increasingly set aside in places separated from the rest of society where, if their parents have money, their incorporation and "development" are closely supervised by adults, but, if poor, left to roam on their own (Olwig and Gulløv 2003, 2). Institutional processes to define and separate children as a group demonstrate the control that concepts of childhood—that is, what is thought proper and correct for children—hold for children's experiences at any point in time (James and James 2004, 21). The dependency that is central to current Western notions of childhood is aligned with changing notions of "home," "family," "nurture," "risk," and "danger," the first two of which are seen as being particularly constitutive of the passive and dependent "child" (James 1998). Arrangements and institutions for children are, accordingly, packed with moral assumptions and understandings (Gulløv 2003, 24).

Anthropologists and sociologists have closely followed what has been identified as a significant shift in patterns of child rearing in North America since the 1960s. But the principal features and underlying causes for this shift differ somewhat from one account to another. Coleman (1987) and Persell (1991), for instance, note that the role of unstructured, home-based or neighbourhood activities for children and youths, which had once been loosely watched over by parents, have increasingly been replaced by highly structured, school-based and community-based activities that are invariably supervised by adults and frequently by professionals. Lareau (2003) focuses on underlying distinctions between two contrasting approaches towards child rearing that she labels respectively "concerted cultivation" and "accomplishment by natural growth." The former, she claims, is characteristic of middle-class parents who seek to transmit differential advantages by developing their children's educational interests and taking an active role in their schooling. These parents also pursue "concerted cultivation" by facilitating their daughters' and sons' participation in organized extracurricular programs in sports, the arts, and other community groups. "Accomplishment by natural growth" is linked with working-class and poor parents for whom economic constraints make it a challenging task to keep their children suitably fed, sheltered, clothed, and ready for school the next morning. According to Lareau (2003, 3), most of these parents do not consider the concerted development of children, especially through organized leisure activities, an essential part of good parenting.[1] Newman (1988, 1991) emphasizes the growing burdens placed upon many parents by widening economic disparities. To remain within the middle class, many husbands and wives have had to find paid employment, dealing as best they can with the additional tasks of raising children and scrambling to find daycare (Newman 1991, 113).

Another perspective on the changing practices of child rearing in North America during the last half century underscores the manner in which precepts and models drawn from developmental psychology have given rise to a practical advice-to-parents "industry" (Knowles 1996, 89–90). At the centre of this rests the practice of defining children in terms of their supposed "needs" rather than of their duties and obligations or economic utility (Woodhead 1990, 60). The authority associated with such "needs" statements, argues Woodhead (1990, 63), derives from their ostensibly straightforward descriptive quality, which serves to convey considerable emotive force, activating a sense of responsibility and even feelings of guilt should these not be heeded. Similarly, the construction and popularization of the concept of "self-esteem" led to it being harnessed to models for parenting and education, moving Ward (1996, 16) to observe that a society with a concept of self-esteem is necessarily unlike a society without it. The resulting reconfiguration of popular notions of what children "need" and what conscientious parents should do to satisfy these needs combine to make the commitment to raise a child today a different and, in some respects, arguably more fraught matter than it was for members of previous generations. This in turn is said to have sparked escalating parental insecurities about raising children, replete with fears and concerns, confusion and ambivalence (Fine and Mechling 1991).

Alongside the psychologization of child rearing lies increasing intervention by state agencies and authorities into the everyday organization of children's and parents' lives, prompting Rose (1989) to identify modern childhood as the most intensely governed sector of personal existence. Thus, the family does not merely reflect individual preferences but is shaped by various legal and social sanctions (Knowles 1996, 11). A child's behaviour becomes a clue that can be read as a means for screening families for signs of "failure" and judging the appropriateness and effectiveness of parents' efforts (Knowles 1996, 34, 89–90). This opens the family, in the case of "defective" or "dangerous" parents, to varying levels of surveillance by agencies (Knowles 1996), but also to self-monitoring by mothers and fathers in the case of "competent" and "independent" families. Juxtaposed to this is a tendency on the part of middle-class parents to mediate their children's experiences and treatment in schools and other institutions, ever ready to intervene on behalf of sons' or daughters' interests (Lareau 2003, 165, 171). In short, what was once taken as constituting a child's education has, since the 1960s, been extended from the confines of the school into play and leisure activities, as well as the family environment itself.

Nevertheless, as Lareau (2003, 239) reports, child-rearing practices often seem quite natural aspects of everyday life to those who carry these out, leaving parents scarcely aware that they are orienting their children in particular ways. This is interesting, particularly with respect to middle-class parents whose emphasis in guiding their children's development is not primarily an effort to reproduce their own childhoods but rather to enlarge and preserve advantages for their sons and daughters (Lareau 2003, 64). Thus, the notion of proper places and outcomes for children does not so much refer back to an idealized past with which parents can readily identify as forward to equally idealized futures that, parents hope, are in store for their children as prospective adults (Olwig and Gulløv 2003, 2–3). In practice, the reality within many two-career families is that parents are simply unable to follow previous patterns of how family "ought to be," particularly given geographic mobility and, thus, absent grandparents (Wolfe 1991, 5). So parents are obliged to find what works for them. Differences in styles of child rearing reflect the fact that not all parents have the same resources to work with, and, therefore, cannot all afford to have the same hopes and expectations. Yet even when levels of family income are not critical factors that necessarily channel choices, differences in what parents may seek in a range of institutional settings may still be quite pronounced (Gulløv 2003, 27).

BUSY FAMILIES, UNCERTAIN PARENTS

A motive force in the reshaping of child rearing in North America in recent decades has been an awareness of the gradually declining fortunes of many segments of the middle classes, not to mention the worries of poorer families with respect to more basic matters concerning the provision of food, clothing, and other life necessities (Lareau 2003, 249). An abiding tendency to under-communicate the impact of social class factors, including levels of education and income, serves to impose upon families a persisting ideology of potential social mobility that, in turn, generates what have been referred to as the "hidden injuries of social class" (Ortner 1991, 171). Notable among these is the manner in which families that struggle to retain middle-class jobs and lifestyles may be skewered by their continued subscription to the tenets of "meritocratic individualism," which assert that occupation is the measure of one's worth, that rewards flow to those who are really deserving, and that individuals are the masters of their own destiny (Newman 1988, 84). A gnawing anxiety for many parents is the possibility that their child or children might well find it difficult as adults to reproduce and retain their mothers' and fathers' class status, never mind to become upwardly mobile. An intimately related but in some ways even more immediate concern emerges from fears that a parent's child-rearing activities here and now might be viewed as unsuitable or insufficient to prepare their child properly for what lies ahead.

In fact, the reshaping of conventional forms of childhood in recent years has been not only accompanied but also compounded by a set of changes in the lives of adults and in societal expectations of what a "standard adulthood" is likely to comprise. The mid-twentieth century has retrospectively been characterized as a Fordist era of relative political, economic, and social stability (Lee 2001, 9–15). Post-war economic growth meant that "growing up" could involve moving predictably at what now seems an early age from the parental home and schooling into a job, marriage, children, and family life. With the dismantling of Fordism and the dramatic rise in "flexible" and part-time employment since the 1970s, permanent jobs along with previous patterns of relatively long-lasting intimate relationships that had once underpinned a more or less "standard adulthood" became less widely available. Henceforth, adults were obliged to become more adaptable to respond to rapid change, both in their jobs and personal lives (Lee 2001, 8). In Lee's view, the greater the uncertainty of individual adults' lives and of adulthood generally, the greater the attractions of placing emphasis upon child rearing as evidence of successful careers and of appropriate family formation on the part of mothers and fathers. Yet, in contrast to the immediate post-war period, when parents supposedly had only to realize their expected roles and to fulfill a manageable range of assigned duties and responsibilities to secure a stable family life and authority over their children[2] (Lee 2001, 15), child rearing has increasingly been transformed into what Gubrium (1988) terms as "family as project."

One of the most tangible and telling outcomes of this approach to child rearing is the escalating "busyness" (Darrah, Freeman, and English-Lueck 2007) that has become endemic within families that subscribe to one or another version of concerted cultivation. In their detailed ethnographic research on the patterns and forms of busyness in everyday life, Darrah, Freeman, and English-Lueck found that families are busy in distinctive, non-standardized ways. Busyness involves not only matters of time, but is also about creating ourselves as moral beings who confront the vital question of how one should lead one's life (Darrah, Freeman, and English-Lueck 2007, 107). Although by no means confined to families, busyness becomes especially heightened when parents have not only their own obligations at work but are also ensconced in and affected by the hectic lives of their children. While planning family activities and commitments is time-consuming, nonetheless, it is seen to make life and lives predictable and meaningful (Darrah, Freeman, and English-Lueck 2007, 82). It involves not simply finding and embracing lifestyles but assembling and enacting them. Dealing with the demands and details of busyness in family life is, therefore, very much about whom we choose to be and what we might wish to provide our children, thereby infusing morality into our every choice and action (Darrah, Freeman, and English-Lueck 2007, 259).

WRITING CHILDREN'S SPORTS INTO
CONTEMPORARY FAMILY·LIFE

An appreciation of the factors that have combined to reshape contemporary approaches to parenting and understandings of childhood can offer insights into the processes by which some Canadian parents and families have become ever more involved in organized sports activities for children and youths. Before turning to the ethnographic materials that inform this chapter, it is, however, necessary to take notice of existing writings on this topic. Touching upon a matter referred to above, both MacGregor (1995, 312) and Messner (2009, xi) express misgivings about the "adults behaving badly" stereotype that is so often and uncritically applied to sport parents. MacGregor (1995, 252–68) also considers in some detail the intensity of the emotions that hockey parents, for instance, may experience when watching their children's competitions.

Several authors (Thompson 1999; Lareau and Weininger 2008; Messner 2009) have focused primarily upon concerns with the gendered division of adult labour in child and youth sports, arguing that women's lives tend to be more entwined with and supportive of their children's sports activities than are those of fathers. Coakley (2006) suggests that recent shifts in American society, including the rise of neo-liberalism and feminism, have obliged fathers to become more involved in caring for their children beyond just earning a salary. In his view, getting involved in children's sports offers them a means of doing this. In a study of Little League Baseball in a Houston suburb, Chafetz and Kotarba (1995) identify such involvement as an ideal leisure-time vehicle for displaying upper-middle-class women's proficiency as mothers through their efforts to create "son gods." In another study of neighbourhood baseball, Grasmuck (2005) tracks the clash of "harder" and "softer" versions of masculinity among male coaches in Philadelphia. Carefully delineating the development of "hard masculinity" in youth baseball, Grasmuck also draws attention to the ways in which some boys engage inconspicuously in providing emotional nurturing for their teammates.

My own work shows that child and youth sports are valued by Canadian parents because these are said to keep children "off the streets," out of trouble, and in character-building pastimes (Dyck 2000e, 2002, 2003, 2007). Furthermore, organized sports offer predictable schedules, provide parents with measurable indicators of their children's achievements, and permit children and youths to gain status with their peers and the larger community. In other countries, however, markedly different structures and objectives for child and youth sport exist. Anderson (2008) explicates state-driven purposes for cultivating citizenship in Denmark through sports activities that children attend and take part in without their parents being present. Richards' (1997) account of the use of soccer as a means of social reconstruction in Sierra Leone documents how young people's interest in the game offers a glimmer of hope for socially reintegrating former child soldiers who have returned home from a murderous civil war with blood on their hands. A fundamentally different set of calculations and arrangements prevails in contemporary Britain where, in the wake of the Thatcher government's decimation of publicly funded schools and school sports, there has arisen a system of soccer "academies" and centres of excellence operated by professional soccer clubs and other for-profit entities (Green 2009). Intentionally designed to discover, develop, and commoditize the talents of promising child and youth players, this system sprang up when the state lowered the age at which boys are legally permitted to enter into agreements with professional clubs from the previous minimum of 14 years to 9. What is more, child football prospects can be "traded" between professional clubs and the boys' participation in any other sports activities is controlled by these clubs.[3]

Returning the discussion to North America with these contrasting ways of organizing children's sports in mind, the nature and extent of parents' and other adults' involvement in this sector come into sharper perspective. As part of what Adler and Adler (1994) have categorized as "afterschool" activities, organized sports here has come to be widely viewed and spoken of as an instrumentality for undertaking the "socialization" of children. What is touted as being positive about such arrangements can just as easily be labelled as problematic. So, on the one hand, sport can be fashioned as a source of fitness and health that permits boys and girls to pursue their dreams while it prepares them for the adult world that they will one day enter. It can also be envisioned as a potential source of cultural capital that might ideally even earn accomplished young men and women athletic scholarships to attend college or university (Dyck 2006, 2011). On the other hand, the intensification and virtual "professionalization" of child and youth sports is shown to have cranked up a level of competitiveness that injures young bodies in alarming ways (Sokolove 2008; Hyman 2009). Moreover, by virtue of being adult-controlled activities, organized sports are said to limit children's opportunities to play and discover on their own, thereby steering them away from developing skills of improvisation and self-reliance (Adler and Adler 1994, 325). Finally, in addition to absorbing substantial amounts of children's and parents' leisure time as well as family finances (Trussell 2009), child and youth sports have been charged with being too often tilted towards elite levels of achievement that fully endorse corporate values (Adler and Adler 1994, 324–5). Like beauty, the benefits and defects of community sports lie in the eye of the beholder.

What does seem to be commonly acknowledged in this literature are the ways in which moral values and precepts are so often brought into play within and through child and youth sports. Thus, Fine (1987, 2) notes that adults tend to view Little League Baseball as a distinctly moral activity that trains boys to be outstanding citizens, while McCormack and Chalip (1988) indicate that a reported 96 per cent of Americans in the 1980s believed that sport taught good citizenship and societal values. Reversing the polarity of the alleged moral dimensions of sport, Andrews et al. (1997) identify youth soccer in suburban America as a "family activity" that affords "White" parents with an inconspicuous means for maintaining an informal but effective racial frontier or boundary that "protects" their children's sport participation from "non-White" intruders. Similarly, after conducting a large-scale survey commissioned by Swimming USA, Dukes and Coakley (2002) concluded that the organization's plans to enlarge and diversify participation in competitive swimming might well run up against the preferences of the overwhelmingly middle- and upper-middle class parents in that sport to maintain its relative exclusivity of membership.

To sum up, if child and youth sports are intended to provide safe havens from unregulated public places and streets that children are supposed to be saved or delivered from, then how are these demarcated and carefully supervised spaces to be designed and managed to ensure appropriate continuities between the family home and the shared space of children's sports?[4] Part of the answer for those who seek to promote and manage these activities seems to involve finding ways to smooth over and draw attention away from differences of social class and styles of child rearing (Grasmuck 2005). For those concerned instead to understand why children's sports are configured and pursued in the ways that they are, Anderson (2008) offers sage guidance: we need to keep in mind the possibility that officials' claims about the nature of parents, children, and organized sports activities might tell us less about the actual attributes of parents, children, and sports than about what these are "supposed" to be.

RECRUITING PARENTS TO COMMUNITY SPORTS

Although the rhetoric of community sports steadfastly presents these as being "for the kids," organizers of these activities recognize that children's participation relies upon parental support. This was made explicit in a sidelines discussion between the coach and several of the parents of a six-year-old girls' team that had just finished its last game in an end-of-season soccer tournament. As the only girls' team competing in the youngest age division, the "Eagles"[5] had lost all three of their tournament games. Yet far from being discouraged, the coach and several mothers and fathers were discussing how they might attract more girls to join the local soccer association when the next season rolled around. Entering into the discussion, I commented upon the special attention they were giving to recruiting girls. One of the fathers corrected me immediately, stressing that the deciding factor was, not so much the girls' interest but the willingness of parents to become involved in soccer. To illustrate this, he pointed to his own daughter, a first-year player, who had been "willing but not desperate" to play soccer. Yet she had, he believed, relished playing the sport, a claim that corresponded with my impressions of several of the team's matches during the Eagle's inaugural season.[6] From what I had witnessed, not only had the girls pretty consistently appeared to enjoy taking part in a season of matches during which the Eagles scored but two goals—one of these an own-goal by the opposing team—but also the Eagles' mothers and fathers seemed to have hit it off with one another, coalescing into an effervescent team of their own along the sidelines.

While parental recruitment to community sports is often actively undertaken by coaches and sport officials eager to attract larger numbers of child and youth athletes, mothers and fathers may also collude in their own "conscription" into these, sometimes in ways that come as a surprise even to them. Vicki, a mother of two sons, recalls how she and her husband Steve could not initially imagine themselves becoming sport parents:

> You know, I can remember when we were first married and we had a friend—that was a teacher friend of Steve—and they had kids from between the ages of 6 and 12 at that time and they were really involved in hockey. And I had to think, "How come they put so much time into hockey? They don't have any time for themselves," you know. It was because this was from naïveté. We weren't there, and it was only once you got your own kids—and they've got two *good* kids—and we saw that was because they supported their kids, they were with their kids. And it became, it was very natural when our kids got involved that we were with them, too. And they [the older couple] laughed at us because when their kids got married recently and they said, "We haven't seen you." And I said, "You know where we are. We're on the soccer field. You were at the hockey rink." And [now]

you can see where they were, but we were naïve and didn't know that at the time. And I can remember saying to Steve, "They are always at the hockey arena. They just don't have any time for themselves." But that was where their life was at that time and I can understand that, and my life's with my kids right now. And that's okay.

When parents explain why they support their children's participation in community sports, considerations of safety, security, and healthiness are often raised. Carla, a mother of three, notes that times have changed since she was a child: "You were always down at the park because that's where you went, and everybody was down there, and it was not a big deal. But I wouldn't be all that thrilled about my kids going down to the park and hanging around there now. So times have changed to the point where that's just not feasible any more. It's too bad."[7]

When asked what his two daughters would likely be doing if they were not involved in community sports, Colin replied: "Probably hanging out at the 7–Eleven[8] with the rest of them. You know, you have a tough time keeping them home. If they don't have the outside activities, what are they going to do? I mean, they both like to swim, so summertime's not a problem. They go to the pool or to the beach and stuff like that. But the rest of the time, what do they do?"

Responding to the same question, Marie, a mother of four, replied: "For sure, they'd be hanging out at the mall. You know, watching too much TV and playing too [many computer games]. I really firmly believe ... my husband and I are both active, physically active. I wouldn't say we're slim and trim necessarily, but we're both in fairly good shape, and I really wanted to instill a lifelong belief in being fit. Just a lifestyle of being fit and hopefully this will continue because they are quite fit kids, I think."

Eric, a father of two teenagers explained that, given his children's personalities,

> my daughter would still be with that group that, you know, wanders the
> malls and that sort of thing. My son would be probably sitting around with
> a few guys, playing [computer games]. When he does have spare time,
> that's where his focus goes to ... I don't know what it would be if they
> weren't into sports or in the back yard shooting baskets ... but I guess it
> would be very, sort of, non-active types of roles.

Steve and Vicki conveyed a more specific and worrisome sense of where their sons might spend their leisure time if not involved in community sports: "Which would be hanging around Hasty Market!" (Hasty Market is a neighbourhood convenience store where a teenager had killed another customer the previous summer in a widely publicized incident.) "Or they would be involved with all the wrong kids, doing the wrong things, B&Es⁹ and drugs and all kinds of things ... and then you see what your stress level is!" Bhaskar and his wife, immigrants to Canada from South Asia, had opted to support their sons' involvement in sport for similar reasons:

> We, as parents, got involved with it because, you know, the standard thing
> is that you don't want them to get into fights and this, that and the other.
> And as they grew up, it became very clear ... I'll give you an instance of
> what I mean, why it was important, not simply for them but also for us.
> The transition from Grade 7 to 8¹⁰ has been sort of traumatic for many....
> The one thing that my son said in the first month of him being in Grade
> 8 at the junior high school is that, "Dad, look, all those bigger kids that are
> around me, I'm scared of them and especially if they find you alone in the
> washroom, they'll beat you up. Especially trying to push drugs." That was
> his fear. And he says, "But look"—this is, of course, a bigger school and all
> kinds of new kids ... from other schools that he had not been to—"but,
> you know what dad, there are soccer kids from all over the place. We either
> played with them or against them." And the camaraderie that they felt
> was a protective device, a circle around them, a protective belt, in Grade 8.
> Right off the bat. I was surprised.

As well as being relied upon to keep children safe, active, and out of trouble, community sports also offer parents templates for organizing portions of the time allocated to family life. Community sports present themselves as child-centred activities, and so they are. In addition, they project definitions of what children are, what they need, what they should become, and what parents ought to do so that their children may "turn out all right." Moreover, they provide reasonably predictable schedules of activities and events to fill in family agendas. By enrolling one's son or daughter in a sports club, longer or shorter portions of weeknights and weekends will be organized for parents and children. Because sport practices, competitions, and related events tend to be intensely social occasions, parents and children will meet a variety of people, some of whom they like and some of whom they would not otherwise or willingly seek out in the run of everyday life.

Each community sport setting offers a somewhat familiar but also somewhat distinctive template of times, activities, discourses, characters, and roles. So children and parents may, if they wish, move from one to another, seeking a sport or a team that particularly suits their preferences. There are costs of various sorts to be borne both in joining and staying on in any given community sport, just as there may be larger and smaller social charges incurred in angrily and abruptly quitting or gracefully departing a particular activity. Families may, if they wish, put together an assemblage of community sports for different children or for the same child. Familiar propositions about sports being "good for kids" and about parents being responsible for the development of their children as well as for the apparent success of their families *as families* can be found in most venues of community sports.

Since families are evolving entities, there is recognition on the part of parents of the contingency and temporariness of any given version, stage or iteration of a family. The commitment of parents to family projects potentially reaches beyond simply meeting minimal parental responsibilities to making more ambitious versions of family a key component of their life, identity, and sense of self. Community sports, along with similar forms of non-athletic but organized activities for children, provide a medium not only for organizing key aspects of child rearing but also for sculpting an ongoing project and story about who one is and what one's life is and has been about. The dutiful and appropriate raising of children is a responsibility placed upon parents' shoulders as well as a responsive and malleable medium with which to articulate a sense of personal purpose, comfort, and worth.

For instance, Katherine, a single parent whose son and daughter had completed more than a decade of involvement in a range of community and other sports activities, looked back on these years with satisfaction:

> We were spending time as a family, and that was really important, and that it would never come again.... So all the soccer games and rugby and God knows what else, including the goofy skiing things where everybody ended up in snow banks or whatever, it was actually a fun, positive way to spend time together as a family. And I guess that was my goal.... I don't know how things would have been had their father not left, but there's no way you can talk about that or predict it. But because there were just the three of us, I just thought, "Well, that's okay. Spend time together because there's only a

set number of years to do that and then after that, everyone's busy getting on with their lives and you only get together at predictable times, really".... I really *enjoyed* what they were doing, too. I really enjoyed spending time with them, so I looked at it as sort of an investment in their future and a history that I could look back on with a lot of laughter [*laughs*] and a lot of fun. We met a lot of great people and a lot of different kinds of people.

Parental involvement in sport does not, of course, generate only pleasant memories. Bernie, who had dedicated himself to supporting his sons' sports activities over several years, attributed the failure of his marriage in part to the extent of his and his former spouse's involvement in community sports:

She grew rather negative towards the end of our marriage about the heavy involvement of the family. She felt that most weekends were totally immersed in sports, and we didn't have enough quality time as a family.... She felt our whole free time was immersed around the children's activities and sports, being we'd come home after work, be rushing off to practice. Weekends come, you're off to some sporting events. Specially, the track [and field] was a total commitment of weekend time, a lot. But I looked at it as it's only how many months of the year, right? And we had a lot of months still free. But she took only the negative aspects.... I found a lot of pluses in it. I liked the social aspect of meeting new friends and having my sons, as well as being involved with other children, also being involved with other adults, meeting new adults because when you're going out into the world on your own, you've got to be a social being in order to excel or just to be able to be a member of society. And it teaches them that there are more people around than just their parents and the family to be able to relate to.

Bernie regrets the loss of his marriage but is not inclined to second-guess the importance of time spent with his athletically accomplished sons in a variety of sports.

Likewise for Karen and Chad, the parents of two young sons, community sports stand as prized activities, notwithstanding the demands these make on their time. For instance, football, observes Karen, is a "major family commitment." When their older son first joined the sport, the coach of the team to which he was assigned told Karen and Chad and other mothers and fathers, "If parents aren't willing to volunteer [to assist with the organization of the team and club], take your son[s] and go home. I demand family participation, and if you can't make the commitment, now's your time to back out." As harsh as that sounded to Karen at the time, in due course she came to accept it as not only a condition for her son's involvement in a sport but also an opportunity for family participation:

> It's also a way for us to spend time with them because, from what I've observed, when kids get to be teenagers—and I see it happening now with our older son, just starting—they're ashamed of their parents, they think we're stupid, and they don't want to be around us. So if they want to join track or hockey or football, we all join because we're the people that have to sell the hotdogs and line the field. So like it or not, and they may not like it, but we get to share some of their life where ordinarily they would turn their back and say, "Oh god," you know, "do you want to do that again?" "Can't you do something with your hair, mother?" I can remember doing it to my parents and just leaving them and not wanting to be with them.

Although expectations of parent participation within community sports enable mothers and fathers to become part of their children's leisure-time activities, sometimes both members of a couple may find themselves pressed into service as volunteers. Demands for parental assistance that might seem onerous to some couples may, however, permit others to combine meritorious public participation with conscientious parenting at one and the same time. In such instances, a marriage may be enacted and experienced as a durable, effective, and committed partnership that can be seen to function smoothly in the public venues of community sports as well as, presumably, within the more intimate space shared by a couple.

A GREAT WAY TO MEET PEOPLE

Participating in community sports involves comfortable forms of social interaction that may be attractive to busy parents who live within otherwise anonymous urban and suburban residential areas. While parents will need to make adjustments to their personal schedules, family budgets, and preferred lifestyles to fit their children and themselves into these activities, the choice to do so remains theirs. Above and beyond whatever community sports actually provide for child and youth athletes, becoming involved in these activities furnishes parents with means for framing, performing, and reflecting upon child-rearing and recreational activities. In short, these may assist mothers and fathers to attach themselves to their neighbourhoods and communities in socially manageable and temporally limited ways.

Just as children who are preparing to enrol in a new school may be preoccupied by thoughts of whether this will or will not bestow opportunities to make new friends, so too are mothers and fathers who accompany their sons and daughters into community sports mindful of the social implications of doing so. This is especially the case in relatively mobile urban and suburban communities such as those found in the Lower Mainland of British Columbia into which many parents have recently moved from another part of the province, another province, or another country. Mobility of this sort often leaves couples starting families with few, if any, relatives living in the vicinity of the home they are establishing. The commitment to support a child's entry into one or another community sport, however, puts parents in touch with their counterparts, at least some of whom may be in a similar situation.

For Bob and Norma, who with two sons moved to Canada from Scotland, joining a community baseball team in a suburban neighbourhood afforded boys and parents with a set of social contacts that the couple finds "amazing." For instance, during a trip into Vancouver, Bob and one of his sons stopped at a fast-food restaurant where his son immediately recognized and said "hello" to someone he knew through baseball. According to Norma, her sons have made "lots of friends" through a sport about which neither they nor their parents had initially known anything. Watching from the bleachers, Norma notices that her eldest son when playing an infield position talks to each of the opposing batters that manage to get on base. And, when running the bases himself, "he'd talk to the guy on first base and then he'd talk to the guy on second on the way around." Although Bob's brother and his wife had preceded Bob and Norma to British Columbia, Norma recalled that they had not known anyone else when they arrived there: "But we've made lots of friends through the boys' playing sports. It was good for us as well as it was good for them to meet other kids outside their own classroom. You know, they got to know other people as well, which was good. So that no matter where they go now, they always know somebody. It's been good that way to have them involved." When their younger son was selected to play all-star baseball, Bob remarked, "there goes your vacation this year. You don't get anywhere [else]. It's just constant, it's all the time." Indeed, when relatives arrived from Scotland for a vacation, "they saw every baseball diamond in the

Lower Mainland while they were here, I think. We'd go up Grouse Mountain [a local tourist site] and shoot down for a baseball game."

Dorothy, who had immigrated to Canada from the Antipodes with her then husband, has a somewhat different view of the social dimensions of community sports, regarding this as something primarily for her son. "I like that he makes the social contact with adults who are very different from me and have a different set of values and stuff. And he meets different kids from what he normally would." Indicating that her involvement in her two sons' sports had always been at a high level, Dorothy observed that "even when my ex-husband was home, I took them to the games most of the time.... Now, I go to all the games pretty well, take them to practices." These occasions do, however, allow Dorothy to spend time with some women she met when her boys attended pre-school: "You know, you see the same parents over and over again, and I guess I've become friends with a few of those. But the primary impetus for that friendship was not the sport."

Ivan, a father of four young athletes active in community sports, does not appreciate the manner in which, as he sees it, some parents come to see community sports as a social event for themselves, "and if they have to drag a kid along, so be it." What Ivan and his wife look to community sports for are activities that offer their children a counterbalance to their schoolwork:

Each [of the sports our kids have played] is a non-academic event that we were hoping would encourage them through the period of time when their academics were not as good as they should have been, that they still had this to look forward to in terms of success or in terms of a new set of friends that would rate them differently than their classroom friends would and provide them with a balance. And in large part it has done that. In some cases, [a couple of our children] did extremely well. In academics they did extremely well, in sports they did extremely well, in music, it didn't matter. [For another child], it was a very important thing because they weren't doing well in school and to be recognized in sport was something that was really helpful. And when they didn't seem to need that recognition, sport and all these other things kind of faded in significance. These became an individual exercise, and that's good.... I have no real desire for them to do anything other than something that they would enjoy and that I could also see as being somehow beneficial some way other than just [providing] babysitting. A lot of people I see, they look at this whole set of extracurricular activities as babysitting, as a social club for themselves, something like this. And that's different than what I have in mind.

For Marie and her husband, who grew up in the Greater Vancouver area, children's sports are not a significant source of new friends, although Marie has become friendly with a couple of the mothers of her children's friends. Indeed, she sometimes arranges with these women and with friends from her university days who have similarly aged children to get them onto the same community sport teams. Also born and raised locally, Theresa distinguishes between personal friends and sport friends: "I've made friends [in community sports], but they've never become really close friends. They're just friends that I say are 'sports friends.' But it's different because you still have your own friends. In sports, because the kids, they come and go with the [different] sports, it's not the same."

The use of the notion of "sports friends" to identify relationships developed by parents with the mothers and fathers of other children who are involved in community sports—or by boys and girls to refer to types of personal associations that might arise for them within sporting milieux—can be further illuminated by use of Sansom's (1980) distinction between formal identities and consociate relations.[11] Formal identities, notes Sansom (1980, 138), are evoked in categorical relationships, "when the people said to be 'all the same' are grouped together with reference to their common subscription to a style made up solely of forms for action." Being a parent who is recognized as being involved in a given community sport—if only to the minimal extent of being seen to accompany one's child to a game or competition—makes one eligible to claim or to be accorded such a formal or categorical identity. Consociate identity, in contrast, is constructed "with reference to a person's history of co-participation with others in happenings" (Sansom 1980, 139). Thus, while parents may, through their involvement in sport activities, interact repeatedly with other unnamed sport parents, consociate relationships and identities are formed only when individuals become capable of (1) putting names to known faces and (2) telling stories about mutually shared experiences in the world of community sports. In consequence, parents who participate in community sports may over time develop different types of relationships within this interactional sphere. They may remain situationally co-present but personally distanced from one another; they may begin to know one another on a casual basis; or they may, in the course of "helping out for the kids," form consociate relationships with other parents. In the latter case, consociate parents may come to know quite a lot about one another, even though their dealings may be largely or entirely restricted to the venues and events of a given community sport.

For instance, Bhaskar recalls the challenges and adjustments to his and his wife's approach to parenting that commenced when their sons began to play in a community soccer league:

> We were new to this, not only as parents raising kids—you know, on-the-job training for all of the parents—but also in a country where we didn't quite adapt to the weather as quickly as we did back in the old country. There would be snow and there would be rain and there would be mud and the kids would be playing in there.... And in that context, for instance, the kids getting wet and being exposed to cold and stuff, we worried more than the local parents did. And one of the coaches set us off simply by saying to my wife one day, "Hey, Lady," he said. "My kid is here on the same team, and not only have we done it since we were children, but do you think I would let my kid get sick?"... And he said, "That's the way they've got to get tough. They've got to learn to live with that." Ever since that happened, there was a bonding between the parents....

Far from being merely co-present yet personally distanced from one another or from interacting with one another in a fairly casual manner, this particular mother, father, parent coach, and some of the other parents on that team together experienced the first of a series of "happenings" that became part of their history of co-participation in soccer. It might have ended badly with Bhaskar and his wife feeling that they needed to withdraw their son from this team, but it didn't. Instead, there developed a set of consociate relations between the parents from that team that lasted during the years that the boys continued to play soccer together, relations that Bhaskar speaks of with fondness. Contextually specific but nonetheless strongly felt bonds can, as Bhaskar and others tell us, develop between consociate parents in community sports. The notion of sport friendships need not, therefore, necessarily designate a superficial or inferior form of friendship.[12]

FIGURING OUT HOW TO FIT IN

A demand for parent participation exists within virtually all community sports organizations,[13] although the nature and extent of what is required varies from one team or club to another. A usual minimum is that parents pay necessary registration and competition fees and get their children to and from practices and competitions. In most sports it is also assumed that parents will want to support their children by attending at least some, if not all, of their games and competitions. Much more than this may, however, be expected, frequently in the way of fundraising to support one or another special project or undertaking mounted by an ambitious coach or club officials. In addition to the formal commitments and requirements that may be communicated to parents when they enrol their daughters and sons in these activities, what else do they have to learn to fit themselves comfortably into these activities?

The first time that mothers and fathers attend a beginning-of-the-season parents' meeting that has been called by the coach or manager of the team to which their child has been assigned, they may be taken aback by the quantity and specificity of the information provided them. In addition to familiarizing themselves with game schedules, practice times, and field locations, they will be pressed to volunteer for "jobs" that range from the tedious to the worrisome. What the team or club needs, they are told, are parents who will, among other things take care of team communications (via telephone, email, and/or a team or club website); prepare and distribute sliced oranges for the players at the half-time break;[14] line playing field boundaries with lime, set up and take down goal nets or other competition equipment; act as minor competition officials; or even serve as an assistant coach. Mention might also be made of future fundraising schemes and the need for every family to get behind these "for the kids." While the particulars of the jobs assigned to or taken on by individual parents may differ from one team or sport to another, the expectation that overall responsibility for supporting the team or club falls to the parents is remarkably consistent throughout community sports.

As well as figuring out these formal organizational aspects of community sports, parents must also find a place for themselves alongside the playing fields, swimming pools, or ice rinks where their daughters and sons compete. Parents tend to be left to decide where to locate themselves, what to watch during the ebb and flow of a competition, and how to interact with those standing or sitting nearby.[15] A soccer game, for instance, will feature two halves of reasonably continuous action on a single field of play and last from 60 to 90 minutes or so. In contrast, a track meet can continue for two days and feature long intervals of waiting between events that take place in scattered sections of a stadium and often finish in less than a minute. Working out what is or isn't happening during a meet or a game and what, if anything, to say to the unknown person who has been standing alongside you for the past 20 minutes are small but persistent matters that confront sport parents. Mothers and fathers who are committed to giving their child a chance to play a sport may be little inclined to acknowledge even to themselves that they sometimes find these events not especially entertaining or pleasant occasions. Striking up a conversation about the weather or asking a fellow spectator to identify which child is theirs might just offer momentary relief from the travails of attending community sports events. It might also, in retrospect, turn out to have been a first discursive step towards the establishment of consociate relations.

The ways in which parents—not to mention coaches and child and youth athletes—shape their individual and collective deportment, discussions, and interactions within what might be metaphorically labelled as the "sidelines" of community sports events will be given further attention in subsequent chapters. At this juncture, however, it is important to sketch in some of the underlying features of social spheres that can be experienced and depicted in such differing ways, depending upon the nature of one's engagement with it. To begin with, parents are expected to "step up and help out" with the organization of community sports, but are warned not to "interfere" with the management of these activities. Since the line between helping out and interfering can be difficult to discern, how are understandings about what is and isn't appropriate arrived at in community sports?

Moreover, how is the participation of parents managed and disciplined by coaches and other officials when none of them are obliged to be there? An ethnographic example illustrates some of the ways in which parents may allow themselves to be organized in community sports. The morning after a five-hour Saturday fundraising event that had mustered the attendance of most of the parents and all but one of the members of a 13-year-old girls' soccer team, an extra practice was staged to prepare the team for the resumption of league play. I arrived five minutes before the practice to find only one other car at the field. Nevertheless, between 9:58 and 10:02 a.m., all of the remaining cars that transported girls from several suburban cities to the practice field wheeled into the parking lot. An hour and a half later, when I arrived at the field to pick up my daughter, there were already several parents waiting in their cars and even more of them convened on the running track, alongside the field, waiting for the practice to finish. This was entirely usual, even though it was raining lightly. The only parent who appeared obviously anxious about the practice running over the scheduled hour and a half was Don, who had to be somewhere else almost immediately following this session. He began quietly but clearly to plead, "Come on, Roger [the name of the coach]. I've got some other things to do today." His message was heard but not acknowledged by those assembled on the track, for Roger's wife was standing only two paces away from Don.

I, along with others, had certainly felt the same way on other occasions. Indeed, before the beginning of this practice, one of the mothers had asked Roger, "How long will it be?" to which he had answered initially with a shrug of his shoulders and then an estimate of "about an hour and a half." In fact, it was Roger's style to have frequent practices that also frequently ran over time, as if to underscore the primacy of the action on the field. Don's irritation this day was merely an assertion of what is invariably the case—that parents do, in fact, have other priorities in their lives. What was surprising about Don's impatience that morning was not what he said, or how he said it, or that it raised any lingering problem, for it didn't. What was surprising was that on this team it was so infrequently said. Part of becoming a member of this particular parental "team on the sidelines" was learning to not complain or challenge the working definition for these situations—namely, that practices sometimes have to run longer because what is happening on the field *is* what really matters. Indeed, coming to accept the inconvenience caused by waiting in the rain for the practice to finish might even be likened to a form of parental communion by which parents collectively register their sacrifices and commitment towards their children's involvement in what is jointly confirmed as being an important sport activity. When a parent learns to wait patiently, it signals his/her recognition of both the value of the activity and the merit of one's contribution as a caring parent who helps to make it happen.[16]

Experienced sport parents often take steps to manage scheduling conflicts and to negotiate the extent of their child's involvement in a team or club. For instance, Nigel, the father of an 11-year-old soccer player, approached the coaches of her team to explain that there would be a conflict on Thursday evenings between one of the team's regularly scheduled practices and her choir practices in another community. Noting ironically that, since these were the two things that she enjoyed most, it was almost inevitable that sooner or later they would come into conflict, Nigel deftly suggested that the coaches not paint themselves into a corner by making a concession for one girl that might create problematic precedents with others. In the end, a compromise was reached that satisfied both the coaches and the choirmaster.

When Vicki and Steve were informed that their son had been tentatively selected to play on an elite soccer team, they too moved swiftly to establish their conditions for their son's involvement:

> When Danny was chosen to go on the team and we found out who
> the coach was, we weren't that happy about that because it was not our
> philosophy of what we wanted a coach to be. And so it had to be Danny's
> decision to be in that [team], and that's fine. But before we even allowed
> Danny to know that he was on the team, we phoned the coach and said,
> "We like soccer, but our life does not revolve around soccer. So therefore, if
> it's going to upset you that we're going to say we want to go skiing one day
> and there's a soccer game or there are going to be other times throughout
> the year where he's not going to be available.... But other than that he'll
> be at all practices and all the games that we can get him to and we'll be
> there 100 per cent to support. But there are going to be times when he's
> not going to be there for *valid* reasons. But *our* life does not revolve around
> soccer. And if you know where we're coming from and you still want him
> on your team, that's fine. But he knew that before he even selected him.

The coach in turn replied that he could accept this as long as Danny would be available for all practices and games during the playoffs, a condition that Vicki and Steve readily accepted.

Thelma, a veteran of community sports and other organized activities for children, has hit upon the strategy of pre-emptively offering to be the "50/50 mum"—that is, the mother who sells de facto lottery tickets during a game to parents and other spectators and then splits the proceeds evenly between the team and the winner—to avoid being drafted into more onerous jobs: "I try not to be too organized within the team because I do find that we don't have time to enjoy our family life if you're constantly volunteering. I used to volunteer. Right at the beginning, I volunteered for everything." Similarly, Jim and his wife, Laurie, who had become mainstays of a local track and field club, flabbergasted another member of the club executive when they declared that they would be missing a weekend meet that they had always attended in previous years. Jim matter-of-factly stated that since it was his birthday, Laurie had this year arranged a party for him and a weekend trip out of town. It had obviously never occurred to the executive member he was speaking with that Jim would ever miss this meet. It took her several seconds to process this message.

GRASPING THE DYNAMICS OF PARENTING IN COMMUNITY SPORTS

As noted above, sport parents often compare notes with one another concerning not only how today's community sports for children and youths diverge from those that existed—or didn't exist—during their own childhoods but also how much their experiences and responsibilities of parenting appear to differ from those borne by their mothers and fathers. Some chalk this variance up to having grown up in another part of the world, while others who were born in Canada might attribute it to the particular circumstances of theirs' and their parents' lives. Yet what else might be happening in these discussions? Among other things, exploring differences between childhoods then and now or there and here may enable parents to grasp some of the underlying features and broader implications of contemporary approaches to parenting as well as of their and their children's involvement in community sports. What is more, to trace differences is potentially to entertain alternative ways of imagining the organization of children's sports as well as of parents' lives.

To join a community sport is to enter a space where the personal and the particular encounter the structures and practices of pre-existing teams and clubs, not to mention the rhetoric of contemporary Canadian approaches to child rearing. To account for why and how individual parents choose to accompany their child into these activities requires not only a listing of their reasons for doing so but also an appreciation of the triggering circumstances that led them to do so: for instance, had friends of the parent or the child told them about a particular sport or club? Had the parent played or carefully avoided a particular sport in his/her childhood? The matter of staying in a given sport activity also needs to be considered. Why, how long, against what costs, and in return for which benefits have parents, children, and families remained involved?

Unlike schooling, working for a living, and paying taxes, participation in community sports remains an optional or voluntary undertaking. Some parents and children will join these while others will not. Since community sports are not mandatory, their creation, maintenance, and continuity are not assured but require continuing attention by those who endeavour to organize and lead these. Thus, the structures, operations, objectives, and circumstances of any given community sport are being constantly worked out. These activities continue only if they attract sufficient numbers of parents and children to sustain them. So community sports have to be responsive to some degree, but they also require some degree of durability to escape having to be debated and reinvented every day.

Community sports feature collective forms of participation. What parents and children seek within these are outcomes that satisfy them sufficiently as individuals to keep them coming back. These activities therefore fuel an ongoing practice of self-consciousness and reflexivity about who I am, who my child is, what she/he needs, what we want from this team or club, and are we getting it. There is always potential for friction between the different views and objectives attached to community sports because collective arrangements imperfectly reflect and systematically risk offending individual participants in one respect or another. Yet precisely because community sports are volunteer activities, they may offer a compelling means for the possible realization of strongly held personal ambitions for one's child, one's family, and oneself. Far from producing total identities for either parents or children, community sports operate on a part-time basis as specified components of otherwise complicated lives and scattered relationships. Yet within large-scale, complex, and often anonymous communities, these activities offer means and venues within which individuals and families may seek to fashion senses of belonging that are particularly suited to their tastes.

Finally, it is important to locate community sports within the larger context of locales, fields, and institutions within which children and parents live their lives. Tracing salient differences between the realms of schooling and community sports provides an instructive contrast. Schooling is compulsory and widely viewed as a primary avenue within which children's future lives and prospects are shaped. There is no doubting or ducking the inevitability of schooling. Within this realm, parents function not as equal co-participants but rather as supplicants who must bow to the legal and professional power wielded by teachers, principals, and school boards. Unruly children and parents are subject to disciplinary practices which they may contest, but which they cannot simply choose to opt out of. The labelling of children's behaviour and character and of parents' responsibilities, duties, and shortcomings falls within the purview of educational authorities. One might choose to contest some aspects of the organization of a particular classroom or school, but the cumulative experience of parents in attempting to do so serves to discourage most from venturing in this direction. For the most part parents try to keep their heads down, not least to avoid doing anything that might trigger formal or informal retribution being directed against their child. Schooling is believed to be essential to the current lives and future prospects of children. Yet the capacity of parents to shape the arrangements of their child's schooling is often quite limited. Nor are they allowed much leeway within this realm to demonstrate the efficacy of their efforts and capacities as caring and able parents.

Community sports are so widely sold as being "good for kids" that they might almost seem to be an inevitable and obvious choice for parents to make, but clearly this is not always the case. Some parents, nonetheless, support their children's experimentation with one or another community sport, raising the matter of what attracts them to meet the necessary costs and endure the inconveniences of supporting their child's entry into and continuation with a particular sport or club? In addition to the considerations discussed above, another factor is that community sports not only invite but demand parent participation, thereby creating a space for the conspicuous display of parenting. In these locales, parents are outfitted with ample opportunity to shape activities and arrangements that are believed to be beneficial to the "proper" development of their children as competent and competitive individuals. All of the worry and angst that parents are not encouraged to give vent to with respect to children's schooling can be given full and enthusiastic expression in community sports—at least to the extent that other parents will tolerate this. Yet given that other parents have likely also been drawn to community sports for roughly the same reasons, there is no denying the centrality of parenting and displays of parental care and competence in these venues. What unfolds is the endless contestation and elaboration of various postures, presumptions, and programs for employing community sports and one's own child's engagement in these as a means for attending to the rearing of one's child but also addressing and resolving the doubts and anxieties that parents have about their own responsibilities and capacities as parents.

In subsequent chapters we shall examine other dimensions of the dynamics of parenting in and through community sports. Before doing so, it is necessary to consider the involvement within this overall field of activities of two other sets of participants: the coaches and other officials who lead community sports and the child and youth athletes who perform within these.

NOTES

1 See Rosier and Corsaro (1993) for an ethnographic case study of impoverished African American mothers who, nonetheless, pursue strategies that rather closely resemble the actions attributed by Lareau to middle-class mothers who are engaged in "concerted cultivation" of their children.

2 It is, however, important to keep in mind that parents who reared children in the 1950s and 1960s had themselves lived through years of global depression and world war. Their adult children's retrospective depiction of the post-war period as a time of stability, predictability, and comparatively light child-rearing responsibilities might usefully be adjusted to take account of these frequently overlooked historical circumstances.

3 These arrangements go far beyond the bounds established by Major League Baseball academies established in the Dominican Republic in the late twentieth century. See Klein (1991) for a detailed account of the workings of these baseball academies.

4 I am indebted to Frykman and Löfgren (1987, 271) for helping me to see these issues in this way.

5 The names of teams and clubs have also been replaced with pseudonyms to preserve the confidentiality of players, parents, and sports organizations.

6 I watched these and many other soccer games that season as the father of a teenaged daughter who was refereeing for the first time.

7 In fact, the neighbourhood where Carla raised her children fell within the larger territory where Clifford Olson, a notorious convicted serial child murderer, had been active during the early 1980s, stalking and abducting children. The palpable sense of danger that this cast over the region left many parents fearing what might happen to their children if left unprotected for any period of time.

8 This refers to a local franchise of a convenience store chain that was initially supposed to operate between the hours of 7:00 a.m. and 11:00 p.m. But in this neighbourhood, the 7–Eleven was operating "24/7" thereby creating a late-night point of convergence that attracted teenagers in an otherwise sleepy suburban community.

9 This is an abbreviation for the criminal offence of "break and enter."

10 Bhaskar was referring to a time when Grade 7 marked the end of elementary school and Grade 8 marked the beginning of junior high school in British Columbia.

11 I have also written about formal and consociate relationships in Dyck (1995).

12 See Paine (1969) for an anthropological approach to friendship relations and Amit-Talai (1995) and Wulff (1988) for analyses of the dynamics of friendship among young people.

13 Exceptions sometimes involve local charitable organizations that raise money to support underprivileged children's participation in sport activities and teams operated by these bodies. For instance, the Sun Youth Sport programs in Montreal provide children with league registrations, uniforms, and basic playing equipment, not to mention coaches, managers, and transportation to and from "away" games. In short, organizations such as this one perform the roles and duties otherwise expected of parents in community sports.

14 Often referred to as "being the orange mom," this and some other tasks are often assigned primarily to men or to women. The dreaded "pooper scooper" job—that involves a member of the "home" team ensuring prior to kick-off that inconsiderate dog walkers have not permitted a playing field to be fouled—tends to be assigned to a father.

15 There are, of course, exceptions to this pattern. In California, for example, children's soccer matches tend to shepherd the parents and supporters of competing teams to opposite sides of the field. Parents accompanying visiting teams from British Columbia can expect to be told in no uncertain terms when they have strayed onto the "wrong" side of the field.

16 When the practice finally concluded, I noted that there were eleven cars to pick up thirteen girls. Only two of them had caught rides there with other parents. Overall, there had been a car and a parent—although not necessarily her parent—there for each girl. And all of this to bring the members of this team to an extra practice held the day after a five-hour fundraising event.

Chapter Four

ORGANIZING AND COACHING COMMUNITY SPORTS

DURING THE SECOND HALF of a Sunday afternoon "away" game that had taken my daughter's team to a playing field almost an hour's drive from our home, I was momentarily surprised to recognize Harvey, the president of our local soccer association, standing alongside the sidelines watching the match. Following the final whistle he came over to say "Hi" and explained that he was there to see his daughter's game, which was scheduled to kick off next on the same field. The trip that had brought him there was only a small part of his engagement with soccer that weekend. Both of the boys' teams that he coached had played "home" games on Saturday. On Sunday morning he refereed two matches in a youth tournament staged in yet another community that was a 30-minute drive from his home—in the opposite direction from the journey that had led him to the sidelines where we happened to meet. On my way home, I thought back to a telephone conversation a couple of years earlier when, as a new coach, I had called Harvey to ask about arrangements for the distribution of team uniforms and equipment. His wife answered the telephone and explained that, "No, Harvey is not home." When I asked whether he might be at the association's equipment shed or one of the local fields, she replied, "I don't know where he is at the moment. All I know for certain is that he is somewhere with a soccer ball."

Harvey was a long-time member of the executive committee of the local soccer association, having served previously as a division coordinator and vice-president. In addition to coaching both junior and senior boys' teams and refereeing many games each season, he sat on the district disciplinary committee that convened monthly to review incidents reported by match officials and mete out suspensions to individual players and coaches judged to have acted in an unacceptable manner. Above and beyond these official roles, Harvey had a ubiquitous presence in the local community soccer scene. He attended each of the technical coaching certification training programs for soccer held within the community and shepherded senior coaches from the local association to higher level provincial coaching clinics. At the beginning and end of each season he spent parts of his evenings and weekends at the equipment shed, doling out uniforms, cones, and a bag of soccer balls to each arriving coach or manager and, months later, checking and counting those eventually returned. Although he held a steady job, I never saw Harvey garbed in anything other than either soccer shorts, boots and a T-shirt, or a referee's uniform, or the athletic warm-up pants and jackets favoured in local coaching circles.

Harvey is not presented here as a typical community sports coach or technical official, even though the general features of his profile would be recognized within most local sport circles. What distinguishes him and his counterparts from most other coaches and officials are the prodigious amounts of time that they seasonally and over many years devote to community sports. The roster of coaches, assistant coaches, technical officials, and organizers active in community sports in any given year includes a diverse range of volunteers with differing levels of interest and personal investment in these activities: novices who have only recently and, perhaps, reluctantly taken up their volunteer roles; others who have acquired a few or several years of experience; and those, like Harvey, who over time have become mainstays of an association, club, or sport. Newcomers must be recruited each year in sufficient number to fill the slots left by those who may not have enjoyed their experience of coaching or who may have been actively discouraged from continuing. They take their leave along with parent-coaches who follow their sons or daughters to another sport or out of sports altogether, not to mention those who move from the area or simply decide that by now they have done their bit. Thus, each local sport organization must devise means to cope with the recurring turnover of volunteer coaches and officials as well as of players.

Coaches of most child and youth sports, along with those who hold executive or less exalted positions in local sport organizations, leagues, and sport bodies, do so as unpaid volunteers.[1] Notwithstanding the match fees that he receives as a referee, Harvey, like so many others, is far more likely to expend an appreciable part of his disposable income—not to mention his leisure time—serving as a volunteer coach and official in community sports. This is, of course, above and beyond the considerable amounts of time and money that he and his wife—along with countless other parents—disburse to support their children's participation in community sports.

Parents with children involved in community sports account for the largest proportion of volunteer coaches and officials in this overall sector.[2] What are the fathers and mothers who take that additional step to help out with the training or management of a team or club likely to encounter? To begin with, they will be expected to balance any paternal or maternal concerns about their own child's participation and athletic success with even-handed treatment of other child and youth members of the team or club. Altruism is implicitly and sometimes explicitly demanded, if not always reciprocated by parents who call for it from coaches. Parents who coach learn that their own performances in competitions and even practice sessions will be subjected to assessments by other parents[3] and coaches, not to mention the individual athletes under their charge. All of this, however, occurs within structured competitive sports events designed to create and demarcate winners and losers, outcomes capable of fuelling highly combustible and sometimes combative emotions among both athletes and spectators.

Much, therefore, is asked of and delivered by volunteer coaches and officials, for better or worse. Yet if challenged or criticized, incumbents to these voluntary positions might just offer to turn the reins over to those issuing complaints to "see if you can do any better." Coaches and officials who issue such "offers" may be suspected by those who feel obliged to "either put up or shut up" of shoring up positions of power within a team or organization. These comprise a few of the underlying features and fault lines that run through the coaching and organizing of community sport. Before delving further into these and related matters, it is necessary to specify some of the logistical dimensions of arranging and directing community sport.

ORGANIZING COMMUNITY SPORTS

Spectators at, for example, a hockey or baseball game can't help but notice the officials and coaches who regulate and direct the play of child and youth athletes. In hockey, competition officials include a referee, one or two linesmen, and a timekeeper, while in baseball a home-plate umpire may be assisted by one or more field officials and scorekeepers. The number of officials and the requisite technical qualifications they are expected to hold can vary considerably from one match or sport to another, reflecting the level of competition and the availability of suitable officials. At the earlier age levels in team sports it may be possible for a coach and perhaps one assistant to direct players during matches and practices. While a preliminary count of the officials and coaches present at any given competitive event might suggest that child and youth sports could, in a pinch, be staged with a limited number of such supervisory personnel, in practice the logistical demands of community sports reach far beyond what might be initially apparent at a single game, match, or competition.

Depending upon the individual, a coach might prefer to look after the various administrative tasks that connect a team to a given sport association or league largely on his/her own, but more often coaches opt to appoint a team manager to deal with routine matters. An additional volunteer or two may be drafted to manage communications between the coaching staff, players and their parents, ensuring that competition schedules, venues, and driving instructions that might have to be changed quite suddenly due to inclement weather conditions are made known in a timely and accessible manner. Game-day assistance of various sorts that may be requested of parents is sometimes formulated into continuing positions or roles, and certain parents may be asked to oversee fundraising ventures. Team games that at their most rudimentary level might be played with one coach per team and a single referee can, nonetheless, be rapidly transformed into more institutionally complex undertakings that conscript a range of capacities and resources.

Teams function within local sport associations or clubs that muster any number of squads to compete either in intramural matches or extramurally in leagues made up of teams drawn from other associations or clubs. Allocation of players to teams reflects factors of age, gender, and the competitive capacities of individual athletes. Girls and boys who join a team sport at an early age are likely to be assigned to what are sometimes termed "house" teams or to less structured introductory programs that are supposed to be "recreational" in orientation. These are, in theory, intended to allow young athletes to be introduced to a sport and to play for fun rather than to stress competition and winning.[4]

The organizational structures and operations of local associations and clubs vary from one sport to another, but the similarities tend to outnumber the

differences. Community sports organizations are required to be legally registered entities that possess a constitution, a set of bylaws, and elected officers,
including, for instance, a president, vice-president, treasurer, and secretary.
In addition to these positions, the executive committee or board of a club
may also include a registrar who supervises the enrolment of child and youth
athletes and their registration with provincial and national organizations
that govern each sport; coordinators who oversee the recruitment, vetting,[5]
and assignment of coaches and players to different teams; schedulers who
map out each team's season of fixtures both for house teams and teams that
play in extramural leagues; a head referee or coordinator of technical officials
who recruits and assigns referees or umpires for each game; a coordinator of
facilities who both liaises with local parks and recreation departments and
school board authorities that permit community sports organizations to use
their playing fields, rinks, gymnasia, and pools and then supervises the allocation of these for team games and practices; an equipment manager; and, a
web administrator who manages online communications for the association.
This is by no means an exhaustive list of the types of executive positions to
be found within community sports organizations. Moreover, some of these
positions and functions—notably those of coordinators—may be too onerous
for one person to manage alone, thereby requiring appointment of several of
these officials, each of whom sits on the executive.

Moving beyond team games to sports such as swimming and figure skating
one encounters activities that for the most part involve individual competitors
who take part not in a single match but a range of different types of events and
disciplines. The logistical demands of hosting a track meet, for example, dwarf
those of staging a hockey game. Specialized technical officials are required
to organize a diverse set of events. Running events will require a starter and
starter's assistants to oversee the fair and orderly beginning of races; track
referees to ensure that runners do not stray out of their lanes or interfere
with other competitors; place judges and timers who record the performance
of each competitor in a race; results tabulators who post the results of every
heat and final and maintain these for subsequent tracking of season-long
performances by individual competitors; and a committee to which formal
appeals of results or rulings can be addressed by athletes or parents. Crews
that can quickly and accurately locate and set to the proper height substantial
numbers of hurdles are essential if a meet is not to be unduly delayed by the
tardy setting up and readjustment of the hurdles.

Off the track in the throws,[6] long jump, high jump, and pole-vaulting areas, other sets of specialized technical officials are stationed. Somewhat less skilled volunteers can be enlisted to assist technical officials in measuring and recording the distance of each long and triple jump and raking the sand in the pit before the next competitor takes off. Maintaining an effective mixture of highly skilled, somewhat skilled, and unskilled but willing volunteers can be difficult to achieve. What is required is a cohesive team of proficient and durable personnel who can work quickly enough to permit each young athlete to have his/her prescribed share of attempts in the particular event scheduled for their age and gender categories. Similarly high-jump and pole-vault bars and equipment constantly have to be reset after most jumps and recalibrated as the height attained by competitors moves upwards. The hosts of each track meet must also set up a public address system and appoint an announcer or two who will alert athletes and parents when the marshalling of various events is about to begin, for the schedules established for each event can be overtaken by growing delays that relentlessly extend the length of a meet. The parents of a club hosting a track meet will be expected to work throughout the weekend in one or another capacity, leaving them little opportunity to watch even their own child's events.

Highly qualified technical officials in individual sports, many of whom began to assist with officiating as unskilled, conscripted parent assistants, often remain active as officials after their children have grown up and left home. They, along with other volunteer officials who come into their chosen sport by other routes, are essential to the organizing of community sports. In addition to completing specialized training courses and qualifying at various levels, they must be willing to give up much of their leisure time. Edward, a senior figure skating judge summed up his experience thus:

> Well, some years I have been really active. While I was on the judges committee, it was unreal. I mean, I was on the phone at least two hours a night, every night. And I was out almost every weekend for an entire year. I think there were probably a dozen weekends that I was at home that year.... Sometimes it's only half a day, but your whole day is disrupted. By weekend I mean it would usually be ... about half the time it would be one day on the weekend.... The season doesn't end. It goes on all year, right? We have winter season, ... spring season, ... summer season, and we have fall season. You just keep going year round. It never stops.

Similar to technical officials, coaches in community sports contribute days and weeks of effort to these activities each year. Charlie, the head coach of a minor football team, kept an exact count of the hours that he spent coaching during a season. His log for that year showed a total of 371 hours spent on sundry tasks, including attending league meetings; holding team tryouts; fitting players with equipment; running team practices during the pre-season and season; coaching during regular season and tournament games; and attending the post-season league banquet and team party. Calculated in terms of a 40-hour workweek, Charlie had donated more than 9 weeks of his leisure time to coaching this community football team. Note that this sum does not take into account the coaching clinics that he had attended in previous years, let alone the additional time during this season that he put into planning practices and analyzing game results—vital matters that a committed coach like Charlie can neither neglect nor add up with any degree of precision.

Whether the amounts of time and commitment that Edward and Charlie invest into community sports are characteristic of or exceptional for technical officials and coaches located across Canada must, in the absence of more detailed statistical evidence, remain a matter for speculation. What is unmistakably evident in both cases is the extent of Edward's and Charlie's dedication to sport activities for which they are not paid but to which they are deeply committed. The seriousness with which they pursue their respective participation in their sports does not, however, exist in isolation. It intersects with and in some respects depends upon that shown by others who similarly contribute in one way or another to sustaining community sports. The capacity of community sports established for children and youth to inspire and accommodate such levels of seriousness and passion among some of its adult coaches and officials stands out as one of its more compelling but also sometimes more problematic attributes.

WHAT THEY SAY ABOUT COACHES

Coaches and talk about coaches figure prominently in community sports. The challenges and complexities of the role assigned to them are, to say the least, formidable. Among other things, coaches are expected to teach technical athletic skills, mould teamwork, contribute to the character formation of young players, and judiciously blend a joy of participation in sport with an appreciation of what it takes to win. Manuals distributed at coaching clinics outline the impossibly wide range of expectations attached to this role. How many of the volunteers who attend such clinics could, indeed, ever satisfy all of these? Be that as it may, community sports are first and foremost cultural constructions, so it is worth noting some of the ways in which coaches as individuals and as holders of a familiar type of role may be categorized and discursively depicted.

Fiona, a teenage soccer player, offers what amounts to a typology of the coaches who have tutored her over several seasons:

> I had a couple who I think were involved in it just because their kids were in it and there was a lack of coaches in the area. So they just went into it not knowing a lot about it, but you don't need to know a lot about it at that age anyway because the kids don't know anything about it. They did their best and they were always positive and it was a good experience. And then I got different guys as coaches, and some of them were really into it. Like, one guy came from England ... but he was so good. I kind of expected him to be over-ruling or really aggressive, but he wasn't. He was really good. He was funny. If we made a mistake, he'd just laugh it off: "Oh, you'll do better next time." He was really positive. And I've had coaches that aren't that positive. Like the coach ... who was really smart in soccer but had no concept of how to teach people to do things. Like, if you asked him, "How do you do that?" he'd just go, "You just do it." And he couldn't break things down to show people, and he made people feel really stupid all the time. I don't think he meant to hurt anyone or anything, but just little things he did, you know.... Some coaches are really—they've had too much soccer. They're like soccer Nazis. [When playing for them] you eat, drink, and sleep soccer. You go home and you have your vitamins, and go for your run. Everything you do is supposed to ... [revolve] around soccer. Like, you don't go out, you don't have a social life. You're soccer. That's too much. Like, we're young and we're supposed to live and have fun.

Dorothy, the mother of a son who has played several community sports, focuses on the range and quality of the coaches who have instructed him:

> I think the balance would be in favour of the good coaches. Especially in hockey, I'm really impressed with the way hockey is organized. There seem to be more adults involved, mind you men—they're *always* men. But when Lee started at age nine, he went to something they called "initiation." So they

have a system whereby kids can drop into that sport at almost any age. A neighbour of mine started even later than nine. He was 13. Whereas I have a feeling that in baseball, if a 13-year-old wanted to start playing, it would be almost too late, you know? At that initiation thing that Lee went to there were almost as many adult coaches as there were kids. It wasn't quite that. It was a one to four ratio or something, which was pretty impressive. And just the whole development of skill. But I guess it's Canada's game, eh? . . . This is Lee's fifth season—he's only had one coach who was a bit of a bully, and of course he was much worse with his own son, but that has an influence on the rest of the team. And that's not bad odds, you know.

Carla, who has both coached and served as an association executive member in two sports, views coaching as being about the kids:

I think basically just developing them as people, as competent human beings who are willing to take on anything.... And it's a really big job, and I don't think a lot of people ... [*long pause*] A lot of people, when they get into it, including myself, you don't have any idea that this is what you're really supposed to be doing, you know. They usually go, "Okay, I'll put them on the field, and they'll kick the ball, and then we'll go home." And it's nothing like that. You've been there. I can remember any number of days being out there and lining the field in the rain with a margarine cup because there was no liner. "God this is fun!" But I don't know, one of the things I like is that when I meet any of the kids that I've coached, they always go out of their way to come and say hi and stuff, and that's cool. I really feel good about that because I don't necessarily feel that way about all the adults that dealt with me when I was younger.

These are but three of a virtually bottomless fund of appraisals and commentaries on coaches and coaching that might be dipped into. Nevertheless, what these three cumulatively touch upon are some of the themes that circulate in the everyday discourses about coaches that can be heard or expressed in one or another venue of community sports. At their best, according to Fiona, Dorothy, and Carla, coaches may be depicted as patient and positive instructors who possess differing levels of knowledge about sports. There is also an appreciation of their commitment to do the best job they can, provided this does not lead them to become "bullies" or the counterpart of "soccer Nazis." A different selection of commentators might well suggest other terms for assessing the attributes and capacities of coaches. But working out a master list of the required qualities or a universal job description for sport coaches is not what is being pursued here.

Instead, I wish to highlight the simple fact that everyone who has been involved for even the briefest of periods in one community sport or another—whether as an athlete, parent, coach, or official—will have dealt personally with at least one and likely many more individuals serving in the capacity of coach. In consequence, anyone and everyone in community sports might, if moved to do so, express an opinion or two about what, in their view, constitutes the good, the bad, or the inescapable in community sports coaching, backing these up with first-hand accounts of what they have seen, heard, and experienced. The upshot of this for those who coach community sports is prosaic yet profound. In effect, they accept an exacting set of responsibilities, the performance of which will transpire mostly in the presence of a mixed set of participants and observers who may well hold differing views about what the coach ought to be doing or not doing at any given moment. The wonder is not that so many parents will do almost anything to avoid being pressed into service as a coach but that, against the odds, sufficient numbers of new recruits present themselves for service year after year.

THE CRAFT OF COACHING

For a few years during my time as a youth hockey player the most talked about coach in the community league was an unlikely figure, an American professor of mathematics at the local university who could barely stand up on skates when he took charge of a team of youngsters. Why he began to coach a sport that he had obviously never played in a community that prized hockey above all else was overshadowed by the novelty of watching him conduct practices at the local rink, where most of the boys that he was coaching could literally skate circles around him. The games that his team played also attracted greater attention and commentary than was usual for squads at this level. People were curious to see for themselves this father, who, though having a daughter but no son, had hit upon a then quite unusual approach to coaching: He assigned each player to a forward line or defensive pair, and then rolled out each line and pairing one after another during every game. No matter the score or the time left in a period or game, each of his players shared the same amount of ice time. This approach flew in the face of conventional tactical thinking that dictated that more skilled players needed to get more playing time to optimize a team's chances of competitive success. Against all expectations, the professor's team managed to finish in first place in their age group during each of the two years that he coached. Then, having apparently satisfied the purposes that had initially prompted him to serve as a coach,[7] he quit while ahead, leaving hockey with a short but distinguished record and imprinting upon myself, at least, some inkling that the fair allocation of playing time might not inevitably lead to defeat.

There had, in fact, been something more in the way of a method to the professor's "madness" than had been initially appreciated: He had studied one of the few manuals on the coaching of the game then available.[8] This was, to put it simply, not the preferred approach to coaching in that era, particularly in hockey. Yet flashing forward to today, volunteer coaches in different sports have access to an abundance of instructional resources. Addressing the technical demands of the sport that one is involved in represents one of the primary concerns for new coaches. Those who have previously played or competed in a given sport should be at an advantage when it comes to demonstrating basic skills—such as skating backwards, kicking a ball, or performing a particular swimming stroke properly. An embodied knowledge of how to do something can be sorely taxed by the demands of working out how to transfer this effectively to a novice. Coaches who dedicate themselves to acquiring some of the embodied skills that they did not previously possess may over time combine this effectively with a studiously acquired understanding of strategy and tactics. Volunteer coaches who are keen to enhance their ability to plan training programs and practices and to improve their deployment of athletes in games and competition can, if so inclined, do so. Some community sports coaches voraciously consume coaching clinic materials and technical publications, seek advice from their counterparts, and analyze their own unfolding practical experience to learn about and experiment with new types of drills and modes of instruction.

Coping with the social dimensions of coaching in community sports can be at least as demanding and sometimes even more daunting than acquiring the requisite sport technical knowledge that permits one to work effectively with young athletes. To begin with, coaches are generally expected to maintain a reasonable degree of personal composure as well as to moderate the behaviour of others associated with their team or club during the course of competitive events that can spark mercurial emotions. Stereotypes of boorish coaches, undisciplined children, and out-of-control parents abound both inside and outside of community sports circles, reflecting the ways in which individuals and small groups may sometimes behave inappropriately and insensitively. The line between what is acceptable or unacceptable can be drawn in sharply varying ways. For instance, spouses Karen and Chad hold differing views of the characteristics of some of the men who have coached their sons. According to Karen:

> Some of the coaches who have crossed my path while our kids have
> been playing football I thought have had a very bad attitude. Something
> very sexist, and I thought they were bullies, and that upset me. And I do
> believe the kids, especially when they are playing a contact sport like tackle
> football, have to know how to tackle and block and hit the right way so you
> don't get hurt. But I don't think they have to be humiliated when after 20
> or 30 or 100 times, they still can't do it right. Not for lack of wanting. It's
> for something else that's missing. Maybe they're a klutz or who knows, but
> I don't think they have to be told they run like a girl.

Shifting the conversation to the case of a particular coach, Chad takes a somewhat different tack in his assessment:

> Yet he was the best fundamental instructor that anybody's ever seen. I mean,
> he could teach the kids exactly what to do in a drill. He might yell at them,
> "No, that's not the way to do it—this is the way to do it." You know, if you
> show them 50 times, eventually they learn how to do it and everybody on his
> team knew how to do all the drills, knew how to do all the hits. Those kids
> are really good football players now. There were a few things that grated upon
> people, the way he coached the kids. But in a game, this guy could see the
> whole field. He could see every player, what they were doing, and he didn't
> have to wait four times for … [an opposing team] to score a touchdown
> around the weak end or something [before making a tactical adjustment].
> I mean it was instant. An amazing head for the game.

At which point Karen pipes in:

> But he was belligerent, and [*turning to Chad*], for your information, he
> was given the heave-ho last year. The executive members from the other
> communities, the [league], and everybody, mid-season [said], "Get that guy
> out or we're not allowing your team to play."

Neil, an experienced youth soccer coach, explains that he has generally been fortunate to work mostly with parents who attend games and applaud the team, win or lose:

> That's a real bonus as far as I am concerned. The negative aspect is where you have a parent who wants to voice his opinion of how the game is going, the way the game is being coached, to everyone because somehow that is important to him. And I appreciate it's important for the parent to do that. However, that's a negative thing in my mind, and I always make sure that the parent knows that. And it can be … a parent can swear and yell and scream and that type of thing. And if they want to do that in their house, I mean, you can do that in your house. But you come onto the soccer pitch, and I look after that environment for the child and for the parents, and there are rules that you don't step across the line.

Another challenge for parent-coaches who have a son or daughter on their team is that of working out how to proceed, all the while knowing that other parents may be watching closely for any indication that the coach's kid might be receiving preferential treatment. Indeed, the frequency with which concerns about fairness or bias arise in discussions of community sports speaks to the prevalence of parent-coaches in this sector and the perceived potential for a conflict of interest on their part. Ivan, a parent of three young athletes who respectively play soccer, ringette, and hockey, wonders whether parents should be allowed to coach their own children:

> We've had examples where the coach's kid could do anything and get away with it, and we've had examples where the coach's kid could not be a kid … they were just stomped on every time that they got out of line. By the coach because he expected more of his kid than he expected of anyone else. At the same time, when you review the commitment in time, could they afford to be a parent *and* a coach and not hopefully double up on some of the travelling and attending games and things like that? So that's one of the things that I don't have the answer to, but it's sure a tough thing. I know that the best coaches we've seen in hockey are people that have coached at much higher levels as well as older ages and then [return to] coaching younger kids. They are the best coaches in terms of skill, in knowing what's likely to be a useful drill. The worst coaches in terms of skill are those that are coaching their kids and taking whatever skill coaching level classes [that] are necessary to

coach their kid. In terms of drills, etc., they're just lost. They know as much as the kids know. But that's not a complete waste because sometimes they just really like kids and they play them in a way that the kids enjoy. So it's not a total loss skill-wise. The worst combination is when a coach thinks he knows something [about the sport] but doesn't and is basically there to look after his kid. That's the worst combination, and however that is eliminated, that's going to make sport a much more enjoyable thing.

Other questions that might be added to those formulated by Ivan concern the "career" paths of these more experienced—and, thereby, presumably older—volunteer coaches who may eventually opt to coach younger kids. How many of these individuals, one wonders, started as parent coaches who accompanied a son or daughter up the age and skill levels and then opted to remain in community sports when their child or children grew out of these? Might not these now experienced and knowledgeable coaches, who are deemed impartial precisely because they no longer have a child on the team, possibly have run the gauntlet of acquiring on-the-job training under intense parental scrutiny in earlier years?

Athletes who are coached by their parent often report being held by him/her to higher standards than are their teammates. They may or may not appreciate this or other aspects of playing under the direct tutelage of mom or dad. Michelle, a softball pitcher who has been coached as a child and youth player by her father, reports that:

My dad and I are very close, so it hasn't been a problem at all. Like, he usually asks me things ... and I kind of tell him, you know, kind of apart from the team to try to make things better. As for other players on other teams, it's never been a problem. But you get more problems from your own players usually because if he does something that they don't like, they take it out on me usually. Or they used to when we were younger. So then it could be hard.

Only one teammate had ever accused Michelle of being favoured by her father:

I was always there before practice. Like, I made sure I worked harder so that could never be said, and I always did my job so that could never be said. But we did, for one year, this girl and I, we were on the same team for quite a few years and then all of a sudden she thought that he was

favouring me, putting me in games so I could win awards and not her.…
But then everyone else on the team stood up for me and not for her.

Marshall, who had been an accomplished athlete in his own right, has gone on to have considerable success as a community sports coach, even though he was initially reluctant to coach at this level. What prompted him to do so was the "absolutely just pitiful" coaching that his sons were receiving in community sports. To ensure that both of his sons will have the benefit of his coaching expertise, Marshall alternates coaching football and baseball between the two age levels at which his sons compete:

So what I'll do is switch between the boys' teams, type of thing. So the
one kid will go through a really just horrible year for coaching and I'll
coach the other boy. And [the next year] I'll come back and coach the
other kid.… Some years I've done two, I've done two baseball teams.…
It was just so badly done that if I didn't step in and do something, then
the kids would have really a poor experience because you don't get to play
forever and you're only young once, so what I did was come into help out
to ensure they have a good and positive experience while they're still young
[*laughing*]. As soon as they're out of Grade 12, then I can go play golf.

The circumstances that permit a coach like Marshall to pick which teams he will guide in a given year are not always available to parent coaches. What is more, the competitive levels at which a given child athlete and her/his parent coach are best suited to perform might not always coincide. Speaking of her youngest daughter, Carla notes that "She was a good player, but I think the problem was that I was coaching a team that was a level above her abilities and that ruined it for her. Up to that point, I think she really enjoyed what she was doing."

The widespread reliance upon parent-coaches and officials in community sports augments the frequency of awkward situations and strained relation-ships between coaches, parents, children, and sport associations. While these may be handled more or less efficaciously within a particular organization, team, or family, the demands of doing so and the likelihood of such attempts falling somewhat short of satisfying all concerned never entirely disappear. In fact, these and other complications are just as likely to be exacerbated by other characteristics or properties of community sports.

MANAGING FUN AND GAMES

Although community sports for children and youths are meant to afford them enjoyment, realizing these hopes depends upon the investment of some measure of seriousness by the athletes, coaches, and officials who take part in these activities.[9] What is minimally required is at least passive acceptance of the rules and conventions of a given sport. Thereafter, the relative weighting assigned to fun and to serious endeavour in community sports becomes a matter for interpretation and negotiation from one sport, age group, or level of competition to another. Coaches and officials, who are structurally charged with managing games and competitions, are never far removed from differences of opinion sparked by these issues.

It tends to be assumed within community sports that fun and serious athletic endeavour ought to complement one another. Yet the ways in which fun and seriousness are defined and pursued in particular settings reflect diverging viewpoints and complicated organizational settings that can easily engender disagreement. Parents sometimes act as though what the kids are doing on the field of play is not in the end all that important. Cute, perhaps, a source of healthy exercise and fun, it is to be hoped. Accordingly, a son's or a daughter's effort and determination may be celebrated, even in the midst of registering a last place finish or chalking up another losing season. Not many parents and adults take this approach all of the time. The alternative stance values the manner in which community sports challenge children to develop the self-discipline and determination needed to acquire embodied skills and to attain results that might initially have seemed far beyond their grasp. Yet applying this approach too vigorously to young children can lead to adults being chided for being excessively serious about athletic performances and results.

At the beginning levels of boys' and girls' participation in community sports, parents are more likely to endorse the notion that children possess a natural need for and affinity to unadulterated forms of fun. Additional commentary on these matters is sometimes prefaced by references to dictums about the social and physical capacities of children at different ages and stages. This may not produce much in the way of agreement about, for instance, what it is that a 10-year-old might be expected to understand or be capable of accomplishing in comparison with a 7-year-old or a teenager. Thus, diverging notions about the "normal" stages and signs of child development—as well as about what constitutes fun and appropriate seriousness and how these ought to be blended—regularly collide in community sports. Striking a workable balance between what parents, on the one hand, want community sports to be and to do for their children and, on the other, what boys or girls seek out or will no longer tolerate comprises an ongoing concern for coaches and sport organization officials.

Ironically, adults' contributions to and involvement in community sports are from the outset accepted as serious matters, no matter how light heartedly these might sometimes be spoken of or enacted. Mothers and fathers are not permitted to play fast and loose with their sons' and daughters' safety or upbringing, but neither are they supposed to let their own earnestness about these matters unduly impede the anticipated fun and flow of children's sport activities. There is also ongoing surveillance and discussion of the manner in which coaches and officials handle games and practices and interact with athletes and other participants in community sports. Assessments of whether a coach takes a game or a sport too seriously or not seriously enough abound within this sector. According to Chuck, a long-time coach and executive member of two local sport organizations, sport becomes a serious matter when the results of competition are acknowledged and recorded:

> When you keep a score—I don't care what the sport is—when you keep score, you have competition. I mean, that's reality. I think they [child and youth athletes] like the competition. I think they ... like to win, but they tend to stay in if the competition is fairly even. Nobody likes to get blown out week after week.... So the skills are important and bad coaching in any sport, I think, does not bode well for a sport. Kids—the ones who are serious about it—pick that up *real* quick. Very young, they don't know. Let's face it, in amateur sport you're dealing with mums and dads who step forward and say, "I'll help out, hey." And in the [executive] positions I've gone through in clubs, we really appreciate that. But the kids, when they get a bit older, start to pick out the expertise or lack of it, and that's important to them.

The management of competition in community sports can be addressed in varying ways. Some involve the scaling down of the size of fields, the number of players, and the length of games, while others dispense with the keeping of match scores at the earliest levels of participation. Team sports are, however, designed to deliver relatively clear-cut results in the form of goals, assists, runs, and touchdowns that produce wins, draws, and losses. League tables record the comparative standings of different teams. Non-team or individual sports tend to measure results attained, for instance, in running, swimming, or figure skating competitions with even greater detail with respect to times, distances, or points awarded for different elements of a performance. Hence, individual sports offer athletes the opportunity to compete against not only other athletes but also their own previous results. Coming in last in a race heat can, in consequence, still be counted as an achievement if the time recorded by the individual athlete represents a personal best.

Another means for managing competition in sports is to divide players and teams according to their levels of athletic proficiency, thereby increasing the chances that their opponents will be neither too far above nor below them in terms of playing ability. Less accomplished players, teams, and leagues may be labelled as recreational ones. More highly rated athletes are then streamed into what may be referred to as competitive tiers that are further scaled in terms of numbers, letters, or colours (i.e., gold, silver, and bronze). At the point that formal streaming occurs in a sport, the debate concerning the relative importance of fun and serious competition often enters a new phase where, in effect, children and parents are expected to choose between one or the other. To accept the offer of a place on a team in a more highly ranked competitive division opens young athletes, parents, and coaches to a presumption that they have taken on board the need to participate henceforth in more serious and demanding ways. This, it is commonly said, leaves those who are not selected or who choose to compete in lower, recreational divisions without the pressures, demands, and often unequal amounts of playing time associated with higher levels of competition. In fact, the approaches applied in higher-level teams tend to spill out of these elite levels of competition and into so-called recreational divisions, not to mention those for younger age groups that are supposed to still be playing just for fun. The naming of different levels of competition does not end debates about how it should be managed in community sports. Nor does it resolve the potentially differing ambitions and expectations of the athletes, parents, and coaches assigned to one or another team.

A GOOD COACH

Summing up the qualities and capacities discursively attributed to good coaches in community sports is neither a particularly difficult nor novel undertaking. He/she should, of course, possess a level of technical and athletic expertise suitable to the needs of the boys and girls being coached. A person like this should enjoy working with children, know what matters to them, and transmit a deeply held love of the sport or game to which young athletes are being introduced. Such a coach is typically a patient and perceptive being who, nonetheless, has the knack of knowing just when and how to motivate athletes to higher and more enjoyable levels of performance. A good coach is a fair and reliable individual who puts the interests of child and youth athletes ahead of her/his own. An accomplished leader of children and adults, a good coach is rarely upset by the vicissitudes of action on and off the fields of play. He/she will manage competition with aplomb, consistently exhibit sportsmanship, but never take him/herself too seriously. Last, but no means least, a good coach demonstrates the superiority of her/his capacities by establishing over time a winning record in directing a team or club and developing outstanding athletes. Men and women possessing these qualities and abilities are exactly the type of coach yearned for in community sports.

Not surprisingly, individuals, who actually serve as coaches in local sport associations, more often than not tend to fall short, in someone's estimation, of satisfying these lofty ideals. A set of well-worn labels is handed down from one generation of community sports participants to the next to attach to coaches and sport officials, characteristically behind their backs. These include the "nice guy who just doesn't have what it takes"; the man or woman who is "just too intense"; the coach who makes the mistake of "trying to suit everybody"; and, the club official who "doesn't get it and won't listen to anyone." These highlight perceived imperfections on the part of coaches and officials that might provoke a bit of discussion but which don't necessarily prompt further action. More seriously regarded issues involve coaches and officials acting in ways claimed to be inconsistent with the purposes and practices of community sports. A parent coach who is deemed to be running a team solely as an instrument for developing and showcasing the talents of his/her child alone might be subjected to more robust forms of criticism that might or might not lead to him/her being superseded by another coach the following season. So, too, are coaches who are observed to be involved in community sports, as one parent puts it, "not for the kids but because they want to be the coach of a team that's won something."

The categorical ambivalence parents sometimes express concerning coaches and sport officials can be reciprocated by these figures, even though the majority are themselves parents. A humorous suggestion that drew enthusiastic applause at one of the first coaching clinics that I attended was that it should not be kids but parents who should be required to try out before being selected for teams. Norm, a seasoned and extremely successful hockey coach (whose son also plays community sports), expresses his reservations about parents in blunter terms:

> In all honesty, I don't like parents at all. I have no use for parents. I have very few friends who are parents. The reason being I have lost a lot of friends over the years. Right now, in this team, I have two families that I would consider social friends. I know a lot of people, and we may go over for a drink or something, but there's only two families who are friends. Some day I may have to cut those boys from the team, and all of a sudden those parents aren't your friends anymore.

Norm's criticisms reach beyond parents to coaches and officials who are, he believes, too often involved in community sports for themselves:

> It's a vehicle for a bunch of adults to control a particular program, and the kids are secondary. The adults seem to come first. The adult rules, the adults totally dominate the kids, totally. The kids have *nothing* to say about the game. They have no say as to where they play or what level they play. They're, in a lot of cases, forced to play at a higher level where they may not be able to enjoy it.

Norm recalls raising these concerns during his tenure as president of the local hockey association: "I said, 'We've had three meetings in a row now.... Not once have we ever talked about a child. Not once. Nobody's mentioned children.' It was always jerseys or the [fundraising] dance or something else, you know."

To sum up, the workings of community sports reflect the reliance of local sport organizations upon volunteer coaches and officials who not only take on demanding roles but in doing so also become objects for continuing scrutiny. They become, by fits and starts, the recipients of appreciation, disapproval, and sometimes both coming from different directions at the same time. Discourses about how coaches and sport officials in general ought to perform their duties are regularly invoked by parents and fellow coaches as a prelude to more detailed and kindly or uncompromising assessments of the performance of particular incumbents to these roles. They are, undeniably, central figures in community sports. They are not, however, all-powerful or alone in shaping the form and tone of these activities. The interests and purposes of parents and governments with respect to the broader field of community sports have, of course, been introduced in previous chapters. The next step is to introduce the children and youths for whom community sports are constructed with such care and contention by adults. They, like parents and coaches, play a more complicated part in these processes than the pre-existing structures and discourses of community sports tend to acknowledge.

NOTES

1 In certain community sports, such as swimming, student coaches are paid for their services, and incomes are beginning to be earned by as yet relatively small numbers of specialist coaches in recently developed, commercially oriented development centres that cater to various sports.

2 Coaches who have a child on the team or in the club they are in charge of are most often encountered at the earlier levels of community sports. I am not, however, aware of records being kept about the proportion of parent-coaches involved in given sports, let alone the incidence of parents who coach a team on which their child plays or an event in which their child competes. The lack of statistical information about these matters belies their practical significance and divisiveness within community sports.

3 Some local sport associations now ask parents to complete online evaluation forms that allow them to assess coaches according to a five-point scale that ranges from poor to excellent. Specifically, parents may be asked to rate matters such as the level of improvement made by your child this season; your child's level of satisfaction playing for his/her team; your level of satisfaction with the level of coaching/training received by your child; the effectiveness of your child's practice sessions; the fairness of allocation of playing time on your child's team; the level of interest your coach shows in your child's welfare and development; your relationship with your child's coach; your child's relationship with their coach; and, your overall rating for this coach.

4 Although these are usually intramural teams, they may also take part in occasional tournaments or festivals that include teams from other associations.

5 Over the past decade sport organizations in Canada have given increasing attention to guarding against suspected pedophiles and persons with criminal records being placed in charge of child and youth athletes. Prospective youth soccer coaches in British Columbia are now required to report with identity

documents to their local police detachment in order to undergo a criminal records check—which may include being finger printed—prior to having their applications considered.

6 This refers to the caged venues for events in discus, shot, javelin, and, sometimes in older age categories, the hammer throw.

7 According to my father, who befriended the professor, he had been attracted to immigrate to Saskatchewan by the political program set for the province by the Cooperative Commonwealth Federation government of T.C. Douglas. Shortly after arriving in our neighbourhood, he became active in the local community association, learned about a shortage of hockey coaches, and offered his services.

8 Again, my source on this was my father. I have often wondered whether the book might have been Lloyd Percival's book *The Hockey Handbook* (1992). This work— first published in 1951—was widely rejected by then-leading Canadian hockey commentators as being "the product of a three-year-old mind" but was credited by a leading Russian coach as having introduced them to the mysteries of Canadian hockey.

9 See Dyck (2000d) for a discussion of the manner in which seriousness is seen to inflect games, bodies, celebrations, and boundaries in anthropological treatments of sport. See also Podlog (2002) for an astute assessment of the seriousness invested into reckoning matters of "success" and "failure" in athletic undertakings.

Chapter Five

BECOMING ATHLETES
AND PLAYERS

DURING DINNER WITH A coach from another district and his family following a weekend of sport, I outlined the objectives of the study I was conducting on community sports. This prompted discussion around the table with enthusiastic participation on the part of the hosts' athletically active children. Picking up on my interest in the relationships and social arrangements that figure within community sports, Norah, a 12-year-old, reported that while she was regularly singled out and praised for being a "hard worker" by her coach, other kids could go weeks without getting any recognition. This, she noted, was "just so unfair." Britney, age 16, mentioned that boys' soccer seems to offer more prestige and status for individual players than is the case for girls' soccer. For her, soccer had always been a game that she plays rather than one she watches on television, but she suspected that this was not necessarily the case for boys. Out of this impromptu colloquium came agreement about the importance of talking with kids about their experiences in sport, as we had done that evening. Britney capped the discussion with a claim that cut to the heart of a previously unmentioned yet crucial aspect of the matters that we had been addressing: surveys of kids, she claimed, could never capture exactly what kids think because kids are so practised in figuring out and responding to what adults do and don't want to hear.

I was initially struck by how infrequently discussion, let alone endorsement, of this possibility seemed to arise in adults' conversations about community sports.[1] What, indeed, would be the implication of adults admitting to themselves that what they might like to believe and declare that they are doing for girls and boys might rest upon less than transparent readings of what children and youths might actually want from and feel about these sport activities? Yet when I rummaged through recollected conversations and listened carefully to new ones in the coming weeks and months, I began to identify comments that displayed signs of uncertainty on the part of various adults concerning what in fact motivated a son, a daughter, or a team member to do or not do something in a given situation. Moreover, attempts to clarify these matters often brought forth sparse and opaque explanations from kids frustrating adult interrogators who may suspect they are being kept at arm's-length from what the kid in question really thinks about a particular activity, event, or relationship. Evidently, children and youths may sometimes be more difficult to read and less eminently knowable by adults than might be presumed by those who leap to apply either developmental frameworks or "simple common sense" to explain kids' behaviours.

The point of taking these matters onboard is not to lobby for the reclassification of children and youths as though they had suddenly and mysteriously been revealed to be inscrutable figures that adults—just because they are adults—can never truly comprehend. It is instead to acknowledge how conventional modes of thinking about childhood and youth, along with the unexamined everyday practices that spring from these, serve to complicate and in some respects obscure relations between actual children and adults.[2] If we take seriously Britney's line of reasoning, then girls and boys need to be recognized as close observers of what various adults might want and expect from them as children as well as skilled social actors in their own right. Viewing children and youths from this perspective offers respite from hackneyed suppositions concerning either the inherent innocence and naïveté of the young or, at the other end of the spectrum, their mooted capacity to act unconscionably on occasion owing to their alleged immaturity.

In short, it involves giving ourselves analytical permission to consider persons who happen to be children, youths, or adults not solely in terms of their age or as stereotypical representatives of different age categories but also as individuals. Envisioned in this manner, any of us might be seen to differ from or to resemble those who are older, younger, or roughly the same age as us in various ways. In everyday life, of course, no one can entirely escape the social roles and expectations assigned on the basis of our age. Yet by allowing for the possibility that there might sometimes be a gap between, on the one hand, the imputed nature and presumed abilities of members of different age categories and, on the other, the manifest capacities of individuals regardless of their age, we will be better prepared to trace the ways in which children as well as—and in conjunction with—adults seek to negotiate our respective involvements in childhood, adulthood, or parenthood. In practical terms, this involves approaching children, youths, and adults in roughly the same manner: that is, by treating each person as a social actor whose particular circumstances, practices, relationships, and interests should not be assumed in advance as a function of her/his age status but instead deemed as matters yet to be ethnographically determined.[3]

ENTERING THE FIELD

To show how and why kids play more intricate parts in community sports than is commonly appreciated, we need to review certain underlying facets of their involvement in this field. The first is that children's and youths' engagement in community sports serves to connect them closely to adults, and, thereby, to subject them to the implicit conditions attached by parents and coaches to their support of and involvement in these activities. Unlike street sports that can be improvised by and for kids when and as they please (provided that they can find accessible spaces for these), community sports reflect the schedules and priorities of adults who in combination have access to financial, transportation, and bureaucratic resources that dwarf those that might be tapped into by children and youths on their own. In effect, kids who play community sports are almost as closely bound to one or another set of adults as is a participant in a three-legged race where two partners have one leg of each tied together and one "free" to run with. To move forward at any speed it is necessary to have a good understanding of your partner's movements and wishes, especially if he/she happens to be the larger and more powerful member of the pair.

A second noteworthy dimension of community sports is the manner in which these bring together elements of relationships, activities, and purposes drawn from other social and institutional settings, including family life, schools, workplaces, and professional sports arenas. As a result, the spaces within which community sports are organized and staged must accommodate a mix of not always readily reconcilable objectives and ways of doing things. Which particular goals and intentions ought to take precedence at any given juncture remains an open matter: should it be the patient nurturing of children; the systematic transfer of key skills; the inculcation of disciplined work habits; or the need to place competitive success above all else? In an ideal world, all of these might, perhaps, be seamlessly arranged to complement one another. The logistics of community sports tend sooner or later to pit adult champions of differing priorities against one another. Tracking incipient disputes between adults and moving either to seek shelter from the ensuing fallout or possibly to take advantage of and to leverage these conflicts to advance their own selected interests falls within the observed social competencies of girls and boys.

A third point is that while community sports attract participation by many children in Canada, they also indirectly affect, for better or worse, a far wider range of boys and girls than are depicted in television commercials that celebrate the stereotypical beneficence and "naturalness" of child and youth sports.[4] Sport organizers are proud to draw attention to the fact that boys and girls who join community sports possess differing body types and come from a broad spectrum of social backgrounds. Having proclaimed the heterogeneity of the children drawn to these activities, there is thereafter a marked tendency to speak less of differences between them and more about what it is claimed that "every kid needs." It is almost as if community sports constituted a sort of melting pot into which youthful "immigrants" from all corners of the community are welcomed only to be recast and poured into the standardized protocols of what it is believed that a child or youth athlete must surely want to do and to be.[5] The attractions to sport organizers of this "one size really *ought* to fit all" approach are obvious. Officials' inclination to speak and act as though this must be the case does not, in fact, obviate critical differences between what different children may seek and, in consequence, experience within this field.

What attracts "natural" athletes to community sports or encourages those deemed to be "star" players to remain in these long after others may have elected to quit is not, as we shall see later in this chapter, invariably pursued or shared by all their teammates. Nor do the younger siblings of athletes automatically or unquestioningly accompany a brother or sister into a particular sport or, for that matter, into sport at all. Alongside the many children in Canada who simply cannot afford to participate in community sports stand a substantial if uncounted number of sport "avoiders" who for various reasons may have little or no interest in joining in. Recognizing the aversion to sport expressed by some children who steadfastly avoid these activities as well as the degrees of ambivalence held by some others who participate in community sports usefully grounds otherwise oversimplified depictions of the nature of both kids and sports. It counsels the need for caution when assessing claims premised upon the frequently professed conviction that kids are for most essential purposes "all the same."

Blanket claims about children's "obvious" affinity for sports tend to focus on moments when young athletes seem thrilled to be involved with one or another sporting activity.[6] In practice many athletically involved children experiment with a range of sport activities over a period of years, some of which they may like and play for several seasons and others that they might try out for a while but subsequently abandon. A given girl or boy might, accordingly, offer equally vivid accounts of both what they love and hate about sports, depending upon which sport in which year they are discussing. Children who become involved in sports often accumulate larger and more varied bodies of experience within sport activities than might occur to the adults who design the operations of a particular team or club on the basis of their preferred models of what the "average" child or youth athlete most likely wants. Kids' cumulatively acquired insights into the differing ways in which sports may be organized and how individual adults are likely to respond to various situations also affords them an increasingly informed sense of how they might endeavour to affect some of the conditions of their involvement in community sports.

Determining what any given kid might want from community sports is not, therefore, a simple matter. In fact, individual kids might want different things from one or another sport played in a particular time and place, including the right to avoid having this or that sport impinge too forcefully into their lives unless they wish this to be the case. Furthermore, what boys or girls want from a selected sport or from sports in general can shift over time, reflecting changing circumstances within their own lives as well as those of their families or communities.

GETTING INTO THE GAME

It is useful to take stock of the assorted preconditions that attend children's entry into and continued participation within community sports. More than a few young athletes recall having been enrolled by their mother or father in one or another sport without much, if any, consultation. Others report having had to lobby diligently to obtain parental support to join a team or club first heard about from friends. Over and above a child's demonstrated interest in or mere biddability with respect to community sports stand the financial costs, transportation requirements, and legal arrangements that must be met on their behalf by parents or other adults. Getting into community sports is not something that children can decide upon and accomplish entirely on their own. Yet no matter how they come to be enrolled in a club or team, once in they are obliged to accommodate themselves to the arrangements they encounter, or take steps that might make their participation in these activities more acceptable, or find some way to extricate themselves from this undertaking.

Becoming a child or youth athlete exposes girls and boys to a succession of physical challenges and social demands that may be experienced rather differently by those setting and those charged with meeting these conditions and expectations. For instance, novice baseball players are expected to learn not only how to throw, catch, and hit the ball with some degree of proficiency but also how to cope with the ever-present possibility of being struck by the ball, a bat, or another player during the course of play. Likewise, in addition to familiarizing themselves with the rules and routine plays of baseball, players are called upon to heed intermittent exhortations from coaches and spectators to "keep your head in the game" during extended periods when nothing much may be happening around them. The sudden arrival of a sharply hit or errantly thrown ball in one's sector of the diamond or outfield can instantly attract the scrutiny of coaches, spectators, and teammates. Depending upon one's level of concentration at that moment, a player may be disparaged for having been "caught napping" or celebrated for "staying sharp."

While community sports can engender excitement and a sense of accomplishment among children, there are also occasions when the pressure of performing up to the expectations laid down by coaches, parents, or other spectators can be a harrowing matter for young athletes. One of the more extreme examples of this that I have observed involved an eight-year-old soccer player who came under loud and sustained criticism from his coach and teammates for missing a tackle on an opposing player. After several moments of being berated he suddenly let out a long and piercing scream that continued as he ran off the field. He didn't stop running or crying when he reached the far sideline. Nor did he ever again turn up to play for this team, as I discovered later.

Interspersed with the fun and games that are associated with child and youth sports are underlying competitive structures and purposes that inject a degree of seriousness into these activities. Girls and boys who join community sports discover that along with repetitive practice drills that are meant to enhance their playing skills come public direction, correction, and commentary by coaches and other onlookers. What is said to child and youth athletes during games and competitions can cover the gamut from the purely technical (i.e., "Be sure to mark the fullback on the overlap") to the motivational (i.e., "Come on, you can do it!") to criticism or praise of an athlete's or a teams' performance. As athletes work their way up the competitive ranks of their preferred sports, they will increasingly be required to try out or qualify for selection to higher level teams or competitions. Since such tryouts or trials are designed to attract more athletes than there will be places for, there is inevitably disappointment for some of them. The prospect of not merely being dropped from a select team to which a boy or girl may have belonged for a year or more but also of becoming an object of gossip in kids' and adults' conversations within sporting circles stands as one of the more miserable experiences that an athlete can endure.

Those selected to an elite team or squad may, nonetheless, discover, as the following example serves to illustrate, that they can be obliged to put up with rather more than just increased competitive pressure. One summer evening I had agreed to pick up Kieran, the son of family friends, from an elite baseball tournament that he and his teammates had been looking forward to playing in. His team had been on the field since 2:00 p.m. preparing for a game that began three hours later. When I arrived at 7:00 p.m., I learned from waiting parents that the game had not gone well for the home team, having ended with a loss not to the powerful American team that had entered the tournament but to a team that was part of the local league. When none of the members of the team emerged from the clubhouse following the game, a waiting parent mentioned being at a game earlier in the season when a loss had been followed by a 45-minute session of wind sprints for the entire team. On that occasion, Kieran and his teammates had interpreted this as "punishment" imposed by the coach on the team.

On this evening the coach insisted upon conducting a lengthy "accountability" session in the dressing room in the wake of what he took to be an unacceptable defeat. The team, which had begun the season with great promise and a string of early wins, had now dropped its first game in the weekend tournament, thus relegating it to the consolation round of the competition. As I suspected at the time, and as Kieran confirmed during the car ride home, the coach had been infuriated by the loss. He began the post-game autopsy by asking his players to be frank, to say whether it was possible that he might be "the problem." The few players who initially responded declined to identify the coach as "the problem." Thereafter he rephrased the question as, "Well, then, *who is* the problem?" According to Kieran, what ensued was a sort of orchestrated "bitching session" in which fingers were pointed and fault was apportioned by teammates to one another. Eventually the coach asked the members of the team to vote on who among them had leadership capabilities. Why this was done or what it was supposed to accomplish was not explained to the players. Finally, an hour and a half after the game on the field ended, the coach permitted the players and their waiting parents to leave the park with tersely issued instructions for them to get back there early the next morning to prepare themselves for the next game.[7]

This particular episode does not in and of itself stand for the underlying truth about all community sports or coaches. It does, however, present a youth player's account of what happened to him and his teammates on a summer afternoon and evening. When compared and combined with reports provided by other participants in and observers of community sports about varying types of sport practices and relationships, it becomes possible to discern more general features of these activities. One of these involves the manner in which community sports oscillate between motifs of work and play, fields that are not typically conjoined in adults' lives. Thus, child and youth athletes are supposed to enjoy the opportunities afforded them to engage in one or another sport, to be with their friends, and to taste the delights of embodied competitive play. By the same token, they are also expected to submit themselves to regimes of bodily and social discipline that sometimes uncannily resemble those found in workplaces. What this suggests is the heuristic value of viewing young athletes' participation in community sports as complex activities that in some respects may be much like jobs, albeit ones that don't happen to provide financial remuneration.[8]

On occasions when Neil, a soccer coach, permits his youth team players to organize part of a practice session, they invariably begin with a scrimmage or game that includes everyone. As a committed coach, Neil is always looking for ways to fit specific drills, demonstrations of techniques, and correction into every practice to improve the play of individual players and the team as a whole. Most coaches and many players tend to view practices that feature only scrimmaging as not being particularly well organized or worth very much. In other words, mere play alone is judged to be less valuable than is some amount of focused instruction. Yet there is often a limited amount of patience among young athletes for directed instruction and repetitive drills within community sports. In consequence, a certain tension between "playing" and doing "serious work" tends to surface in training and practice sessions at almost every level of sport. The distinction between striving to play a sport well rather than "just goofing around" continues to be observed, thereby investing child and youth sports with an expectation of some measure of "work" in ways that street or pickup games, which are free to focus on enjoying the immediacy of performing and playing, can forgo.

THE PLEASURES AND PAINS OF CHILD AND YOUTH SPORTS

When asked what they like most about their sports, young athletes more often than not refer to the embodied action, excitement, fun, and sense of accomplishment that they experience during games and competitions. Although 12-year-old Belinda doesn't much care for the smell of the rink dressing room following a match, she loves the speed of ringette. When asked what it is like to play this sport, she responds: "Fun. It's exciting. Gets the blood pumping." What Fiona, a teenager, enjoys most about soccer are "the games, the competition, and meeting all the new people and travelling." Fiona is not especially fond of fitness training sessions where "all you do is run," but she guesses that this pays off in enhanced match performances. What keeps her coming back, however, is, "the competition, just the rush of scoring. Participation by everyone and how everyone is so keen to go after a point. That's all you're thinking about." Twelve-year-old Corey competes for a local track club and also plays football, but his favourite athletic activity is skiing: "I like going fast, and I like it when you go up [the mountain] early and there's no people there. That's good and I love the moguls." He goes on to observe that, "When you get into the higher levels [of competition], you race a lot in teams. That gets really boring, but that's what I got lots of ribbons for.... The best thing about skiing? I don't know, just getting some powder and having snow going fast into your face. That's real fun. And the worst thing is you have to take lessons, and they get sort of boring sometimes."

For 15-year-old Caroline, the best part of synchronized swimming is its physicality and variety:

It's very, very physical. Nobody realizes [this] unless you do it. And there's a lot of variety. You have to do your compulsory figures, and we have

20 figures that we have to learn, and that's almost the same as a figure skater, compulsory figures. And so I think the best thing is definitely the variety. The worst thing is that it's not a sport like karate or soccer where you can go twice a week and win the world championships. You have to dedicate a lot of time because you're upside down [in the water] and you have to get your whole, your balance and orientation and everything like that. So I think … the worst thing about it is that it's a really, really big dedication [of time] and people don't realize what it entails.… [N]obody understands what it's like until you've been in there, and it is one of *the* absolute most physical sports, I'm pretty sure.

Although Caroline is a member of a team that has done well at provincial and national competitions, the importance of this to her is balanced by an unadorned assessment of her own abilities:

Yeah. Um, success is pretty … I mean, of course it's going to be important—I shouldn't say "of course"—it *is* important to me. I'm not great. I'm kind of in the middle, but in any sport, as in anything, you get discouraged and you don't like something that you're not good at. So success is important in that regard, I think, but I know I'm not the best and I've just accepted that. And you just have to alter your standards and your goals. So success is important, but right now, it's really just for the love of the sport. And, of course, you're always going to be working really, really hard for success and that's the only reason that you do work. It's important, but it's not the whole thing.

Laurent, a 19-year-old veteran of community hockey, soccer, and swimming teams identifies basketball as his most satisfying sport due to its non-stop action: "Just always moving, always action. I'm kind of biased towards stuff I am good at, I guess. I am good at basketball. I like watching it on TV a lot, college basketball, not NBA so much. And, I don't know, it's kind of glamorous. It's probably, I think, the most popular amongst the kids these days." The downside of basketball—like other sports that Laurent has played—are some of the coaches that he has encountered: "There's always been coaches that bug me. Too competitive, just mean. It seems like they're a coach so they can be mean and have power and that really bugs me." Yet throughout his playing career in child and youth sports Laurent has attended practices fairly faithfully because he loves playing, albeit "the games more than the practices sort of thing."

Keith's initial foray into community sports as a seven-year-old soccer player was not particularly satisfying, and that experience along with a lingering medical condition combined to keep him out of sports and physically inactive for several years. This lasted until he was 11 years old and a doctor told him, "You're too fat and you have to do something about it." This prompted Keith to take up swimming, an individual sport. When Keith began to swim competitively, he "totally slimmed down and totally got more fit":

> ... My energy went straight up. And yeah, I used to get really nervous at the swim meets, like just to the point of like major nausea and stuff. And then after a while I learned to kind of deal with that and started to get a sense of competition in a way that I could internalize and that I was okay with because it wasn't [*pause*] ... if you wanted it to be, it could be competition against other people, but it didn't necessarily have to be because the primary competition there emphasized getting your times down and becoming a better swimmer and working on your stroke and stuff like that. And the practices are good too because there's always the social aspect to it, and you make a lot of friends and stuff like that. And yeah, I think it was a big ego booster for me physically.

In the process of seeking out and attaining various pleasures and benefits from sport, young athletes may also have to confront and endure what are for them unpleasant experiences. Quinn, a nine-year-old football player, doesn't like being knocked flat on his face, especially when the pointed end of a football is driven into his stomach. Evan, a teenager, recalls that he was reluctant to start playing hockey for similar reasons:

> At the age of five, which is the first year I could have played Termite [level], I chose not to. My parents were really trying to persuade me to do it, trying to encourage me, but I didn't. I was worried about getting a puck in the groin. I was really quite frightened. But finally, my second year [of eligibility] I did it, and I wasn't very strong for the first half of the season. And I don't think I knew all of the rules.... I definitely didn't know all of the rules.

Brandon, an 18-year-old, played box lacrosse for part of a season but was put off by the violence he came up against: "It was crazy. Like the rules are so different and it's just such a hacking game. Like the stick that you use to score goals, you can use it as a weapon. You're allowed to cross check, right?

It's just silly.... I think that if you get what you call a sports implement, you shouldn't be allowed to hit other people with it. You should only be able to use it for scoring goals." Other types of factors conspired to make Brandon's experience as a hockey player less rewarding than he would have wished it to be: "I was discouraged by a lot of people saying that I'd never make it to the pro leagues and stuff like that.... [The purpose of sport] should be to get the kids out doing activities. Get the kids involved.... Finding out what the kids like to do. Don't make it so they have to make it to a professional level. Some kids might want to do that but the time and effort you have to put into it to make it to the professional level is just too high." Community hockey, argues Brandon, should strive to accommodate players with differing body types and talents:

> An all-round player has to be sturdy and have really good agility. Quick thinking because it's such a fast game.... You have to be very strong now because of the body checking. It's a really rough game. Most teams, some teams are even looking for fighters.... Since I am more of a fast skater, I kind of look at players that get picked. I see other players that aren't as fast as me or aren't as quick thinkers, but they're good fighting checkers, and I see them get picked. It kind of develops and you kind of talk about it with other guys and it catches on, you know. The coaches don't really need to say anything. The kids know what the coaches are looking for.

Although growing up in a different province than Brandon, Laurent had a similar journey through youth hockey. When he was 11, says Laurent, his coach at the Pee Wee level, "wanted people who were just aggressive, he wanted big, strong people. Not really skilled people":

> ... And he threw a bag of pucks at my friend because he thought he was being lazy or something, even though ... [the friend] is the biggest hustler you'd ever meet. It just seemed like ... [the coach] had a real problem with the two of us being on the team. Because we were young and I think because we played a little differently. Generally, we were just really good skaters. We weren't very big. Good passers and goal scorers and stuff but not rough, not big players.... An NHL team is what I think he wanted to coach.

As a pre-teen,' Mike switched baseball leagues, hoping to find a better team. What he walked into was a more intense level and different form of competition than he had been prepared for: "There was a lot of competition—not just to beat the other people. I always got worried when I went up to bat because this or that kid had just hit a home run and I didn't know if I could do as well. There was a lot of competition within the team besides the entire game itself." That season marked the end of Mike's involvement in baseball. Evan, however, had a somewhat different response to the prospect of competing against his teammates in youth hockey. He did not look forward to team practices as much as to games since practices were so much harder, but there were other attractions to these training sessions:

> You had to skate. You'd do some skating and if everything was going well, you'd get a scrimmage in the last 15 minutes which was always fun. You'd play against your own teammates, and if you scored a goal, it was sort of showing off to them. And you'd work on different drills like the three-on-twos. And that's where maybe you'd get accustomed to playing with a partner. They'd try to keep the same lines if everything was going well. I remember the practices being pretty well organized for the most part.

What Evan didn't like was being cut from his team at the beginning of what should have been his second season at the Bantam level, when he was 14:

> I was very angry. I was really crushed because I really didn't think I deserved to be cut. I felt I was one of the stronger players entering the last tryout. And they cut me on the last tryout, and that really bothered me.... And then finally I got a call about eight games into the season. They had lost every game and I think they were just trying new things. One player had left. And they brought me in, and in the first game I scored a couple of goals. So I played every game from then on and I wasn't like a star, but I think I sort of—both myself and another player that they did bring back—helped jump-start the team and from the tenth game on we really played well.

What can also be difficult for young athletes to deal with are unanticipated scheduling conflicts generated by their commitments to different community sports in addition to those connected to schooling and their social lives. Fourteen-year-old Cassie was thrilled to be selected to a provincial-level soccer team until it became apparent that this squad held unscheduled practices and played exhibition games long after the normal soccer season ended. This disrupted her long-standing involvement in softball, forcing Cassie to miss over half of her games in this sport, which in turn incurred the displeasure of her softball coach. Twelve-year-old Tamara could not in the end bring herself to offer a full explanation to her coach when she informed him that she would not be attending that week's Friday night soccer practice, the first one that she would miss in four years spent with this team. This created an awkward situation for both coach and player.

What her father later told the coach was that Tamara had accepted an invitation to a classmate's birthday party, the first such social event to include both girls and boys since she and her friends had entered elementary school together six years earlier. Although the coach turned out to be unexpectedly magnanimous once informed of the circumstance, it was noteworthy that both player and parent expected that her playing time would be much reduced during the team's next game, an anticipation that was duly borne out. Eleven-year-old Alisa, whose father coached her team, found herself caught between a regularly scheduled team practice and a school concert that would, she feared, count for a significant proportion of her final grade in music. Her distress was compounded when one of her teammates who was also a classmate simply left a message on the phone to inform the coach that her mother wouldn't let her miss this school event.

The pleasurable aspects of community sports that young athletes identify and describe with such enthusiasm are, thus, never too far removed from certain discomforts and drawbacks that do not figure as prominently as the former in discursive celebrations of child and youth sports. Nevertheless, this latter set of factors—which can include, among other things, the fear of and actual incidence of physical injuries, the taxing nature of practice sessions, the sometimes arbitrary treatment extended to athletes by coaches, the violence intrinsic to some sports, the pressures of competition, and the demands made upon children's and youth's time—are no less a part of sport than the joys of playing and of possibly winning. Sport officials, coaches, and parents are sometimes inclined to label such matters as being just a normal part of growing up or as the types of predictable challenges that when tackled forthrightly by young athletes can serve to enhance the benefits they derive from participating in sport.[10] The kids who actually grapple with these and other predicaments may harbour a less sanguine view of these when reflecting upon and steering their way through community sports.

YOUNG SPORTING CAREERS

Community sports can, as was shown in previous chapters, evoke markedly differing responses from adults. Men and women who contribute substantial amounts of their own leisure time and disposable income to sustain child and youth sports, whether as volunteer officials, coaches, or as supportive parents, can become highly involved and sometimes overly invested in facilitating the competitive success of particular teams, clubs, and athletes. In contrast, other parents and coaches, who may be no less active in nor supportive of child and youth sports, may express and conduct themselves in ways that indicate that what the kids do or don't manage to achieve on a playing field or at a rink on any given day should not be taken too seriously. From this perspective, girls' and boys' efforts to acquire athletic skills and play different sports may be regarded as "good wholesome stuff" and treated as a source of fun for participants and occasionally as comedic relief for spectators. The general impression given off by those adopting this stance is that the outcomes of young athletes' games and competitions and of their playing of sports in general should not be allowed to matter too much. Ironically, this ostensibly "laid back" and "child friendly" approach to community sports can sometimes prove to be nearly as vexing to young athletes as the over-the-top antics of "mean" coaches who will stop at nothing to win. Neither of these approaches pays sufficient attention to the possibility that child and youth athletes might not be just passengers who are along for an adult-navigated ride through community sports but committed participants who attempt to prioritize their own objectives by means of the careers they construct for themselves in community sports.

During a car ride back from a non-sporting event, 11-year-old Talia mentioned that she would soon be finished with individual figure skating and was looking forward to starting keyboard lessons and possibly trying out some other sport. Although she intended to carry on performing with her precision skating team, she outlined her reasons for giving up on singles skating, an activity in which she had previously had some success. It had, said Talia, started to put too much pressure on her, for she estimated that she was probably nearing the limits of her skating ability since her individual routines were not improving much anymore. Given the time demands of individual skating and the costs incurred by her travel to competitions across Canada and in the United States, Talia was no longer enjoying an activity that would, she conjectured, not be likely to have anything to do with the rest of her life.

Similarly, Sean, a 14-year-old soccer player and middle distance runner opted to give up soccer when a couple of his teammates suffered serious injuries during games. The prospect of not being able to compete in track and field due to an injury sustained while playing soccer made it relatively easy for him to walk away from a sport that he had played since he was seven. Persuasive evidence of young athletes' sporting career calculations also became evident to Oren, a coach whose soccer team reached the finals of a provincial soccer tournament. He subsequently learned from various sources that the team's successful season couldn't have come at a better time since several of his more skilled players had been quietly contemplating quitting the team at the end of the season to play other sports that offered them greater possibilities of individual athletic success. Getting to the finals served to keep Oren's team intact for another season.

Fiona's belief that playing sports should be "something you do for yourself"—not like "playing the piano, which I was only doing to please my parents"—is echoed by Mike: "I think that at a younger age, most people just want to play sports because I guess everybody else is doing it. And when it comes down to the game, they want to win. But I think what really singles someone out as being someone who really, really wants to play is if parents don't have to push you in order to be interested in the sport." Nevertheless, kids, says Mike, love to play well when their parents are in attendance:

> … someone whose parents are interested and come to every single game, they kind of want to say, "I want to win this because my parents are here, they're interested in this, let me hit a home run for them," or something like that.… I think if a kid doesn't care about the sport, maybe it doesn't matter at all. And if the parents only come to one or two games, I don't think it will bother him. But if the kid is involved in the sport and he likes the sport and he wants his parents to see if he's improved or something like that, then I think he will be disappointed if his parents don't take an interest. Because it's not only not taking an interest in the sport, it's not taking an interest in the kid as well. It's something he's accomplished.

When asked how much he likes playing sports, Quinn replies that he only plays the sports that he likes, a tendency that has frustrated his parents. His steadfast refusal to join in an athletic activity that all other members of his family enjoy participating in has complicated their weekend outings. Belinda's measure of how much a kid really likes a sport hinges around whether a kid would be willing to pay a part of the costs, something that she does in ringette. Caroline, who began synchronized swimming at age 11, had previously been an overweight child. Swimming, she says, turned her into an athlete, and the 24 hours per week that she devotes to swimming has become a "pretty major part" of her life. Although Laurent has found himself at odds with some of his coaches, he nonetheless devotes some time every day to taking practice shots with a basketball. Kieran phones friends on other teams after each of his games to update them, find out about the outcome of their games, rehash particularly good and bad plays, and discuss controversial calls by umpires and decisions by coaches.

Many young athletes make a point of saving medals, ribbons, or trophies that they have won along with photographs and other sport memorabilia, and some have their bedrooms conspicuously decorated with these. Evan's parents still have a photograph of the first goal their son ever scored on display in their hallway, as do the parents of Quinn. Denise prizes the scrapbook that preserves newspaper clippings from the two years in which she was selected as an all-star at a provincial soccer tournament. Michelle, who subsequently went on to win an athletic scholarship due to her talent as a softball pitcher, delights in the experience of wearing club apparel in sports settings because "when you walk around everybody knows where you're from." When she was selected for a provincial team, Fiona was suddenly showered with prestige: "Within the city, everyone gets to know you, too. As soon as you've been on a provincial team, they see the jacket and they know. They know who you are." Vaughn, whose entire sport career comprised only a couple of years in a Saturday morning bowling league, observes that schoolmates involved in "real" sports tended to dominate the key spaces in his high school, despite the otherwise effective shunning of conspicuous accomplishment by students: "Anybody that kind of was doing any real achievement wasn't really seen as all that cool, unless it was in sports."

While young athletes generally enjoy the prestige and recognition that can be obtained from playing sports[11] and appreciate the support that parents and other family members often provide, they can also offer incisive commentaries concerning certain aspects of the behaviour of some fathers and mothers at community sport events. Caroline identifies the characteristics of the "synchro moms"[12] that occasionally pop up in her sport by referring to the mother of one of her teammates:

> There are people, there's one girl that I swim with, that if she didn't keep
> swimming, she'd be sent off to boarding school. And she came second at

a meet and her mom was mad at her because it wasn't good enough, she didn't come first. And that's just awful and this girl is the most—she's not unhappy when she's around us when she's actually swimming.

She's unhappy when she's around her mom. Her mom will sit there for a three-and-a-half-hour practice. Three and a half hours sitting watching us. She won't take a book or anything. She lives for her daughter and her daughter's success. And if her daughter is paired for a duet with somebody of a little bit lesser ability, she raises heck. And one time, or [on] a couple of occasions, okay, she grounds her daughter if she doesn't work hard enough in practice. And on a number of occasions, if her daughter hasn't worked hard enough in her workout—her mom sits there watching her—she will make her stay after practice to do extra lengths. And that is absolutely ridiculous because that totally defeats the purpose of a sport, I think. It's supposed to be to enjoy it, and the coaches get really, really mad. It got to the point where parents weren't allowed on deck.

Speaking of his own parents, Brandon begins by noting that they have always been good about helping out with scorekeeping, serving at the concessions stand, and assisting with fundraising in hockey. With respect to his performances on the ice, Brandon observes,

My dad's been really [*pause*]—sometimes he'd expect a little more out of me and stuff. If I did not have such a good game, sometimes he'd wonder why, but there was nothing that I could really do about it. He did some good things, like he'd always try and give me pep talks and stuff like that, but then sometimes they'd get out of hand and he'd get frustrated with the way I play sometimes.... But my mom's always been supportive. Never anything bad. I don't know, many other parents might be that way too, either way.

Commenting about parents' antics at her ringette games, Belinda suggests that, "when they're watching the game and cheering, sometimes they get going a bit too far. Ringing bells and cheering and screaming the whole game." Fiona likes having her parents at her games, "so they can tell me what I did. Even if they don't know a lot about the game, they can still pick up a lot and figure out what I was doing and whatnot. I like having feedback other than just the coach's. I know kids that have never had their parents at a game and some of them say they don't mind, but you know once in awhile they'd like their parents to see what they're up to." Michelle too appreciates the backing and cheering that parents provide but doesn't like it when some become angry and "affect if you are having fun or not, just the way they act."

SPORT FRIENDS AND SIBLINGS

Another dimension of young athletes' engagement in community sports involves the types of social and personal relations that they form with team-mates and other children and youths who participate in these activities. Parents sometimes speak as though the connections established between age-mates in one or another sport might be regarded as potential, if not yet fully formulated, "friendships."[13] In part this reflects the depth of middle-class parental anxiety within Canadian society about whether "my child" will acquire the capacity not only to make friends but also to learn how to make the "right sort" of friends as he/she grows up. Mothers and fathers sometimes proudly recount just how many "friends" their son or daughter has made and emphasize "what great kids" their progeny are coming into contact with through a particular club or sport. This presumed capacity of community sports to furnish children and youths with new and appropri-ate friends is recognized by sport organizers as a feature that is particularly appealing to parents. Indeed, much of a child's life outside the home remains effectively beyond the parents' ability to monitor or to shape, unless, of course, they possess the financial resources required to remove their children from universally accessible public institutions like the neighbourhood school and resituate them in an ostensibly more select institutional setting of the sort marketed by private schools.[14]

Supporting or perhaps even initiating a child's participation in a community sport that a parent deems to be socially suitable offers a means to supervise and select which types of child participants and adult tutors a son or daughter will spend this portion of their leisure time with. After all, community sports are scheduled and staged at times and in places that permit parents front-row seats from which to oversee what a son or daughter is involved in both on and alongside the fields of play. Given this degree of adult concern with the types of relationships and social capacities that young athletes are expected to acquire through their participation in organized sports, it is important to listen carefully to boys' and girls' explanations of the nature and relative closeness of these types of relationships. It is also necessary to specify the factors that affect young athletes' interactions and relationships with one another, not the least of which may be the intensity of parental interest in these matters.

The sociality that occurs within community sports takes several forms. Coaches and sometimes parents introduce new recruits to the routines and roles designed for young athletes and explain what is expected of "good team players." For athletes, joining a new team or club usually involves interacting with some strangers. Being accompanied by a friend or acquaintance or two may relieve some of the unease frequently associated with such undertakings. Slipping into whatever it is that a coach wants a collection of boys or girls to do—something that is familiar to veterans of day-care centres, pre-schools, or elementary school classrooms—may offer an initial measure of comfort and collective security. Thereafter, young athletes begin to acknowledge one another's co-presence and shared involvement in this particular situation. In time they learn one another's names, work out the distribution of pre-existing and budding friendships among them, and become privy to some, if not all, of the insights, comments, and judgements that may begin to circulate concerning coaches, teammates, and other athletes. In short, joining a sport is not unlike moving into a new workplace. A good deal of time is spent with others in these settings, and the arrangements that bring them together oblige them to take account of and to work with one another. There are good reasons for striving to foster workable and, if possible, reasonably cordial relations with teammates. Moreover, workplaces and community sports can and sometimes do provide more personalized relationships and friendships that, nonetheless, reflect the circumstances within which these unfold.

Belinda explains that playing ringette has been "how I met most of my friends." These friendships include not only teammates but players from other teams as well. In addition to practising, competing, and travelling with them, Belinda likes to "go over to their houses and go places with them." Soccer has provided 18-year-old Fiona with a social scene within which she has met kids from a much broader area than her local neighbourhood or high school. It has become an important source of friends:

> Most of my friends are soccer friends now. Most of my best friends
> anyway.... I had really good teams lately and we do a lot of stuff together.
> The coaches promote us doing stuff like going to movies and stuff, so we
> get to know each other better, and it seems to make it easier to play on the

field. And we just went overboard on this one. This summer I spent most of my time with my soccer team and we became really good friends.... And we go wherever. Mostly just partying.

Quinn reports that, "Most of the team are my friends because I'm the quarterback. And usually if I get sick and I go to the game, they come up to me go, 'Come on Quinny, we need you. You have to play.'" In fact, all of these friendships came out of playing football, for Quinn "never knew any of them" before joining this community sport: "Well, mostly in my first year, I never knew anybody, so my second year all the fast [i.e., speedy] guys came along and I started making friends with them." In contrast, Denise joined a community soccer team made up of friends with whom she went through junior and senior high school. They remained teammates and classmates throughout this period.

For Caroline, synchronized swimming has become a large part of her life and social relationships: "Oh, it is 50 per cent of my life. The other 50 per cent is academic, because I'm a really, really serious student with very, very high standards. And sport, like swimming, plays so much in my life, it has such a huge role in my life because my best, best friends are the people I swim with. And it's really introduced me to a lot of new kind[s] of people. People that I wouldn't be drawn to regularly at school." Michelle distinguishes between her "sport friends" and "school friends," noting that she rarely saw those whom she swam with or against weekend after weekend over a period of several years except at swimming functions. While Vaughn made friends through membership in a bowling league, these too were specific to a time, place, and shared activity: "They're bowling relationships, but I didn't realize that at the time. It never really continued on after that. I think at the time it sort of seemed more like they were just ... you don't really think that you're not going to see them again after this thing's over."

The relationships that young athletes report as involving "friends" in community sports cover a range of types. Some of these overlap with co-participation in other institutional spheres, such as school, but others do not. Although the ties that connect friends and other participants in community sports may, as long as these last, bring them together frequently and with considerable intensity over significant periods of time, both types of ties tend to be restricted to particular times and activities. There are, accordingly, "sport friends," "school friends," and many other types of friends. Children and youths who form consociate relationships rather than becoming "best, best friends" through their participation in sports may, of course, make use of these should they happen to meet or wish to spend time with each other in other contexts. Close personal relationships forged through participation in sport can and sometimes do continue beyond the activities that gave rise to them, but this is not inevitably the case. More than a few of the teammates or fellow club members that a young athlete may come into contact with in community sports will never become or remain friends, even though they may have shared some memorable moments and good seasons. In these respects, the types of relationships that young athletes fit themselves into, form for themselves, enjoy, or endure in community sports would appear to have more in common with those of the work world than tends to be acknowledged in some adult discourses about this field.

One other aspect of young athletes' social relationships with members of their generation that receives less attention than it deserves concerns the impact of a given child's sport involvement on siblings.[15] Besides sibling rivalry that can be inflamed by the unequal distribution of athletic success and parental attention among brothers and sisters stand the logistics of family organization. It can be difficult for parents to sustain simultaneous participation by two or more children in clubs or sports that clash in terms of scheduling and the distances between different venues. One family member's participation in a particular sport may, accordingly, lead to pressure being placed upon a sibling or siblings to also play that sport, whether or not it happens to appeal to them. Siblings who don't play sports may be obliged to spend many evenings and weekends accompanying their parents to games and tournaments in which a brother or sister is competing. Within these settings the interests and achievements of non-athletic sons and daughters can be overshadowed by their parents' preoccupation with an endless round of games and competitions involving a sibling.

WORKING OUT COACHES

Young athletes' dealings with coaches, trainers, managers, and sport instructors constitute an essential but by no means standardized feature of community sports. This is scarcely surprising, given that athletes, coaches, and the sports that bring them together may possess widely differing styles, dispositions, and forms. That being said, relations between athletes and coaches are not simply personal encounters but intensely social ones that are organized in terms of the roles of coach and athlete. Coaches are charged with teaching athletes the rules and requisite skills of one or another sport as well as directing and enhancing their performance. In addition to providing technical instruction and shaping the moves and tactical understanding of their charges, coaches may also be expected to supervise their athletes' behaviour before, during, and after competitions. Those who accept the responsibility of serving as a coach are expected to have—or at least act as though they have—a greater knowledge of a game or sport than do those who are being coached. The extent of this expected differential in expertise can vary substantially depending upon the level at which a sport is being played and the inducements offered to those who might be prepared to coach. More specific agreements about what it is that coaches and athletes are supposed to do in the course of their joint participation in sports remain matters for ongoing discussion and negotiation. Sport organizations, parents, and state officials are not, however, the only parties interested in reflecting upon and fine-tuning the terms of these paired roles and working relationships. When listened to, young athletes can provide incisive insights into coach–athlete relationships both as these happen to be performed and might otherwise be arranged.

Belinda liked playing soccer from age seven to nine with a community team but did not enjoy switching to a higher calibre club team because, she said, "my coach wasn't a very nice guy." His penchant for giving his best players the lion's share of playing time did improve their play but prevented their teammates from following suit. Even when Belinda became one of the players who began to get more time on the field, "then it was just someone else who joined that didn't get to play. So he wasn't very fair." The best type of coach, for Belinda, would be, "someone who loves the sport, not [just] winning. Someone who's out to play the sport and play the sport well." She contrasts this ideal with an actual coach who "plays soccer himself … knows a lot of little stunts, but he's not after having a good team. He's after having a winning team." To create a good team, says Belinda, coaches must "like the players and the sports. I think that's what you have to like to make it comfortable…. You have to not be prejudiced in any way to the players if it's for not being good or being small or tall or whatever…. I mean, if you're not a dedicated player and you don't come to practice, you deserve to play less. But have the same punishment for everyone…. Everyone pays the same to buy their shirt. You paid your fee, you should play." Corey also speaks about the unfairness of unequal playing time for members of a team: "I think it's really boring, though, if you play football and you're not one of the good players. All you do is stand around during the game." Even league-imposed minimum playing time rules do not, according to Corey, come close to evening out participation by different members of a team.

Caroline offers a detailed account of her own experiences and of what a good coach would do and be:

A good coach is someone that will push you really, really hard but makes practice fun. Because I remember I used to be really scared to come to practice and I would be really, really nervous and I wouldn't want to come to practice because it was just so hard. So a really good coach is someone that pushes you ... and makes you realize you have potential and makes you feel really, really good about yourself. But also doesn't push too hard. You just say, "I can't do it." One of the coaches in our club now just pushes too much. Just too much. And it's like, people are starting to say, "Hey, we're human beings. We're not just athletes and machines that pump out performance." And so I mean, okay, you have a set workout and if people aren't going as fast as you think they ... [ought to], "Okay, we'll cut back or add a few seconds so you can do it and you can keep going but we'll improve on it"—that makes a good coach. Someone who will compromise with the swimmers because the swimmers are the ones that are in the water shivering and going, "*Hello,* I'm in pain!" And there's one coach in our club that just says, "No, you're just going to do it. Come on you guys. Let's get going," even if you only just took a breath. And, "Come on you guys. You're wasting time." Well, you can't push, push, push all the time. A good coach is also someone who has a sense of humour and is your friend and who kind of lessens the gap between coach and swimmer. They kind of come together. And you still, you recognize the difference and you get in the water. There's a difference, but you also know that they are your friends and you can go to them if you need to.

Mike itemizes some of the differences between the coaches that he worked with during his childhood years in community sports and those who are paid to coach teams at his private school:

Well, school coaches I found a lot different from the community coaches. They're a lot more competitive. [My community sport coaches] ... were laid back, and most of these coaches were, if they were fathers and had a kid on the team, they didn't feel too pressured or anything. When the [community] recreation department staff member would teach us or be our coach, it was even more laid back. Like, nothing really mattered, you're just here to have fun.... But school coaches are working for the school, and the school wants them to win, so they're pushing you really, really hard. So there's lots of variation there.

While Mike can't remember ever saying, "That was a really good coach, I really like him," he does remember "being on a hockey team with that one coach who was just too serious, too competitive, and I didn't like it at all. I tend to like having a laid back coach who appreciates that, although he has a team, it's nice just to play. But he still pushes us a little bit to win the game. I like that because I guess it's like the happy medium."

For Michelle, a good coach is:

... obviously someone who wants to be there and who's there for the kids. And doesn't get mad all the time. Like, they can get mad, but if somebody does something and you get mad at them, you have to be able to leave it there and go right on to the next thing and not hold grudges. A good coach, if you're down, they'll get you up. They'll just get you motivated, wanting to do good and that. Bad coaches, usually you just don't want to do anything for them, from my experience. Like they ask you to do something and you don't even try.

What Michelle would wish to have recognized in community sports is that the primary purpose of these activities must be to let kids have fun:

Sometimes there's too much competition and that put in sports. And some kids just want to be in the sport for the social things and that, so when you push them for the competition, it just makes the whole sport not fun anymore, not enjoyable. So if they want to compete and that, they will do it on their own. So just have it there for them to do what they want to do and if they want to be pushed, then you push them. But if they don't, then you don't.... Like when I was swimming, there were people in the club who their parents pushed and pushed and pushed them and they hated it and they didn't want to be there. And some of my other friends wanted to be there, and we weren't pushed by our parents, you know, because we did it on our own, you know, and we got more enjoyment out of it. And it wasn't a miserable time for us.... All the coaches I've ever had have been there for the kids. Umm, I have seen other coaches who, they just want to win and they'll yell and scream if anything goes wrong because they're there for themselves to win.

After describing a couple of coaches who had moved several of their players to quit because these men had favourites who garnered most of the playing time, Evan spoke about the approach taken by another coach:

I had one coach all the way throughout ... Atom and my first year of Pee Wee. So three years, and he was probably my favourite coach up to date. It wasn't all winning. In inter-city [competitive hockey] you do have the option of playing the better players more. It's just something that goes with it.... In house league you're supposed to stay away from it.... But for inter-city, he was a very fair coach.... He was as fair as I think he should have been and winning wasn't everything, and we still had a really fun time most of those years even though I think only one of those years did we actually win the majority of our games. The others we lost most. But it was fun and I learned a lot. Those were my favourite years of hockey probably.

The comments of Evan and other child and youth athletes about particular coaching styles that they individually like or dislike are accompanied by general suggestions about how dealings between coaches and athletes might be configured to enhance their enjoyment of community sports: ensure fair treatment of all athletes; make having fun the first priority; don't insist upon pursuing higher levels of performance unless that is what individual athletes want; keep competition within community sports but don't let winning become the only thing that matters. What their accounts also illustrate are the ways in which young athletes may seek to reshape some of the terms of their involvement in community sports.

FUN AND GAMES

Parents of children who are still relative newcomers to community sports sometimes feel called upon to instruct their sons or daughters concerning various social expectations popularly associated with athletics, presumably because these children are thought to be not yet familiar with these. Expressions of this type of concern as well as the responses these sometimes elicited from young players figured in several under-seven[16] soccer house league games that I observed one season. These events were recorded in my fieldnotes as follows:

———————

A member of the Tigers scores a goal. The father of one of the Tigers has been dispensing directions to the players on the field throughout the game, even though he is standing next to the team's coach. After the goal [is scored] he calls out to the Tigers as they return to the halfway line for the ensuing kickoff: "Come on, give him [the scorer] a pat on the back."

There is no response from the players on the field. The Tigers simply walk back to the halfway line to resume the game.

"Come on, give him a pat on the back. *Show* that you are a team." Still no response, and the game resumes.

Ten minutes later the same Tiger scores another goal. The same father calls out again from the sidelines, "Give him a pat on the back." Again there is no response.

"Give him a pat on the back. *Be* a team."

Finally a response comes back from the players on the field, indeed from the son of the father who has been attempting to orchestrate the on-field congratulation of the successful scorer: the boy calls back to his father, "He [indicating the goal scorer] hit me here" [pointing to his chest].

Immediately the father replies, "Oh, that doesn't matter. Play like a team and give him a pat on the back."

"No, he hit me here."

Five minutes later, another member of the Tigers scores a goal on their hapless opponents. This time the father on the sidelines remains silent. Yet as the Tigers head back to the halfway line, two of them give the scorer high-fives.

———————

Three minutes before the end of a 6–0 match, an enthusiastic father and assistant coach of the losing team yells out to the players on the field: "Come on, guys, let's salvage some pride. Let's make it 6–1."

Following the final whistle, the same assistant coach, who has been expressing himself in generally encouraging but highly directive terms throughout the match, walks on to the field to greet his son, a member of the losing team. The father remarks: "Well, at least it is a nice day to play soccer."

"Yes," replied the son, "and we played well."

"No, you didn't," replied the father.

"Yes, we did."

"No, you didn't."

"*Yes, we did.*"

"*No, you didn't.*"

The boy walks away from his father to join his teammates on the sidelines.

———————

[Young soccer player, with his mother, just after being replaced on the field by a substitute player.]

Mother to son: "What's with this 'kick the ball and then stop,' eh?"

Boy doesn't respond, but leaves to join his teammates after his mother finishes tucking his jersey in.

———————

[An exhibition game between a strong local team and an out-of-town team that as a reward for its good season has come to the city for a "fun weekend." In the first half it becomes clear that the local team is much stronger than the visitors. At halftime, the two coaches agree to swap some players for the second half, thereby roughly evening up the strength of the two teams. By the end of the game all of the players—but especially the visitors, who had no substitute players—are exhausted from playing on a large field.]

The mother of one of the visiting players—a midfielder who has played herself almost into the ground—calls out to her daughter: "Keep going, there is still time!"

Daughter: "Mom, the Ref[eree] said there are only a few minutes left [flashing a big smile]."

Mother: "It ain't over till the fat lady sings!"

Daughter: "Oh, Mom!"

Instances such as these demonstrate how easily and, perhaps, unselfconsciously adults can slip into trying to choreograph young athletes' understandings of how they ought to participate and express themselves within sports.[17] What is also revealed is the independence that young athletes may display in registering their own interpretations of what a particular incident or relationship actually does involve or ought to involve. These debates occur not only between young athletes and adults but also between teammates. For example, at the end of a hard fought soccer match between a pair of under-14 girls' teams that had become fierce rivals over several seasons, the members of the winning team returned triumphantly to their side of the field. Brimming with excitement and decrying the physical roughness and on-field trash talking that had, they claimed, been engaged in by some of their opponents, the players took turns giving voice to just how much they collectively disliked the other side.

As the players and their parents headed towards the parking lot, Nicki, one of the team's midfielders, observed to those around her that somehow she always ended up playing against "nice" opponents. Her claim matter-of-factly eschewed the tenor of partisanship that had been adopted by most of her teammates and some of their parents. Nicki went on to explain that when she is on the field she often talks to herself, and this usually causes the individual opponent whom she is marking or being marked by to laugh. And from there they begin to talk during the game, and Nicki always ends up finding out things that she likes about these other girls. Although a skilled and enthusiastic player, Nicki prefers to construct for herself less agonistic approaches to playing sport than do some of her teammates. A similar preference for a non-confrontational approach to community sports was symbolically conveyed during a soccer match that ended suddenly when the coach of one of the teams disagreed vehemently with a referee's decision, threatened to order his players off the field, and then, receiving no satisfaction from the official, did so. Initially stunned by their coach's decision, several of his players remonstrated with him, indicating their desire to continue playing. Faced with an intransigent coach who insisted upon abandoning the game, these boys stubbornly made their way across the field to shake hands with their erstwhile opponents.

The care with which individual child and youth athletes deliberate on the purposes and meanings of their participation in sport can be no less significant to them than the physical and technical training that they undertake. In the hours and days following games and competitions, young athletes often ponder their performances, disappointments, and achievements, discussing these with one another as well as sometimes with parents and coaches. By themselves, competitive results never tell the whole story about an athlete's or a team's performance on a given day, even in a sport like track and field that measures and records results in fractions of centimetres and hundredths of seconds. For instance, a long jumper who finishes behind the event winner but who fouled his last jump by only a very small margin—a jump that would otherwise have won him first-place and a personal best mark—may initially be distraught when confronting what might have been. Yet some time later a friend or a parent might just circumspectly help the athlete to reframe what had initially been experienced as a crushing disappointment into a harbinger of progress. Nevertheless, to intervene when an athlete is wrestling with the implications of her/his performance can be a tricky matter. Well-meaning parents who rush in too quickly to say something that they hope will relieve the athlete's dismay can find themselves on the receiving end of a blunt assertion from their child that "You just don't understand!" What was meant to provide solace can be experienced as something that patronizes a young athlete's sense of what he/she hoped to achieve but failed to do so.[18]

Another source of tension that arises regularly in community sports emerges out of struggles between athletes and coaches about the levels of seriousness that they respectively believe ought to be observed during practices and games. According to Corey, these types of situations happen because coaches "are trying to encourage strict behaviour like 'do what you are told' and 'don't goof off,' but players are not perfect." Ken, a watchful father, further teased out the dynamics of "goofing around" while we looked on as his son's team stumbled its way through an early evening soccer practice. Kids, suggested Ken, have their own sense of what is meant to be "fun" and what is meant to be "serious." If games are meant to be "serious," he surmised, picking up what he took to be kids' line of reasoning, then shouldn't practices be "fun"? While we watched, Xavier, the coach, attempted to introduce the team to a moderately complicated overlapping pass drill that had been featured in a coaching clinic that he and I had taken the previous summer. Exasperated by the shambles that ensued from his efforts to have his eight-year-old players conduct the drill properly, Xavier was reduced to threatening the boys with a couple of disciplinary laps of running unless they paid attention. After a few minutes of further frustration, he surrendered himself to imposing that sentence, and the lads headed off at a slow trot towards the far goal posts.

This episode took me back to a flurry of impromptu cartwheels from the players that had interrupted, to my dismay as a coach, a practice session I had staged a couple of weeks earlier. The underlying problem is, in part, that coaches, and especially those who are keen to improve their coaching and their teams' performances, tend to approach practices with serious and worthy purposes in mind. They have completed coaching clinics, read instructional manuals, consulted with other coaches, analyzed their team's and players' weaknesses, selected appropriate drills, and come to practice with serious purposes and plans. Kids, on the other hand, have more often than not already put up with a full school day of serious purposes and quite possibly some additional hours that might have been claimed by swimming or dance lessons, a Brownie meeting, or practising the piano. It is little wonder that they might hanker for at least a bit of relief from a surfeit of seriousness by late afternoon or early evening.[19]

When coaches are unable or unwilling to adjust the form and tempo of practices to suit what is desired by or is minimally tolerable to their athletes, "goofing off" and "messing around" can give way to more deliberate campaigns of "pissing off" the coach. Brandon outlines one such instance of this: "A coach that I had said he never wanted to see us take a slap shot when we were younger. He only wanted to see wrist shots. Well, that didn't really … it kind of took our spirits away from us. We never understood it. It kind of got us where some of the players wanted to take slap shots just to piss him off, right? He got on our backs for it." Brandon reports a similar pattern of resistance being applied to a coach whose priorities were not shared by his players: "If you don't like it at all, it drains your energy. If you're just wasting energy fighting the coach or something, you just get lazy, I guess. And, I don't know, everyone feels they've got to do everything just to piss off the coach because no matter what you do, he'll be pissed off anyway. Like just dragging around during practice."

The line between playful "goofing around" and instrumental "pissing off" can, indeed, be a fine one. Whether it is read as being innocently or deliberately crossed at any given moment depends on one's point of view[20] and, perhaps, level of exhaustion. Specific instances and accusations tend to remain shrouded in conjecture. These recurring forms of friction that are generated by the differing priorities of athletes and coaches serve to illustrate another way in which boys and girls seek to alter the conditions of their participation in sports. They also lead us to the vital matter of how various forms of discipline enter into community sports.

DISCIPLINING SPORT

The pursuit and application of discipline have become near ubiquitous elements of contemporary social life and parlance, in sports as in so many other areas of life.[21] I have elsewhere specified some features of contemporary anthropological perspectives on discipline that are pertinent to this concern:

> Broadly speaking, discipline may be invoked to refer to a range of overlapping activities, relationships, and outcomes. It may comprise programs of training, especially pertaining to mind and character, which aim to reproduce preferred forms of conduct. By the same token, discipline may be identified as the product or result of such training, as in the "suitably

ordered" behaviour of school children or soldiers. Or discipline may be located within sets of rules established for the purpose of exercising control over people, be they prisoners, coreligionists, or fellow practitioners such as physicians or lawyers. So too may discipline be depicted in terms of the application of particular forms of punishment. (Dyck 2008b, 2)

Our examination of young athletes' participation in community sports has to this point touched upon instances where one or another form of discipline—be it swimming additional laps, receiving reduced playing time, or being made to run around a field—has been meted out to athletes by coaches or parents as punishment for failing to comply with adult-imposed requirements. Yet an arguably even more powerful dimension of discipline in child and youth sport emerges when it is not primarily or solely something that is applied by coaches to athletes but instead becomes a way of doing things that athletes choose to apply to themselves and to incorporate into their participation in sports. The value of self-discipline has, of course, been much celebrated in sport in general. The prospect of child and youth sports inculcating habits, postures, and beliefs that are thought to embody this way of being is often touted as one of their principal benefits.

Where discipline that is applied by others ends and self-discipline begins can be difficult to determine, even in retrospect. Keith appreciates the ways in which his involvement in swimming has enabled him to accomplish things that he had not thought he was capable of doing. Yet he remains ambivalent about the manner in which he acquired the discipline that came to shape his involvement in this sport:

[I never liked] ... the fact that you became really dependent on other people's discipline, and it was, I guess, kind of authoritarian. Like you were told what to do and you had to do that and you couldn't really question it or anything. You just did it. I guess that ended up, in the long run that obviously contributed to the positive effect of it. But I could see, if I was to be a coach, getting kids to make up their own workouts and stuff because obviously if they want to be there and they want to work hard, then they should be setting personal goals for themselves and trying to achieve them in practice as well as in competition. So yeah, the worst thing would be the lack of independence and I guess the best thing would be the independence that I gained from it.

Keith also remembers:

> ... that one particular coach who, he was a really driving, discipline coach.
> I remember he once made me get up [out of the pool] and do push-ups
> because I was fooling around or whatever, and I just left. And he was, "No,
> get back here." And I'm, "No, forget it." We always had this turbulent rela-
> tionship, but I think he did a lot for me in getting me in shape and then
> saying, "See, you can do it." And I think he was one of the people who
> really disciplined us, strenuously, but mainly to prove that we *could* do it....
> And it was cool. Because we all knew that we didn't *have* to do it, but that's
> why we were there.

Yet the power that can be generated through the application of discipline in
child and youth sports does not inevitably lead to positive results and grati-
tude on the part of athletes. A year and a half after I had first interviewed
Caroline, who was then a highly committed member of a synchronized
swimming club, I was contacted by her mother who told me that her daughter
had something that she wanted to add to what she had told me previously
about her involvement in this sport. Shortly before our initial interview, her
club had appointed a new coach who had arranged extensive physiological
testing of all the athletes. Caroline explained what happened thereafter:

> I was overweight as a kid, so weight was a big issue with me, and then we
> did physiological testing ... and I was told that I needed to lower my fat
> composition, like my fat percentage. I wasn't told how to do it. I already
> was a really, really healthy eater. I stayed away from the junk foods, the fats,
> all the fatty condiments and everything, but this coach just said, "Well, I
> want you to, like, lose 3 per cent fat," or whatever. And I was just devastated
> because already I had lost 15 pounds just training normally with the club,
> like 15 pounds in three months and that's fine because I wasn't on a diet.
> So that's basically when it started and I remember that day. Just starting
> from that day there was no way that I was going to let her boss me around
> because if somebody tells me something, I say, "Well, look I'm going to
> show you then." I know there was a button to be pushed, but that's when
> it mostly started.... I think we were going to go back and do physiological
> testing within the next few months. This was December and she wanted
> me to do it again at the end of April.

Caroline became severely bulimic and found that she was "really, really good at hiding it." By the time she began to receive treatment of this condition, she had been forced to drop out of "basically everything" except her schooling. Ironically, a year later, when that particular coach had moved to a more prestigious club—although not before several other of Caroline's former teammates had followed her out of the sport—Caroline was contacted by her old club: "They needed me back at the club because they had lost another swimmer and they were begging me to come back. I wanted to go back, and my Mom, very wisely, said, 'No, you're not going back.'… And so that pretty much is when it ended because I had to take care of myself." Reflecting back on this experience, Caroline suspects that:

> … coaches see a person and they want to transform that athlete into the ultimate athlete. A lot of coaches use athletes so that they themselves can work their way up because, if your athletes do better, then you'll be considered a better coach so you'll get a higher coaching position.[22] … I think definitely coaches just see an athlete and kind of think of what can be done with that athlete, with the body, not the mind. They definitely see it [i.e., the athlete's body] as their own to mould and put through hell and just do whatever they want with it. And it's up to the athlete too, in that case, to kind of know when enough is enough. But coaches have immense power over their athletes…. I would do anything because if they told me something to do, half the time I would look at them and go, "Are you nuts? I can't do that." And they would say, "Do it." And amazingly enough, I could do it. And so when I think back on the training last year, I'm amazed at what we were doing. It's like some of the stuff that if there isn't a coach out there to tell me to do it, a coach standing on deck, I physically cannot push myself to do it. And you just have so much respect for your coach, you want to be admired and respected by them. So, I don't know what it is. Basically because without them, you know you're not going to get where you want to go and they're going to help you to get there. So I can't put my finger on it, but I just know they have an immense power over their athletes.

The general features of Caroline's experience are by no means unique to her or restricted to synchronized swimming. It is important to take account of instances such as hers at a time when sport is being enthusiastically and sometimes rather uncritically promoted as a means for responding to increased levels of obesity among children in Canada and elsewhere. Sport activities and relations that directly or indirectly give rise to eating disorders, the illicit use of steroids and other banned substances, serious sport injuries,[23] or sexual abuse have immediate and disabling impacts upon young athletes that may continue to plague them long after their playing careers have come to an end. Hence the importance of recognizing the double-edged nature of discipline and the adverse effects that can result from the unrestrained pursuit and application of this powerful form of social technology in community sports.

Nonetheless, acknowledging that these types of problems unfortunately do sometimes arise within community sports should not be taken as a rationale for jumping to the conclusion that what young athletes really need is greater regulation and management of their sporting activities by responsible adults or experts who are presumed to know what is in their best interests across the board. Exercising vigilance to guard against unsafe or repugnant practices should not be confused with assuming control over determining the purposes, "best practices" and preferred orientation of child and youth sports. The first strives to protect young athletes, the second serves to infantilize them.

The argument presented in this chapter is that we need to regard young athletes not primarily as immature and dependent beings but as individually competent, albeit young, social actors who play an indispensable part in community sports. What is more, they do so in ways that take account of some, if not all, of the varied interests of parents, coaches, and sport officials in these activities without losing sight of their own. Having completed, with this chapter, the task of identifying the principal roles and actors that figure in community sports, we can next turn our attention to the ways in which their respective enthusiasms intersect to create an expansive and varied field of activities that inspires equal measures of passion and controversy.

NOTES

1 It struck me that this is probably also the case in conversations between adults involved in other fields of leisure activity besides community sports that are organized by adults for children.

2 Fine and Mechling (1991) have also commented on the tendency of this pattern to appear within adults' relations with actual children and youths.

3 Anderson's (2003) account of her study of a recreational badminton program for children in Copenhagen makes a compelling case of paying careful attention both to what children say and do with respect to their participation in sport activities.

4   Television viewers in Canada are familiar with advertisements that feature nostalgic depictions of children's sports as a valued part of family and community life. These have become prominent elements in the "branding" of Tim Hortons coffee shops and McDonald's restaurants in this country.

5   Anderson (2003) reports a similar instance of this tendency in a program that was launched to provide inner-city children in Copenhagen with access to sports.

6   Conversely, a similar (although negatively weighted) approach can be employed to frame a particular child's dislike of sports.

7   The team went on to lose each of its remaining games in the tournament. Kieran noted that, while the squad had started the season well, other teams in their league simply improved their level of play while his team had not. He also observed that he and his teammates tended to commit more playing errors during the second game of weekend doubleheaders. From his perspective, notwithstanding the many and gruelling practices held between games, not to mention the lengthy pre-game and post-game sessions called by the coach, the team did not end up playing better ball. Kieran suggested that his teammates were beginning to "tune out the coach," who was, in his view, "not a very positive person." All of this led me to wonder whether the coach might perhaps have given up on the team's chances for success that season and turned his attention to shifting responsibility for a disappointing season onto the players.

8   See Donnelly (2000) for a discussion of the amounts of time devoted to sport by young athletes and a suggestion that they may be in need of child law protection.

9   Mike was 14-years-old when I interviewed him.

10   Grasmuck (2005, 4) observes that a parent's experiences and observations about children's sports tend to be affected by the level of their child's skill in playing sports.

11   See Fine (1987) and Grasmuck (2005) for analyses of the dynamics of sporting prestige within the ranks of Little League Baseball players.

12   Caroline took care to point out that there are also some "synchro dads" who act in a similar manner.

13   See Amit-Talai (1995) for an assessment of some of the types of prevailing adult assumptions in Canada concerning child and youth personal relationships and friendships.

14   More selective and, hence, more locally prestigious institutional settings may also be provided by public schools that offer special programs in, for instance, French immersion or that require children to pass entrance examinations or to be interviewed before they are admitted and, if successful, to wear what amount to school uniforms.

15 This matter is, however, considered by Trussell (2009, 28) who also notes that at
    the level of families, children's sports tend to affect not only child athletes but all
    members of a family.

16 The "under-seven" designation means that all players must be younger than seven
    years of age at the time of the cut-off date that is established for registrations in a
    given sport.

17 MacGregor (1995) makes the interesting suggestion that if parents were from time
    to time to miss some of their children's sports competitions, then a daughter or
    son could have their own stories to bring home, rather than always having to listen
    to their parents' stories about their games.

18 Parents and coaches, along with friends and teammates, may volunteer or may be
    implicitly conscripted to assist an athlete to sort through not only the meaning of
    particular athletic performances but also their overall status, potential, and worth
    as an athlete. The difficulty that a parent faces in such situations is that sons or
    daughters may seek to evaluate their own performances by "reading" parents' (and
    others') estimations of how well they should do in any given event. Perceptive
    parents come to appreciate that young athletes need to be left to set their own
    goals and standards; they also learn how difficult a disappointed athlete can be
    to deal with. So the trick is to be encouraging and optimistic without setting a
    too specific or "realistic" goal or expectation for the young athlete's performance.
    The circumspect parent in these situations might seek to offer a fairly positive
    but non-specific assessment-cum-support statement to the athlete before the
    competition, thereby leaving a bit of leeway for post-competition reassessment to
    accommodate either success or failure.

19 Nor is this type of desire to "mess around" limited to eight-year-olds. The
    highjinks that erupted among teenaged members of a provincial youth team that
    was spending long hours travelling in vans to matches staged across and outside
    the province eventually brought the team's van to an abrupt halt on a mountain
    highway. Lined up on the side of the road by a fuming coach-driver, the guilty
    parties were dispatched to retrieve shoes and articles of clothing that had been
    tossed out the windows by bored and boisterous players.

20 Ben-Ari's (1997) study of a Japanese day-care centre makes an interesting point
    about the manner in which children's disruptive behaviour in this setting tends
    to be labelled as "senseless" by adults, thereby effectively permitting boys and girls
    with some leeway to engage in it precisely because it is not perceived by adults as
    threatening the "serious" order of the preschool centre.

21 See Heikkala (1993) for an overview of the rationale of discipline in the logic of
    athletic competition.

22 The coaches at this and other synchronized swimming clubs are not volunteers but are paid for their services.

23 See Hyman (2009) and Sokolove (2008) for critical assessments of the increasing problems posed by sports related injuries, especially for girls and young women.

Chapter Six

PULLING TOGETHER AND APART IN COMMUNITY SPORTS

ARRIVING AT A TRACK and field club's practice session on a summer evening, I spotted a gathering of coaches, parents, and athletes of various ages waiting in front of the locked equipment room. Uncharacteristically, none of the three senior club coaches who held keys to the room had yet arrived. As the minutes ticked by, the impatience generated by lack of access to equipment needed to set up the throws practice areas and the high jump and long jump pits became perceptible. Several teenaged athletes dribbled a soccer ball to an adjoining grassy area, prompting a father to observe, "I didn't drive him all the way here just to kick a ball around. He could do that across the street from our house." The hurdles coach, a schoolteacher, added that had he known the equipment room wouldn't be open, he would have brought along a set of exams to mark.

When the president of the club arrived, he was met with suggestions about how to ensure this holdup would not occur again. Fifteen minutes later one of the three key-holding coaches rolled up, actually somewhat ahead of his usual time of arrival, having driven directly from work to the field. Within moments equipment was disbursed and the practice session assumed its usual pattern. A few of the older hands in the club stayed on a bit longer, noting how viscerally the response to this irritating but atypical delay had departed from the bonhomie and good humour long prized within this community sports organization. Joining them, the club president declared with some exasperation that this was, in actuality, just another instance of the sort of complaining that he and other senior club officials had had to put up with that season.

Although not mentioned by the president, this spate of complaining coincided with the transformation of a modestly sized community sports club for children and youths into a larger and more ambitious organization. The club had not only grown in terms of the numbers and quality of its athletes and coaches but had also taken on the task of hosting a major athletics competition scheduled for later that season. As a result, club coaches and officials on occasion found themselves struggling to meet the various challenges that accompanied these initiatives. Indeed, as I learned later, the head coach and other equipment room key holders had been delayed by a last-minute request to resolve certain arrangements for the forthcoming competition before a meeting to be held later that evening with provincial sport officials. Those waiting in front of the equipment room were unaware of the backstage developments transpiring that evening. What some of them were beginning to comment upon were the ways in which, as they saw it, club officials appeared to be moving away from the organization's previous objectives and ways of doing things. What had been a fairly close-knit and unified club seemed to be morphing into a divided organization. According to some, there was now an inner circle that included those directing an ever more complex set of athletic initiatives. Across from them stood an out-of-the-loop set of others, some of whom harboured growing concerns about the relative ranking of their interests and those of their children in the club's shifting priorities.

By the time the head coach's wife arrived at the field with another key, the immediate problem had been resolved. The grumbling heard that evening resurfaced in the coming weeks and months, continuing even after the club's successful handling of the competition that had preoccupied senior club officials throughout the season. A veteran club member recalled wistfully that in previous years an annual picnic had brought together athletes, parents, coaches, and officials in a purely social event. This, she said, had served to ensure that everyone knew one another as individuals, thereby forestalling the creation of cliques and divisions within the club. By her reckoning, the decision to skip the picnic this season had been a costly one.

The particular issues that figured in that evening's events raise more general questions that confront those who seek to sustain community sports for children and youths. As noted in previous chapters, community sports involve not only organized forms of athletic performance but also differing modes of social participation by children and youths, parents, and others who opt to join in, support, and run these activities. Engaging in and with these optional, leisure pursuits—whether as a parent, coach, official, or athlete—involves not only a voluntary allocation of time and other resources but also the shouldering of some amount of unpaid work of one kind or another. In return, those who involve themselves in community sports hope for outcomes that will reward their choices and render their efforts worthwhile. How are the differing purposes and expectations, roles and relationships that figure within community sports articulated, and what happens when these cannot be readily reconciled? Given the structures of competition fundamental to organized sports, how, indeed, can the interests of "me and mine" be balanced discursively and practically with those of the team, club, sport, or community? In what ways might jealousy enter into and inflect community sports?

COMPETITION AND JEALOUSY IN COMMUNITY SPORTS[1]

Although jealousy and envy are sometimes treated as being synonymous, these feelings can and should be distinguished from one another.[2] While envy derives from the desire to acquire something possessed by another person, jealousy is grounded in the fear of losing something already possessed (Foster 1972, 168). Within community sports, neither jealousy nor envy tend to be freely confessed or self-attributed, although rumors of the susceptibility of others to these are by no means rare. The public display and acknowledgement of emotions remain ambivalent and complicated matters within children's sports, in no small part due to the manner in which these types of sport activities seek to combine two otherwise separate and diverging fields of social endeavour. Rearing children rests at the heart of domesticity and family life.[3] Mothers and fathers are expected to establish a family home as a private setting within which intimate responsibilities for ensuring the well-being of and for guiding the rearing of infant, child, and adolescent sons and daughters is undertaken. In contrast, sport typically occupies and resides within public venues. It entails diverse forms of rule-governed physical and athletic performance that are performed not merely for the personal satisfaction of athletes but also for the enjoyment of spectators or fans who need not be personally connected or known to the athletes. Indeed, the anticipated presence of an audience comprises an essential factor in the social construction of selected physical activities and games as organized sports (Dyck 2000d, 29).

Concerns about the appropriate management and display of emotions that surface within community sports afford a vantage point from which to trace certain complications that result from connecting child rearing to competitive sports. Family life is commonly taken as the primary locus within which children are supposed to receive the care, guidance, and security that will enable them to learn how to manage and express their emotions in healthy ways. Children who fit easily into activities organized outside the bounds of family life are judged to have developed (or to be developing) an ability to get along with others, a capacity especially valued in community sports. Suitably behaved children, in turn, imply conscientious and effective parenting.

The enrolment of sons and daughters in community sports activities involves them not merely spending time companionably (or at least peaceably) with other children, coaches and officials but doing so while engaging in one or another form of competition. Designed to distinguish the athletically proficient, the more determined, the better coached, or simply the more fortunate of competitors from others, organized sports function relentlessly to register wins, losses, ties, records, championships, triumphs, and failures. Competition is supposed to be taken seriously; athletes are enjoined to do their best to win or at least to improve their competitive performances and standing. The prospects of perennially losing in athletic contests or, even worse, of not particularly minding doing so are problematic matters within organized sports.[4] Indeed, Canadian children are often implored to "show some emotion" when participating in sports. Giving vent to anger over an off-target shot at net, an unsuccessful at-bat, or the outcome of a game or race will not only be tolerated by some adults but may even be positively interpreted as a sign of an athlete's desire to win.

Ideally, child rearing and organized sports for children might be arranged in ways that would sustain a nuanced and balanced reconciliation of the principal objectives of both spheres. Within this scenario, parents would prepare their daughters and sons to become socially adept, emotionally adroit, and highly "coachable" individuals. For their part, coaches and other officials would endorse and observe the values and objectives of parents while augmenting the athletic capabilities and competitive spirit possessed by boys and girls under their charge. Yet no matter how often parents and coaches might declare their commitment to fostering one or another rendering of this preferred state of affairs, the taken-for-granted priorities that they fall back on when participating in and determining the shape of community sports for children are not always compatible and, hence, sometimes collide in telling ways. Resulting frustrations and conflicts tend to inflate the currency of stereotypical claims about the suspected motivations of various "types" of parents and/or coaches who are implicitly held responsible for such outcomes.[5] Clichés don't take sufficient account of the ways in which complicated instances of jealousy contribute to these consequences. To grasp this it is necessary to recall the attractions that draw parents and coaches to children's sports as well as certain underlying dynamics that can threaten their enjoyment of them.

Games, matches and competitive events stand at the centre of sport, showcasing the movements and performances that exemplify athletic endeavour. Routine plays along with sometimes-exceptional feats accomplished by individual athletes and teams remain focal matters for spectators and athletes alike. The social behaviour exhibited on and alongside the fields of play by children, youths and adults acting in various capacities can also be observed at close hand. Whether community sports ought to be approached strictly *as sports* and enjoyed and valued in their own right or, conversely, be treated as pliable social instrumentalities that can be harnessed to more fundamental projects of child rearing marks a basic cleavage. An ongoing tug-of-war between these two positions persists within the operations of many community sports associations. Depending upon one's point of view, how individuals behave within the ambit of community sports may be construed as being at least as important as the athletic outcomes totted up on scoreboards.

Roughly similar sets of activities and role repertoires exist across a broad range of these sports. Athletes take part in games and competitions and dedicate themselves more or less zealously to enhancing their athletic abilities to attain competitive success. Coaches provide training and direction for athletes and are expected to devote as much time and energy as they can muster to improving their teaching of skills, understanding of athletic tactics and strategy, and proficiency in managing and motivating athletes to prevail over their competitors. Referees and umpires preside over the officiating of athletic events; their knowledge of the written and unwritten rules of a sport and the finesse with which they interpret and apply these during games and meets is essential to competitive sports. Other sport officials register athletes and coaches, arrange the use of athletic facilities, and schedule competitive events—mundane but necessary tasks that build and maintain the infrastructures of sport. Parents and whoever else happens to show up to watch community sports events provide an invaluable audience whose presence helps to transform running, jumping, and throwing into athletic events.

Each of these forms of involvement can be performed in varying ways, permitting some scope for the realization of personal styles and preferences. Girls and boys might join teams simply to spend time with friends playing games that are fun to play. Alternatively, they might wish to work towards one day competing at the Olympics. The coach of a youth soccer team might be a father or mother conscripted just before the beginning of the season so that there could be a team for his/her child to join. Yet after that child has grown up or stopped playing soccer, the now veteran coach might still be working to complete the higher levels of the national coach training program[6] to be eligible to mentor an elite youth team that represents an entire league or city in regional or national competitions. Those who agree to serve as club or league officials might initially approach this assignment rather like jury duty: just taking their turn to help out for a season or two. Yet officials who discover that they enjoy engaging in these activities may transform their involvement into a veritable calling that becomes the equivalent of an unpaid second job. Spectators who attend children's sports events may spend this time chatting sociably with other onlookers or can make it their mission to provide professional-calibre cheerleading in support of "our team."

Audiences at community sports events tend to be made up primarily of parents and other family members. In contrast to the social distance that separates athletes and spectators in professional sports, boys and girls who compete at the community level are not just financed, transported, and accompanied to their sports events by mom and dad, but may also at some point be coached by their own (or a teammate's) parent. The athletic successes or failures chalked up as well as the shows of social aplomb or immaturity evinced by young athletes are not, therefore, those of unknown figures but of girls and boys whose parents might well be standing or sitting along with other parents on the sidelines. Whose child is this can, if it is not already known, be determined easily enough. In the absence of anonymity, the deeds of children and youths tend to be linked discursively to observed styles of parenting.

Community sports provide mothers and fathers with venues where their performances of parenting can be witnessed and validated by other parents. The responsibility that Canadian parents are increasingly expected to shoulder with respect to the eventual outcomes of their sons and daughters as adults makes child rearing a long-term and challenging venture. What community sports offer is a set of structured events and activities that accommodate and valorize publicly performed acts of parenting in ways that schools, for example, generally do not. By doing what parents are asked to do in community sports, mothers and fathers can openly demonstrate their care and concern for their children. Implicit and explicit recognition by other parents of the conscientiousness and effectiveness of one's efforts is immediately forthcoming, especially when a daughter's or a son's enjoyment and success in sport are plainly evident to other dads and moms who are looking on. While this might be interpreted as prima facie evidence of an underlying instrumentality that guides parental involvement in community sports, it should not lead us to lose sight of the hazards and risks that parents might also encounter within these settings.

The pleasure that sport can generate takes many forms. To begin with, community sports can offer a welcome change of pace from the everyday demands and rigours of adult employment as well as of child and youth schooling. Scheduled sports events permit parents to allocate a certain amount of time each week to accompany their children to recreational activities. The time spent driving to practices, games, and tournaments represents not only shared journeys to positively anticipated occasions but also a significant proportion of the practical opportunities that parents and children might have to touch base with one another. Once at the field, pool, or rink, girls and boys come under the supervision of coaches, enabling fathers and mothers to step back and watch the action with other parents. Although parents and children remain mostly within sight of each other, they get to observe and interact not just with their generational counterparts but also, in the case of children, with adults who are not their parents or, in the case of parents, with girls and boys who are not their children. In consequence, family members can spend extended periods together without being constantly on top of one another.

Community sports are regularly mobilized to support endeavours that range from the pursuit of personal dreams to family projects to enterprises that enlist the support of entire teams, clubs, or leagues. A child or youth athlete's wish to excel within a sport can be nourished or even initiated by a coach or parent. Alternatively, a mother or father might wish to ensure that the competitive imperatives of sport won't be permitted to threaten a son's or daughter's satisfaction of simply being a member of a team and playing a sport as well as they can without worrying too much about winning or losing. Amateur coaches might seek to emulate the exploits and win the recognition that leading coaches and managers receive within professional sports. So, too, can ambitious club and league officials give free reign to previously hidden organizational talents by mounting campaigns to increase the membership of a club or to pressure municipal politicians into providing more and better athletic facilities.

These and other attractions draw child and youth athletes, parents, and other adults to attach themselves in varying ways and for differing reasons to the activities of community sports. The rewards such varied involvement might yield cover the span from moderately satisfying ones to moments and matters of intense joy. Yet however pleasing these may be, their attainment and continuation remain utterly dependent upon what others also seek to accomplish within these settings. In short, that which parents and others involved in community sports come to love and depend upon can be undermined and extinguished by the enthusiasms and designs of others engaged in this field. The inescapable vulnerability that participation in community sports entails, feeds feelings of jealousy that can and do complicate and sometimes corrode activities that are meant to bring health and happiness.

FEAR OF LOSING

Jealousy arises when that which is particularly valued is damaged or threatened not by accident but because of the known or suspected interventions of a rival. Thus, the loss or impairment of any of the various types of attractions afforded by community sports can stoke up the anxiety, vigilance, and suspicion commonly associated with jealousy. Because parents are well positioned to appreciate the benefits that community sports can bestow upon not only their children but also themselves, mothers and fathers may be doubly susceptible to experiencing jealousy when they fear that the operations of a team or club may be shifting in ways that will negatively impact their daughter or son and, thereby, them.

To enrol one's child in a team or club is to assume that he/she will receive instruction on how to play the sport and have sufficient opportunities to do so. Disputes about unequal allocation of playing time during games and competitions are endemic within community sports. This may be less of an issue on teams established to introduce young children to a sport. Coaches of novice teams who adopt a policy of providing every athlete under their charge with more or less equal playing time explain it in terms of their chosen priorities: for instance, they might announce that primary consideration is to be given not to competitive results, but to "letting the kids have fun" and "letting them get to know the sport." Proceeding in this manner, at least at the outset, can serve to nurture a sense of camaraderie and "being in this together" both for children and for parents.

Some children, however, develop proficiency in a sport more rapidly and fulsomely than do others, and sooner or later someone will question the wisdom of always providing teammates with equal amounts of playing time. When a team is not winning more games than it loses, then a coach's abilities and/or methods can begin to attract criticism, more often than not expressed behind his/her back. Rationales for making changes of one sort or another begin to circulate tentatively along the sidelines. It might be contended that "always losing is no fun," that kids have to find out about the "hard facts of competition" sometime, or that it is unfair to "hold back the development of the more talented kids." Provisions implemented by leagues and sport associations for streaming or separating child and youth athletes according to their athletic abilities are supposed to resolve the difficulties of enabling all kids who wish to play sport to do so while also permitting the more talented among them to enhance their skills by joining elite teams or programs. Even measures such as these cannot prevent the unequal treatment of child and youth athletes from re-emerging again and again as a divisive issue within clubs and teams, whether at elite levels or within recreational or house leagues that are supposed to ensure that less talented players' opportunities to play a sport will be protected from the ravages of untrammelled competition.

This can be illustrated by looking into actual instances. In the first, a 12-year-old girl who was the leading scorer on a championship soccer team was surreptitiously recruited by the coach of the championship team at the next highest age level to join his squad the following season so she could improve her game by playing with and against slightly older players. Her parents, who were interested in boosting her prospects of eventually winning an athletic scholarship to a "big" university in the United States, agreed with this proposal, and she switched teams. Her previous coach was initially quite disappointed by her departure. Nevertheless, he moved on to design and implement a rather different style of play for his team that made better use of the talents of his remaining players. That season his team once again captured the championship in its division, largely as a result of the new tactics that showcased the abilities of several players who had previously been viewed as "hard workers" and who had provided a solid "supporting cast" for the erstwhile scoring star.

As it happened, the team to which she bolted recorded a "decent" season but did not repeat as division champion. Shortly after their daughter's former team won its second consecutive championship, the parents of the player in question contacted her former coach to inquire delicately about the possibility of her rejoining his team for the coming season. The parents of the girls who had remained loyal to the team and who had shone in the absence of the former leading scorer now contemplated the prospect that the gains their daughters had individually and collectively achieved might be undermined by the return of a player whose preferred style of play would most likely lead to a turning back of the clock for the team, both on and off the field. The impact upon team parents when the coach opted to let the prodigal star return was immediate. While the player subsequently made a sustained effort to accommodate herself to the team's new style of play, she once again became the leading scorer. There was a discernible discomfort and stiffness among the familiar faces along the sidelines when her parents took up their place there at the beginning of the next season.

A second example comes from a championship match in football for 10-year-olds. To ensure that all team members would, in fact, be allowed to have an active part in this match, league rules required that every player must take the field for a minimum of 10 plays. One of the teams dressed all of its players for this prestigious final game and made certain that each of them got into the game for at least 10 plays. The opposing team, which in the end triumphed, similarly observed the formal rule. It did so by dressing a roster of players from which six team members—who were identified by those familiar with the team as being its weaker players—were absent. When questioned about their absence, the winning head coach produced signed notes indicating that each of them was either injured or ill that day and, hence, unable to take part in the game. Parents from the losing team were furious with what they interpreted as a cynical fabrication and unsporting stratagem on the part of the victorious coaches. Some of them felt that by honouring the letter but not the spirit of the league's regulations that the opposing team had stolen their sons' chance to engage in a "fair and square" competition for the league championship. Several of them also wondered aloud just how those six young boys whose contribution to the championship victory had been to be declared sick or injured might have felt about their place on the winning team. One might also have asked how the parents of the missing six viewed this episode.

Complications sparked by the collision of social class differences can also erode enjoyment of community sports activities. Teams and clubs often draw participants from different neighbourhoods and from varying income and occupational categories. Recognizing the potential sensitivity of these differences, care is often exercised within clubs and teams to undercommunicate or simply steer clear of discussions or situations that might involve explicit admission of matters pertaining to class, ethnicity, religion, or politics. Nevertheless, social class differences can surface unpredictably and problematically within community sports.

Evidence of middle-class parents' concerns regarding the social prospects of their children and the chances of them being able to reproduce, if not surpass, their parents' class status (Fussell 1983; Newman 1988, 1991) is not difficult to find within community sports. For instance, Janet, an immigrant mother whose teenage son and daughter belong to a sport club that she views as being solidly middle class in its membership cheerfully identifies as its most attractive feature the fact that it brings together "kids who are going somewhere in their lives." In a similar vein, Quentin, a track and field coach whose daughter had recently graduated from the club, observes that among the boys and girls he mentors, "it is not a matter of them asking each other, 'Are you going to university?' Instead, they're asking, 'Which university will you be going to?'"

These are not the only readings or interpretations of middle-class styles of participation in sport. Steve, a self-identified "working man" who stepped down from a successful run of coaching boys' hockey in a region that spanned both working-class and middle-class neighbourhoods, explains that a large part of the frustration he had increasingly encountered was caused by "kids from families with a lot of money" who came to practices or skipped them as they wished. In Steve's view, kids from families that haven't much money tend to make hockey far more of a priority in their lives. Interestingly, Eric, a "dad coach" of a girls' soccer team in an upper-middle-class neighbourhood in another city, substantially corroborates Steve's observation, albeit from a rather different point of departure. Speaking about the "special challenges" of coaching a team such as his, Eric explains, "Our kids all come from families that have money, so these kids could be doing a lot of other things besides kicking a soccer ball. Most of their folks go skiing or have cottages, so many weekends it's not easy to ensure that we have a full team." Eric goes on to cite the affluence of children on a team such as his as a rationale for streaming soccer players into elite programs at a much earlier age than is permitted by league rules. This, he argues, would make it possible to identify and recruit the best athletes to elite soccer programs in a timely manner, thereby permitting this sport to compete more effectively with others in the drive to corral superior athletes.

Unanticipated sources of friction may be generated when taken-for-granted social practices stumble over class differences that can scuttle the best-laid plans for "getting everyone to pull together" on a team or in a club. Lorraine, a mother whose two children clearly enjoyed taking up track and field, was dismayed to learn midway through the season that each family with a child in the club would be required to "sell" two small advertisements for the printed program that would be distributed at the club's annual meet. A member of the club's executive explained to those present at a parents' meeting that "it should be no problem to ask your lawyer or accountant to make a contribution in return for a bit of advertising." Families that neglected to "sell their ads" would, he advised, be expected to contribute the $100 advertisement charge themselves. As Lorraine confided to one of the other parents she had befriended at the club, she didn't know any lawyers or accountants and the family's budget was already fully accounted for. She worried that this might force her kids to drop out of the club. A behind-the-scenes intervention initiated by that other parent with the club executive resulted in an unannounced exception being made in the case of Lorraine, but she and her children did not return to the club the following season.

No less awkward was the situation created when the coaches and parents of a girls' soccer team drawn from a socio-economically mixed suburb decided that purchasing warm-up jackets in team colours (with the name and playing number of each girl on her jacket) would give a much-needed boost to team morale. To offset the cost of jackets, team parents organized a "bottle drive,"[7] but the returns realized from this fundraising effort still left half the cost of each jacket to be covered individually by parents. On the pre-arranged afternoon when the jackets were brought to the field for distribution, one member of the team, Sylvie, was missing. All of the parents present were reminded that they would have to pay the team manager the balance of the cost of their daughters' jackets.

When Sylvie also missed the following week's practice and game, the team manager telephoned her mother to advise her about the time and place of the next scheduled game and to remind her about the payment owing for Sylvie's as yet unclaimed team jacket. The mother replied that her daughter did not need the jacket since the family had already purchased winter wear for her and her siblings. Since the team had accepted delivery of the jacket and could not return it, the team manager, wishing to avoid a situation in which Sylvie would be the only player without a team jacket, made an on-the-spot "executive decision" to "forget" the outstanding payment. When Sylvie appeared at the next team practice, one of the coaches took her father aside to explain that the team had never wanted the jackets to be a problem. Sylvie's father, however, insisted on paying the amount owing on the jacket. He and his wife had decided to get the jacket for their daughter "as her Christmas present." He went on to detail just how much his daughter seemed to have benefited from playing soccer that season. Sylvie's teacher had identified her as a "discipline problem" the previous year, but this year the same teacher had asked her parents what had led to the startling and positive change in her classroom deportment. Although he and his wife credited Sylvie's participation in soccer for this change, from that point on neither of them came to watch her games.

Any formal or implied acceptance of disparities in the status of young athletes or of their parents within a team or a club can cause grief, even in situations where social class differences are not significant. Awards ceremonies are often rather tense occasions, for these oblige coaches (or whoever is called upon to determine who will receive particular awards or honours) to make decisions and draw distinctions that might thrill winners but that may well be seen as invidious by those who feel spurned or slighted. For instance, during the awards ceremony at the year-end banquet of a local sports club, the parents seated at one table started the evening in good spirits. They had become friendly with one another over several seasons and all had made substantial contributions to the operations of the club. When the daughter of one of the couples at the table won the club award for her event specialty, hearty agreement was expressed. When the son of another couple seated there was overlooked for an award in his event, the geniality that had engulfed the table began to disappear.

The disappointed father, Brad, turned his attention directly to another parent who was part of the group of coaches that had decided the awards. Brad cited the multiple first-place finishes that his son had recorded that season and argued that his results were at least as impressive as those of the award winner. He turned then to his own highly successful and well-known efforts to raise funds on behalf of the club, the assistance that he had afforded in organizing several of the club's meets, and his wife's work as a coach who had filled in as an instructor at the novice level the previous year. It was, in Brad's view, unlikely that either he or she would play very active parts in the club in the future.

These examples illustrate some of the ways in which jealousy enters into community sports. The pains so often taken by participants within this sphere to avoid appearing to be the type of person or group that might be baldly pursuing his, her, or its own interests without regard for those of others speaks to the difficulties involved in seeking to accommodate the plurality of objectives entertained within community sports. Taking note of the dynamics of larger and smaller disagreements, disputes, disappointments, and conflicts that unfold within community sports clubs and teams is important, especially when those involved seem so determined to mute or cover over the extent of their differences.

Once there, however, parents, coaches, and sport officials must confront the possibility of being obliged to surrender or compromise their own values and ventures by virtue of being overwhelmed by those of others. This might, conceivably, reach far beyond the prospect of having to put up with the personal foibles and penchants of one or another individual for an afternoon or two. Having to grit one's teeth for an entire season and endure a stream of assumptions, comments, and projects that appeal strongly to some, but not all, tastes is entirely another matter. Accordingly, camaraderie and jealousy rest cheek by jowl in community sports, situated uneasily alongside one another, supporting and contesting the direction of child and youth sports activities as well as of family life.

DOING IT FOR THE KIDS

Those who venture into coaching and organizing community sports take on the prospect of substantial interaction with athletes, parents, other coaches, and sport officials. The circumstances and motivations that prompt individuals to volunteer as a coach or assistant coach can vary significantly, not only between individuals but also over a period of time for a given volunteer. Similarly, those who commence by assisting with the mundane organizational work that community clubs and teams need to have done by someone, may—if they don't slip away at the earliest opportunity—find themselves encouraged or personally drawn to assuming an executive position. Improving the operational procedures of a club or league might be experienced as a worthwhile activity in its own right or become the gateway for developing a more fulsome "career" as a voluntary sport organizer. Teams and clubs may extend the scope of their ambitions far beyond routine schedules of competition to undertake trips to compete in tournaments in other provinces, countries, and continents. Alternatively, sport organizations might strive to host major athletic competitions on a one-off or continuing basis. To establish an annual sport tournament that attracts visitors from faraway is to exhibit the resources, sophistication, and prestige possessed by its organizers. Perhaps the epitome of such special projects on the part of local sport organizers would involve them as key figures in the promotion and construction of new sport facilities such as hockey rinks, stadiums, pools, or playing fields, all of which are expensive to construct and maintain. To play a key part in obtaining government support and private donations of the order needed to see projects of this scale through to completion is to earn potential recognition as a "builder"[8] in local sport circles.

In return for the countless hours that such highly dedicated community sports volunteers invest into these activities, they as individuals gain access to organizational opportunities and resources that would most likely otherwise remain beyond their reach. An acclaimed (or even a not-so-acclaimed) community sports coach can, indeed, devote hundreds of hours each season to training and supervising the athletes or team that he/she directs. Yet, as essential as his/her contribution is, that time and effort represents only a small proportion of the overall total of such resources that is invested into the operations of a particular team or club by the young athletes, parents, and others who also sustain its existence. Just as love requires lovers, ambitious coaches require athletes to realize their own wishes to become accomplished coaches. In the case of community sports, however, coaches and club organizers also need conscientious parents who will underwrite club fees and equipment costs and provide transportation to get young athletes to and from games and practice sessions. To the extent that volunteer coaches and organizers not only contribute significantly to the construction of community sports but also derive personal opportunities and social benefits that may become vitally important to them as individuals in doing so, their participation needs to be recognized as something that might well involve something more than mere altruism and selflessness. To note this is not to imply any sort of impropriety or to discount their contributions. It is, instead, to acknowledge the ways in which the individual aspirations of every participant in community sports constitute active ingredients of these activities.

Ironically, the existence of conflicting interests in community sports on the part of parents, coaches, and officials is confirmed by the frequency with which personal interests and aspirations are discursively eschewed and excoriated. Most notably, the phrase "it's for the kids" shows up again and again within public and private discussions of community sports. Framed in slightly differing forms—"everything we do is for the kids," "it's all for the kids," or, more simply "it's for the kids"—this is not so much a summary accounting of what actually happens within community sports as a moral directive that, according to the speaker, ought to guide and regulate the involvement of adults in this field. As frequently and as earnestly as it may be declared, the phrase still elicits uncertainty and some skepticism among those who are familiar with it.

Theresa, a mother of two young athletes, suggests that parents who make this claim in support of one or another organizational measure often "get so wrapped up" with what is happening that they lose track of the possibility that what they are advocating is "not for the kids. It's for *their kid!*" Katherine, a mother of two teenaged athletes, has heard it many times, but is still not certain about its meaning:

Well, people stay in marriages "for the kids" [*laughing*]. "We're doing it for the kids".... Well, I have a problem with that statement if it's used to continue a negative activity. I'm okay with it if it's a reminder on the field or whatever—any kid group activity—that is reminding parents that it's not.... The kids aren't supposed to be living for them. You know, it's like this is their experience. This is their activity. They should be getting out of it whatever they can. Yeah, it's a weird statement. I guess I'd be suspicious of someone using that statement because I'd wonder, "Why do you have to say that? Who the hell else would it be for?" But in some cases, I think people say it's for the kids, but it's actually for them. I've met a significant number of people that are actually trying to relive their youth through their children. Or it may be their misspent youth or their mis-set goals or misperceptions or whatever. But they're trying to sort of recreate their own glory days or whatever through their kids, but they don't actually see the kids. They say it's for the kids, but I'm suspicious that it's maybe for them. So I don't know what that statement means. I guess it means a lot of things.

Chuck, a long-time coach who has held executive positions in several local and provincial sport organizations, explains how this claim tends to be used within these circles:

I'm very suspicious when I hear it sometimes [*laughing*], depending upon who's saying it. I sit on a board right now and, you know, "Well, we're getting too competitive and this is just for the kids." I'm thinking, "But you're keeping score. Aren't you more concerned about fairness?" And I think they get confused with what's fair and what's not. I think sometimes they're talking about their own child instead of the group. And there's an idea sometimes when I hear this that "it's all for the kids" [means] that "you're *not* for the kids." And I've heard it directed at me, but I've heard it directed at other people [too]. You go around and you hear it. I've heard the question, "Well, do they not care about the kids?" "Well, I didn't mean it that way, but, but, but." So, when I hear it I wonder about it because I'm sort of in it, I thought, because it *was* for the kids and that was understood so I don't have to say that. So, I don't know. People who are successful, you never hear them say that [*laughing*]. They're just there for the kids. I don't know, maybe I'm all wet. I assume we're there for the kids. We're sure as hell not getting rich doing it, I'll tell you [*laughing*].

Norm, an accomplished hockey coach who has also served as an executive member of various sport organizations, approaches the matter of how this phrase is used in community sports with frankness:

"Why are we here?" The rhetorical question, "Why are we here?" "It's for the kids!" I'm not so sure it is for the kids. The overall sport is not for the kids. It's a vehicle for a bunch of adults to control a particular program and the kids are secondary. The adults seem to come first. The adult rules, the adults dominate the children totally. The kids have *nothing* to say about the game. The kids have really no say as to where they play or at what level they play. They're, in a lot of cases, forced to play at a higher level where they may not be able to enjoy it. Instead of being adequate, they may want to be superior and play at the lesser level. Adults, in a lot of cases, don't understand that. My feeling on the phrase "it's for the kids," I use it quietly with myself. I'm saying it's for me. But when they say they've enjoyed it, that's where I like it and I go into it saying, "it's for the kids." And we just got a write-up there in the local paper [points to an article that has been framed and mounted on his wall]. It matters not what level. It matters not. I can coach wherever I want. I can go and coach junior hockey or at the "A" level. I prefer to coach at the "B" or "C" level and make those kids happy. I feel, my own philosophy is, yeah, "it's for the kids." Everything is for them. Just leave me and these fifteen or seventeen kids alone and we'll go out and have a great time. I guarantee it. But yeah, I feel it's for the kids. The sport isn't for the kids. The sport is for the adults, but the game is for the kids.

Reflecting upon the more than 20 years that he has spent coaching in various sports, Norm is explicit about his reasons for doing so:

I enjoy it. It's a hobby. Without being egotistical about it, I am good at it, so I feel good about myself, it's good for my own self-esteem. And it's just the ability to communicate with children, whether they be five-years-old or thirty-five—not just children, but people. And over the years, I've had a lot of good teams and very, very few poor teams.... And the kids always say, "It's the best year I ever had." And that's what I like. Well, my motives are selfish, and it's something that I really enjoy. I just *really* enjoy it. I don't mind getting up early in the morning, and if my boy can't make it, it's not a big deal. I'll go without him. It's very, very selfish of me, but it pleasures me to have kids enjoy themselves.

Edward, a technical official in figure skating, notes, "I guess we'd all like to think that 'it's for the kids'":

A lot of judges will say, "I do this for the kids." Parents that run things and organize things will say the same thing all the time as sort of justifying their own participation as if just doing it isn't enough. I don't know. I guess you could have all kinds of base motives for being involved. So by saying it's for the kids, you basically say you're there for a noble purpose so you feel good about being there, I guess. A lot of people look at it and say, "I must be crazy spending all my time doing this when I could be doing something more productive," or whatever. So I must be doing it for the kids. You know, it's almost like a default kind of answer in some ways because, you know, they can't think of any other good reason to be there [*laughing*]. In fact, they can think of lots of good reasons not to be there.

What emerges from these reflections on the meaning and usage of the customary assertion that "this is all for the kids" is acute awareness of the contradictions that exist between this commonplace rationale for these adult-directed activities and the varied personal interests and objectives that motivate parents, coaches, and officials to support community sports. There is a widely shared suspicion among those active in community sports that, in the words of Carla, an experienced coach, sport administrator, and mother, that "you hear that from people who give you every indication of it not being for the kids." Detailed accounts of situations in which advantage was allegedly taken or self-interest pursued by someone or some group under the guise of "doing it for the kids" can be produced at the drop of a hat. Nevertheless, even the sternest critics of this credo cannot simply or entirely jettison it from their explanations of what, at its best, community sports might entail. There are, after all, countless instances of parents and other adults diligently seeking to do the right thing with and for children through community sports, whether defined by reference to the prevailing wisdom within a particular club or sport or in terms of their own reckoning. Good intentions in and of themselves cannot, of course, guarantee the efficacy or appropriateness of these efforts, but it is essential not to overlook or dismiss these summarily.

What also needs to be noted is that parents and community sports coaches and officials are not the only ones who claim to be "doing it for the kids." The policy documents and published analyses concerning child and youth sports pumped out in profusion by government agencies, recreational departments, national and international sport organizations, entrepreneurial sport experts, and the burgeoning public-private sport industry in Canada habitually wrap their undertakings in related versions of this claim. Yet far from acknowledging any possibility that unexamined conflicts of interest might just be attached to their collective and corporate undertakings in this sphere, these voices seem bent upon reclassifying community sports as a site for public policy, commercial benefits, and for-profit schemes. The awkward but compelling candour shown by parents, community coaches, and officials in reflecting upon their own complicated involvement in community sports contrasts fundamentally with the simplistic claims about what sport involves and how and by whom it must be managed that issue forth from the self-appointed "stakeholders" who aim to colonize community sports.

PLAYING THEIR PART

Norm's claim that in community sports "the kids have *nothing* to say about the game" might be the case within the restricted confines of club and league executive meetings. But allowing for this does not mean that children and youths can or should be invariably regarded as subordinate and dependent figures whose interests and ability to act rest solely in the hands of parents, coaches, and officials. To adopt that approach would be to take on notions of children and of childhood that willfully ignore the extent to which kids' participation in sport—as in other areas of social life—might also reveal their capacities to work with and around adults. A better way of proceeding is to consider the ways in which children and youths might also engage in sometimes pulling together with and sometimes working at cross-purposes to other participants in community sports.

The tendency to characterize community sports as a field that is utterly dominated by adults who ought to be "doing it for the kids" but who are prone to running these activities for their own "vicarious purposes" creates a curious but not entirely uncomfortable cultural space for young athletes. On the one hand, they are discursively positioned in this view as being fully deserving of *all* of the efforts and expenditures taken by parents, volunteers, and communities to enable them to engage in these activities. This is to be done in expensive sport facilities to which they and their state-of-the-art sport equipment and uniforms must be conveyed by conscientious parents and attentive coaches. Their athletic performances should be watched and applauded by mothers, fathers, and assorted other family members who will duly organize their own lives around the dictates of team or club schedules. Since adults are implored not to place undue expectations upon the on-field performances of young athletes, any son or daughter who feels aggrieved on this score deserves a sympathetic hearing from someone who will intervene on his/her behalf. On the proverbial other hand, the responsibilities assigned to child and youth athletes in this iteration of community sports tend to be rather modest and ultimately forgivable because they are, after all, defined as being "just kids." In this vision of child and youth sports, self-sacrificing adults ought to be prepared to do anything and just about everything for boys and girls who are notionally left to determine which sports they might wish to play, when, and with what degree of seriousness and intensity.

This composite portrait of what it is said that child and youth sports entails does not, of course, automatically or wholly dictate the real-life organization of these activities. But to the extent that one or another version circulates among at least some parents in community sports, it constitutes a set of cultural propositions that is hardly kept secret from children. The downside of appearing in a cultural model as a dependent and immature being who is defined as not yet able to determine what is in his/her own best interests is fairly obvious. Yet a potential upside of occasionally slipping into or accommodating some, if not all, of the premises of infantilization is the manner in which this ultimately places the onus for responsibility upon surrounding or attending adults.

Playing the part of the "kid" in community sports permits boys and girls who enjoy the financial wherewithal and parental support needed to participate in this field some leeway in interpreting and performing the role assigned them. What counts as exemplary behaviour on the part of sons and daughters and what most definitely does not is known from an early age. Parents', teachers', and coaches' unceasing attempts to ensure that kids will "know where I am coming from" and have "no doubt" about what is expected of them too often attribute non-fulfillment of such expectations to children's lack of understanding or immaturity and too seldom contemplate the possibility that non-compliance might be fuelled as much or more by resistance or differing priorities than incomprehension. Working beneath this dense canopy of sundry adult beliefs and purposes with respect to children and childhood, young athletes find spaces within which they might renegotiate some existing practices and explore new possibilities in community sports.

Fourteen-year-old Mike relates the story of how, when he was in Grade 5 he took part in a public-speaking contest at school in which his classmate Nicholas had focused his presentation on the ways in which parents sometimes become too animated when attending community sports events, thereby embarrassing and placing unwanted pressure on their children. Several of the parents who heard Nicholas' speech, but who also knew him and his parents from community hockey, concluded that he had most likely been referring to his own father. Mike and his classmates soon caught wind of this interpretation. Mike was subsequently able to confirm that Nicholas' parents did, according to their son, "really, really push him":

> But oddly enough, Nicholas didn't mind at all. He didn't care. And his speech wasn't about his parents pushing him or about other people who push them. And he said that maybe some kids like to be pushed by their sport, and I think that's because he really, really enjoys playing hockey.

I think if his dad hadn't pushed him, he wouldn't be as good as he is today. I don't know if he's amazing, but he's happy with the way he plays, I guess. He's satisfied. But if his dad hadn't pushed him, he wouldn't be. So I think he's grateful for that. And I think that's interesting because I didn't think anyone could see that [when Nicholas made his speech]. Because if someone was pushing me, I'd say, "Back off. I don't want to be pushed."

After initially being registered in swimming lessons by his mom, Andy requested that she accompany him to unorganized, recreational swimming sessions at the local outdoor pool. In the weeks that followed, a lifeguard told her that Andy was swimming well enough to be competitive in club competitions and encouraged her to let him join a local summer swim club. This she did, and her son soon began to return from meets with ribbons. Up to this point, Andy's father had little part in this endeavour. Indeed, by his own admission, he was becoming concerned about how his son's entry into club swimming might conflict with the family's usual summer pastime of camping expeditions. He simply assumed that all of the children who went to a swim meet received ribbons. Nonetheless, his son and wife urged him to attend a swim meet. Upon arrival he was amazed to see how well Andy performed and to hear his son's name called out repeatedly over the loudspeaker to come forth for ribbon presentations. From that point on, Andy and the rest of his family became steadily more involved in the world of community sports.

Young athletes may—or may not—discuss with friends or teammates their concerns regarding the stands that individual parents sometimes take and the ways that particular coaches treat them and other kids. While some mothers and fathers proudly claim that no secrets exist between them and their child, a parent may not find out about an issue involving their son or daughter until well after it has been resolved. Abby waited almost a year before telling her father, who coached her soccer team, that she had been devastated during a game the previous season when an assistant coach with the team had threatened to take her off the field unless she tried harder. She had, as she eventually explained to her father, been trying her hardest and playing the best she could, so the criticism stung her badly. That assistant coach had, Abby further revealed, later apologized to her before resigning from the coaching staff without explanation. Thus, Abby's dad, the head coach of the team, heard about this incident and learned why his former assistant had unexpectedly departed only when his daughter deemed that the time was right for him to do so. Another soccer player, Denise, explains that by the time she and her teammates hit the age of 16, some had become enthusiastic participants in a high school party scene that involved "a fair bit of drinking." Unbeknownst to their parents and coach, the players established and enforced an unwritten "Sunday morning sobriety" policy that kept in check excesses that might otherwise have compromised the team's championship seasons.

For Keith, the best part of belonging to a swim club was the social attractions of swim meets:

> Swim meets are where it all comes together socially because it is not just one club [involved]. Because what happens at a swim meet is there's a pool, right, and there's usually a park around the pool, and it's *really* kind of neat because what happens is all the tents go up either the night before or everyone gets there really early that morning before the warm-ups. And everyone, the different clubs put up their huge big tents, the big pavilion tents and stuff, and then individual families or whatever put up their little tents, and it's really kind of medieval or something. You go from tent to tent and people are resting in it for their race or whatever and it was really neat. It was cool because in between races, if you had a few hours, you could go and play in the park or whatever or just play cards in your friend's tent. It was cool. Like, I liked swim meets for that.

In contrast to this "backstage" world located around the competition area, Keith points out that the deck and the pool where competitions were held is where all the adults convene: "The kids hang out in the backdrop, in the tents, and all the adults, like the starters and the coaches and the stroke and turn judges and stuff, they're all serious. And the announcers, they're all on deck. It totally is a different world, because you always get nervous as you approach the deck."

Yet when I have asked young athletes what sport might be like if adults were not involved in it, most have expressed some doubts about such an arrangement. Nine-year-old Quinn observes that sport without adults would be "boring." Twelve-year-old Corey suggests that adult-free sports would be "really hard … because most kids need their parents to cheer them on if they're really down and they're losing. And I don't think it would get anywhere. The team wouldn't get any money, and you wouldn't get any trophies at the end of the year." Eighteen-year-old Brandon is a keen participant in street-hockey games and other informal sport activities that he and his friends organize for their own pleasure, so he has considerable experience of sports without adults: "Well, it might be okay. If adults weren't involved at all, it would be pretty much fun. But that depends upon what sport it is because if you're playing basketball, all you need is a ball, right, and you just go out there and have fun with your friends. But if you're talking about hockey and stuff that requires money, that's where you need the adults, you need their support."

Realizing the varied aspirations that lead child and youth athletes to join community sports teams and clubs in the first place and keep them coming back depends upon the support rendered to them by parents, coaches, and other volunteers, not to mention the taxpayers who underwrite the cost of building and maintaining municipal sport facilities. Their involvement in community sports remains contingent upon the continued participation of adult others. Just like their parents and the coaches and volunteer sport officials who also sustain the activities that bring them pleasure, the varied dreams that they pursue and sometimes achieve through community sports remain thoroughly interdependent with and vulnerable to those of others engaged in this social field.

NOTES

1 Portions of this and the following section are taken from Dyck (2010c) and are included here with permission of the publisher of the original article, Wiley-Blackwell.

2 Jealousy, according to the second edition of the *Oxford English Dictionary* (1989), designates "the quality of being jealous," which refers variously to an "anxiety for preservation or well-being of something," "vigilance in guarding a possession from loss or damage," and a "state of mind arising from the suspicion, apprehension or knowledge of rivalry" either in love or in respect of success or advantage.

3 See Allison James (1998) on how the presence of children is symbolically required in order to transform a "married couple" into a "family."

4 See Dyck (2000d, 22–5) for a discussion of informal versions of sports organized for children by children that violate the rules of organized sports.

5 Such stereotypes include the parent who lives vicariously through the achievements of his/her child; the unscrupulous coach who will do anything to win; the "dad coach" who runs his team primarily to develop and showcase the talents of his kid; the "stuck-up" parent who doesn't want to help out with

fundraising; the out-of-control parent, kid, or coach who can be expected to "lose it" sooner or later in closely contested games or situations; and the parent who is determined to see a given sport team or club organized to suit "my kid's schedule" and interests.

6 The National Coaching Certification Program (NCCP) is a coach training and certification program for 65 different sports in Canada.

7 A bottle drive is a familiar although not especially lucrative means of fundraising for sports and youth groups that involves children (accompanied by their parents in cars and trucks) going door to door asking for empty soft-drink and beer bottles and cans that are subsequently returned by the team for the compulsory deposit charges that are charged at the time of sale and refunded upon return by retailers.

8 See Walker (2009) for a discussion of the role of the "builder" in community sports.

Chapter Seven

SPORTING DREAMS

A FEW MINUTES AFTER a hard-fought match between two leading under-14 girls' soccer teams, a Lower Mainland league official met with players from both squads to tell them about tryouts for the provincial team. In making his pitch, he stressed the opportunities for travel and partaking in top tournaments against American teams that lay ahead for those who made the cut and joined the provincial squad. Tournaments such as these, he noted, bring out scouts from American universities who offer good players athletic scholarships to attend their institutions when they complete high school.

While this was the first official presentation to young athletes regarding athletic scholarships that I witnessed, I had been aware of musings within community sports circles concerning this possibility since my daughter's preliminary year of playing soccer, when she was seven. That season a parental "team" of sorts had gradually coalesced along the sidelines during a string of mostly cold and rainy Sunday afternoons. Our reasons for being there varied. A few fathers and mothers, who identified themselves as having been athletes in their younger days, wanted their daughters to have the chance to see whether they might also enjoy playing sport. One mother, who had cajoled her child into signing up for soccer, hoped that lots of running around might have a salutary effect upon her daughter's slightly plump figure. Others with little or no personal background in sport were merely enabling their daughters to tag along with friends who had enrolled in soccer. One couple injected a qualitatively different tenor into ongoing parental discussions. They spoke of the prospects of highly accomplished Canadian youth players receiving athletic scholarships that would take them to top American universities and pay for their entire college education. Nor was this idle speculation on their part: some 10 years later their daughter did, indeed, win a "full-ride" athletic scholarship to a large American university.

A community sport is, among other things, a social field replete with talk about dreams and dreaming. Yet here dreaming departs in some important respects from conventional psychological approaches that tend to define dreams as successions of images, thoughts, or emotions that pass through the mind during sleep. While sport dreams certainly involve mental activity, these are also thoroughly social phenomena that are engaged with during waking hours within interactions and undertakings that are pursued consciously, collectively, and with diligence. Nascent sport dreams may initially feature some degree of imaginative fantasy, but what is notable is just how readily hopes can be hitched to demanding regimes of discipline that seek to transform aspirations into more or less realizable ambitions. To trace how this happens with respect to athletic scholarships is to obtain a fuller appreciation of the processes that underpin the construction of community sports.

DREAMING ABOUT "GOING SOUTH"[1]

Child and youth athletes familiar with the news media's fixation with Canadian professional athletes such as Sidney Crosby (National Hockey League), Steve Nash (National Basketball Association), Joey Votto (Major League Baseball), and others might all too easily slip into imagining that athletic prowess might just lead to a lucrative professional career. Parents of youngsters competing in these sports are frequently reminded by media commentators and others of the rather long odds against even a highly proficient player making it to the professional ranks. To encourage one's son to commit himself solely to the pursuit of a professional career is generally reckoned to be foolhardy. The principal risk associated with failing in such a venture is the possible or even likely neglect of educational training, an outcome that, it is feared, may severely constrain the future life prospects of admittedly outstanding youth athletes who ultimately may not prove to be professional-calibre athletes. Cautionary stories about the disappointing outcomes of kids who *almost* made it to the big leagues" are legion.

It is within this context that the manifest attractions of athletic scholarships—and particularly those offered by American universities and colleges—become apparent. To begin with, there are vastly more openings for student athletes in intercollegiate athletic programs in the US than exist within professional sports. Moreover, scholarships are awarded for a broad range of sport disciplines that reach far beyond those featured in professional sport leagues: athletic scholarships are offered for rowing and field hockey as well as for ice hockey and football. Girls as well as boys are eligible to win athletic scholarships.[2] Most of all, athletic scholarships ostensibly combine high-level sport competition with post-secondary education, thereby sidestepping the risk of athletic participation jeopardizing one's education. Accordingly, the ideal outcome for many young Canadian athletes would be to receive a full-ride scholarship (that will cover the full costs of tuition, books, subsistence, accommodation, and equipment) at a "prestigious" American university. To accomplish this is interpreted as converting athletic excellence into a form of continuing prestige, not to mention the acquisition of a "free" education. Whenever a local Canadian athlete is "being recruited" to attend one or another American college or university on an athletic scholarship, this is a matter for discussion in the venues of community sports long before and after news of it appears in community newspapers.

Given the traditional absence of full-ride athletic scholarships in Canada,[3] promising young Canadian athletes have long been targeted by recruiters from the US. Young Canadians who do opt to "head south" are locally celebrated as recipients of athletic scholarships that, it is said, will permit them not only to get a "free education" but also to "move up" to much higher levels of sport competition than are believed to exist in Canada. Not surprisingly, the prospect of winning such scholarships has become strongly associated with high achievement within child and youth sports in Canada both in schools and in more extensive community sport clubs and leagues. Indeed, a common means of recognizing individual achievements by young Canadian athletes is to proclaim them as possible candidates to receive an athletic scholarship from an American university. To be spoken of in these terms, whether or not one has an actual interest in such possibilities, is to be acknowledged as a superior athlete.

It is important to situate the coordinates within which the discursive construction of athletic scholarships occurs. Since the legal age of majority in Canada is 18 or 19 (depending upon the province), entry into intercollegiate athletics coincides with the socially demarcated transition from childhood to the world of adults. In the years preceding this juncture, children and youths exist as minors, under the care and protection of parents or guardians. From the perspective of parents, another way of framing this period is to regard it as the time when they are (or were) mostly actively involved in raising and nurturing their children. Within this peak period, the domestic pursuits of parents *as* parents take form and are played out.

Because sons and daughters depend upon their parents for the support required for participation in community sports, the athletic careers of boys and girls unfold and intersect with the domestic careers of mothers and fathers. Child rearing within community sports entails the practice of highly intimate activities and relationships within often glaringly public settings. Indications from time to time of the apparent success—or worrisome lack of it—registered by sons and daughters as they move towards adulthood and (hopefully) begin to demonstrate an inclination and capacity to support themselves offer one sign of the possible wisdom and efficacy of any given parent's efforts (Dyck 2000e). Any certainty about how a son or daughter will in the end "turn out" is not, of course, available until long after the most active and visible phases of parenting have ended. In the absence of any such conclusive evidence of likely outcomes during those hectic years when children grow to become teenagers, the attractions to parents of a son or daughter who might be regarded as in the running to receive an athletic scholarship become obvious. Although mothers and fathers freely admit that a parent's assessment of a son's or daughter's accomplishments might not be entirely impartial, the awarding of athletic scholarships by college officials carries with it the imprimatur of objective assessment. Accordingly, learning and talking about athletic scholarships and speculating about whose son or daughter might win one can become absorbing pastimes for many parents.

Discourses about athletic scholarships are constructed and consumed primarily by those engaged in or connected to child and youth sports in one capacity or another, including child and youth athletes; parents; coaches and trainers; community, provincial, and national sport organizers and directors; media personnel who cover youth sports; and, individuals and agencies involved voluntarily or professionally in the recruitment of Canadian athletes to American intercollegiate athletic programs. It is, thus, necessary to take account of varying ways in which discourses about athletic scholarships are shaped and shared.

An item that appeared in the sports pages of one of Vancouver's daily newspapers provides an instructive example of how athletic scholarships tend to be treated in media accounts. It reported the situation of a young local sprinter who was, according to the title of the piece, "weighing her track options." Briefly, "the race to recruit" the young woman, who had been a triple gold medallist at the provincial track and field championships the previous year, was said to be "coming up to the finish line." Although the girl had "talked to dozens of NCAA[4] schools," she had short-listed Hawaii, Illinois, Arizona, and Notre Dame and had already made official visits to each campus. Scheduled to compete in a major track meet in California the following weekend, she expected that all of her prospective coaches would be on hand, thus enabling her to meet with each of them again before reaching a final decision.

What this report contained were the key ingredients of most media discourses about athletic scholarships: a local athlete who had registered first-rate athletic results and one or more American colleges and universities that were said to be eagerly recruiting her to join their athletics programs. Reports such as these often list the names and accomplishments of high school athletes who have received athletic scholarships. What is also stated explicitly or strongly implied in such a summary of an athlete's career-to-date is evidence of the talent, hard work, and maturity that the athlete in question is said to have exhibited, claims frequently corroborated by the testimony of a coach or teammate. While exact dollar amounts and terms of athletic scholarships tend not to be reported, readers are usually left with the impression that the recipient will have his/her post-secondary education paid for entirely.

Moving beyond media reports of athletic scholarships and into the ethnography of community sports, roughly similar sorts of stories and claims are frequently encountered. Driving his 12-year-old daughter and one of her classmates to a track and field practice for the first time, a father who himself never attended university casually explained to the two girls what their participation in this sport might earn them: "That will be your ticket to get your way paid through university, to have fun attending track meets all over the country, maybe even to travel around the world." Discussion of athletic scholarships can also serve to reveal the knowledge and sophistication of the speaker about these matters. Thus, Nelson, a youth football coach, advises parents who might hope that their sons would one day win athletic scholarships to consider enrolling them in lacrosse. Ivy League teams are, he reports, scouting extensively in Canada for skilled lacrosse players. Conversely, Lynette, a young ringette coach, feels it necessary to advise prospective players from the outset that this sport is a lot of fun for girls, even though there are no athletic scholarships offered to its graduates because it is not a sport that has been adopted in American universities and colleges. Invoking the likelihood of athletic scholarships being won by athletes in "our" sport or club can also be a means for declaring the relative social distinction of "us" compared to "them."

Yet familiarity with popular discourses about athletic scholarships does not necessarily render one a captive or adherent of them. Frank, the father of a highly accomplished runner, does not concur with the view of his daughter's coach that she will suffer by opting to attend a local university and continue living at home. While allowing that his daughter could be turning down an offer that might take her to an Ivy League institution, Frank states simply that his daughter is not yet ready to be that far away from home. Inga relates the sobering experience of her best friend's son, who after receiving an athletic scholarship to attend Stanford dropped out a short while later due to the incredible demands made upon his time by the coach of his sport: "They were just *too* serious for him!"

In fact, intercollegiate athletics constitute a vast and complex system of highly competitive sport programs and activities that have a prominent but in some respects quite controversial place within American post-secondary education. A summary account of the nature and features of this densely constructed and diverse athletic establishment falls beyond the scope and objectives of this chapter, but it should be noted that there exists a grow-ing scholarly and polemical literature on the merits and problems with intercollegiate athletics.[5] Tagged by some observers with the sobriquet of "the peculiar institution"—a term used in antebellum nineteenth-century America to refer to slavery—intercollegiate athletics are generally agreed to constitute a very substantial set of activities. Depending upon one's point of view, these programs may be depicted as making positive and strategic contri-butions to the universities and colleges that sponsor them as well as to the young athletes who compete within them. Supporters of athletics programs argue that universities' efforts to recruit students and obtain donations from alumni are decisively enhanced by the operation of high profile, successful athletics programs. Alternatively, critics charge that big-time college sports have become parasitic "businesses" involving major television contracts and the commoditized sale of athletic wear that exploit the myth of the student athlete, not to mention actual student athletes who may have precious few educational benefits or accomplishments to take away with them when their eligibility as college athletes comes to an end.[6] Even "Ivy League" universities are accused of having a much deeper dependence upon intercollegiate athletics programs than they might readily acknowledge.

Be that as it may, athletic scholarships remain a prominent feature of the rhetorical and organizational landscape of child and youth sports in Canada. Ethnographic evidence that more than a few of the Canadian athletes who "head South" are not actually in receipt of full-ride scholarships for all or for any of their years in college indicates that some Canadian parents are quietly making up the difference.[7] In view of the generally much higher costs of post-secondary education in the United States, the supplementary support required to permit a son or daughter to take up a partial scholarship can easily amount to more than the total cost that would otherwise be incurred in attending an academically comparable Canadian university. This practice poses intriguing questions about the factors and motivations that shape certain contemporary Canadian middle-class approaches to child rearing. It also raises the possibility that sport organizations, educational institutions, and parents may be inconspicuously working together to harness the growth and training of children and youths to a set of disparate yet conditionally reconcilable interests, all of which revolve around sharing in reflected forms of prestige[8] attached to and derived from the pursuit of American athletic scholarships.

LIVING THE DREAM

The circumstances that lead some young Canadian men and women to take up athletic scholarships in the United States and the ensuing experiences they report during or following their college years vary in many respects. Nonetheless, ethnographic interviews conducted both in the United States with Canadian student athletes and intercollegiate athletics officials as well as those conducted in Canada with former athletic scholarship holders and the parents of current and past student athletes also reveal certain striking similarities in the paths and processes by which athletes move to and through the role of varsity athletes in the United States.

Although electing to leave family, friends, and country behind constitutes a vital change in young lives, in another sense the receipt of an athletic scholarship continues and extends activities and relationships within which these young Canadians have been ensconced since childhood. Athletes of the calibre recruited by American intercollegiate athletics programs typically have extensive sport histories. What is more, the parents of these Canadian athletes tend to have been involved at least as strong supporters and some-times as guiding figures in their children's sporting endeavours. Garth, the captain of his varsity team, began to play hockey at an early age: "I started skating when I was four, and I played hockey when I was five.... It was my dad who got me into it. Like most parents, probably, it's usually the father that gets them into hockey. And my dad coached me growing up until I was maybe, you know, thirteen. Then once you get to kind of the higher levels, you know, your dad doesn't really keep coaching you." Paige, a volleyball player, reports having sampled a broad range of sports with the unceasing support of her parents: "I started out doing gymnastics, I did like, artistic gymnastics and didn't really like that. And then I did rhythmic gymnastics for a while and didn't really like that. I did track [and field], I did baseball ... a lot of sports. [My parents] were like, very supportive all the way along, always willing ... to drive wherever. And like, they never, never complained, always very supportive." The parents of Pete, a college baseball player, consis-tently attended his games and accompanied him during his many years of youth competition: "I started playing sports ... [during] elementary school and high school, [and my parents] were always there. Especially, you know, [when] playing for [the provincial baseball team], there's a lot of travelling involved. So they were always there with me, travelling around to all the different ballparks and everything."

These levels of parental involvement in community sport for children and youth are, as shown in previous chapters, by no means unusual in Canada. Indeed, parental provision of financial and logistical support has become a mandatory requirement of most community sports organizations as well as some extramural school athletics programs, eliciting concern in some quarters about the impact of arrangements such as these on sport participation by children from low-income families. Within this social realm, determining the extent to which children autonomously chart their own courses through sports activities or instead may be led to, encouraged, and guided within these activities by fathers and mothers remains a complicated matter. It can be difficult to determine whether decisions made by teenaged sons and daughters to pursue an athletic scholarship are essentially their own undertakings or a step within and validation of larger family "projects" rooted in shared domestic sporting histories in which the athletic accomplishments of children become components of the child-rearing performances of mothers and fathers.

Fran, a varsity basketball player, appreciates the unstinting parental encouragement and support provided for her youthful ventures into hockey, volleyball, and basketball. Her father, a doctor, was "very excited" about the process that led to her winning an athletic scholarship. Her high school coaches had also been integrally involved in this process: "They contacted schools and stuff, um, would talk to [American college] coaches, would during games say, 'You know, this school is here to watch you, Fran.' Just little things like that. They were good coaches, they recruited, like, good players to come play for them. So we always had a very strong team."

Lane, a member of a national youth sports team during his high school years, decided at age 17 to drop out of that sport and to fly to the United States where he hoped to focus upon another sport that he had played casually since childhood. Growing up in a small community, Lane had been desperate to leave his hometown after high school graduation and "to get far, far away." Staying with relatives, he spent a year elevating his game, participating in amateur tournaments and preparing videos of his performances to send to athletics departments across the US. To aid his efforts, his mother drove Lane's car more than a thousand miles from Canada down to his relatives so that he would have the use of it during this preparatory year. Daley, a hockey player, also benefited from his mother's assistance during this period, albeit in another capacity: "Luckily, my mom helped me out a lot with it. She did most of the paperwork. I guess I was kind of a baby on that one [*laughing*], she kinda did most of it." When asked whether his parents have been supportive of his decision to go to university in the United States, Daley observed: "Yeah, they're very supportive and, you know, they don't make my decisions or anything, but they help me out a lot and give their opinions and also I take them into account. So, they've helped me out a lot." In contrast, his older brother, identified by Daley as "the smart one," had chosen to remain in Canada and attend a local university.

Naomi received her athletic scholarship as a result of an impromptu venture launched by another father who, wanting to ensure that his own daughter would be seen and considered by American college coaches and recruiters, had organized on his own initiative a hastily assembled team to travel to and compete in a major American tournament. Naomi's parents agreed to finance her travel and accommodation on this trip, and she and several teammates subsequently received offers of athletic scholarships. The circumstances that led Elise to be admitted to an Ivy League university with sufficient financial aid to permit her to attend were hardly a spur of the moment matter. She had been enrolled since Grade 9 in a specialized fee-charging sport academy attached to a local public high school. Through this arrangement she and her classmates received on-ice coaching sessions four times a week as part of the school curriculum, as well as a weekly life skills training class within which students were shown how to prepare university applications as well as personal résumés and videos of their sport performances to be addressed to athletics directors and coaches at American colleges and universities. Yet, notwithstanding the measures taken to increase the likelihood of young Canadian athletes being noticed by American college recruiters and coaches, making final decisions about which scholarship offers to seek and which to accept is sometimes a rather haphazard affair (Dyck 2006, 73–5). While Elise had little difficulty in choosing an offer from an internationally known East Coast university over that of a non-descript state university in the Midwest, when doing so she put particular weight upon the lower ranking of the women's hockey program at the latter school. In other cases, Canadian athletes found it quite difficult to assess and balance the relative merits of the academic and athletic programs at different schools. The personal attention that they received or didn't receive from prospective college coaches and athletics officials often played a critical role in their final selections.

The college experiences reported by Canadian students who take up athletic scholarships in the US serve to illuminate the challenges that arise when a young person moves away from home to another country, enters into higher education, and strives to find his/her place in a demanding athletics program. They generally report having been warmly welcomed by their coaches and teammates and of settling into a packed daily round of classes, training sessions, practices, games, or competitions. While the standard of coaching that they encounter may not always be better or even necessarily as good as that which they had received previously, almost invariably the levels of competition facing them both within their teams and in their intercollegiate competitions is much, much higher than these young athletes had expected it to be. The importance placed upon not just winning games but also of working as hard as possible at every practice session, lest an athlete become the object of a coach's wrath, emerges again and again in students' narratives. Although fully appreciative of the state-of-the-art athletic facilities, equipment, physical training, and therapy services made available to college athletes in the United States, nonetheless, they must cope with the recurring levels of physical fatigue that soon visit most of them. At the same time, the sheer thrill of being suddenly at the centre of sport programs and events that typically receive levels of attendance and fan adulation virtually inconceivable within Canadian university sports can be seductive.

In the classroom, Canadian athletes frequently discover to their relief that they have, in fact, been reasonably well prepared by high schools at home to meet the academic demands made of undergraduates even at Ivy League institutions. A certain number of athletes engaged in sport programs such as football, basketball, baseball, and ice hockey—sports that might well lead to subsequent professional sport careers—appear to decide at a relatively early stage to give their "academics" only as much time and attention as is necessary to remain eligible in terms of NCAA, university, and team requirements to continue to compete athletically. Others strive to observe, at least in some manner, parents', coaches', and administrators' repeated injunctions that they must take care to balance their academics and athletics. In many schools varsity athletes are required during their first year of university to attend study hall sessions to ensure that they don't fall behind in class assignments. Athletics departments also frequently arrange and pay for the services of tutors to assist individual athletes who encounter difficulties with particular courses. Athletes who possess greater academic ability are eligible for release from mandatory study hall attendance as soon as grades are reported at the end of their first semester of studies. A few of these young Canadians set their academic sights considerably higher than do most of their teammates, enrolling in demanding programs such as engineering or pre-medicine studies. To do so may complicate their college lives in ways that may not initially be apparent. Since athletic scholarship holders are obliged to take part in daily practice and training sessions, they are sometimes unable to enrol in essential prerequisite courses due to academic and athletic scheduling conflicts. In this respect, a somewhat more convenient means of reconciling academics and athletics may be to enrol in whichever program fits well with an athlete's schedule. One or another assistant coach is likely to be well-versed about programs of studies that readily suit team practice schedules as well as about instructors on campus who are known to be "friends of the athletics program."

When asked about the athletic and academic challenges that she encountered during her college years, Naomi recalled:

> Freshman year was rough. I cried every day.... Well, you're so far away from home and you're young. Like I'd just turned 18 when I went. And you go from living with your parents and practising twice a week or whatever ...

to [university] where you study all day. We had classes from 8:00 [a.m.] to about 1:00 [p.m.]. And then we had a break. From 2:00 to 3:00 we had [physiotherapy] treatments, 3:00 to 6:00 [team] practice, 6:00 to 7:30 was dinner and a shower. And then 7:30 to 9:30 we had to go to study hall and tutors. And that was every day, like six days a week. We had one day off and they [coaches] usually used it for travel. So there was a rule that you [could] only practise 20 hours a week and then you [would] have to have a day off. But, like, it [could] be on the road....

Like if you have a bad practice, you're not going to start [the next game]. Like even if you're the best player on the team, it doesn't matter. Like you have to prove yourself every practice. And like, they don't tell you the starting line-up until an hour and half before the game. So like all week—and it gets really catty and competitive on the field. 'Cause even though you're a team, you're trying to be better than your teammates 'cause you want to start. So, yeah, they make it hard, like in drills. It's always a competition. Like you're not just dribbling through cones: you're racing ... and if you lose, then you have to sprint a lap of the field. Like you get punished for everything.[9] Not punished, but you know ... the motto of our team was "It pays to be a winner." So everything we did was either a race or a competition. And if you lost, you had to pay.... And that was like, that was the roughest thing I think [during] freshman year. And the coaches are mean. Our head coach ... was like super tough. And we had like two assistant coaches ... and they were super harsh. And we got yelled at. But that was freshman year, and when you're not used to it, obviously it's very hard. And then, you know, the older you get, you don't learn to ignore it, but you ... you don't let it affect you. And then, like the older you are, then you're responsible for the freshmen. So like you, even if you're unhappy, you have to pretend to be happy and to agree with the coaches, 'cause you can't give a bad impression to the freshmen. So ... [*whispering for emphasis*] it's very psychological. Like it's a, it's a head game. Like everything is mental. And that's like what, yeah, that's what I hated. 'Cause they screw around with your head. And even if you think you have had a good practice, they'll bench you on purpose just to see how you're gonna react and if you're gonna let it bring you down or if you're gonna fight and, you know, try and be better. They just, yeah, they play with your head.

Persuaded by her parents to stick with the program at least until Christmas of her first year, Naomi managed to complete her career as a varsity athlete and to earn a degree. As demanding as her experience had been, she judged it to have been preferable to that of a younger relative who had followed her example, taken an athletic scholarship at a smaller university with a Division I sport program, suffered a major injury and subsequently was forced to forego a second year of competition. Turning to her academic experiences, Naomi recounted:

> Freshman year, I was like a "no-preference" major. So I just sort of took whatever random classes you have to, like math and whatever. And I didn't try. So I got a 2.5 [grade point average] ... And I never went to class, and if I did, I was sleeping. 'Cause I was so tired. I was *sooo* tired. Like I rolled out of bed every morning, threw on my sweatpants, and went to class and took a nap. And then sophomore year, I decided I wanted to be a Kin[esiology] major. So I was that for one semester, and then I decided it was too hard and I couldn't handle it. And then, yeah, I changed it to merchandising management. And that was easy [*laughs*].

Ironically, Naomi had selected this university in part because of the balance between academics and athletics that she had been told it offered. Indeed, when the university had brought her to campus for one of her permitted recruiting visits,[10] she had spent an afternoon meeting with academic counsellors to verify that this would be the case. When asked whether her coaches had wanted her to do well in her studies for herself or primarily because they wanted her to remain eligible to compete for the team, Naomi replied:

> I don't know, it's hard to say. I think both. Like for sure—it's really hard to ... [mess] up and not be—like I think you need to have like a 1.6 [GPA] in order to not be able to play. And like honestly, you'd have to be pretty dumb to get a 1.6 [*laughs*] ... So, like they knew we'd be able to play. I think they actually cared. And like you know our team always had awards for [high] GPAs and stuff like that. So I think they cared. But yeah, they wanted us to play. But I think they just take so much pride, like in everything in the States. There's so much pride, like yeah, I'm an athlete and, you know, it looks good when you can put in your media guide that, you know, ten of your athletes are academic [high achievers]—like it's a selling feature.

Although ethnographers of American college life (Moffatt 1989; Nathan 2005) have confirmed the enthusiasm with which undergraduates away from home and the watchful eyes of parents throw themselves into partying and other forms of socializing, athletes like Naomi are restricted in the time and opportunities they have to do so:

We were friends with other athletes, just 'cause, like it's really easy, right? You just meet at study hall and ... athletic functions ... But really I didn't have that many friends [*laughs*]. Mostly the team. The girls on the team. Yeah, and other athletes.... So, like I tried to make friends in my classes, but I really didn't have time to have friends. And I didn't care.... And like I knew I was leaving there anyways, so ... it sounds kind of snobby, but I was like, well I'm never going to see these people again. So yeah, like the athletes just hang out with each other and we go to parties. You know, there's like the hockey house, football house, soccer house, like we were just hanging out.

Other Canadian athletes related similar sorts of experiences, although some of them struggled to maintain friendships with a few non-athlete students whom they met in their classes or in their dormitories. Some athletes found it particularly important for them to foster social outlets and relationships beyond this circle of teammates and other athletes, but again their unyielding schedules often frustrated their attempts to do so. Many universities extend varsity athletes special privileges in recognition of their packed schedules. Thus, one line at the campus bookstore may be reserved for athletes to deliver them from the otherwise lengthy waits endured by other students at the beginning of a semester. Athletes are also entitled to wear sweaters, hoodies, and sweatpants with team insignia that identify them as varsity athletes and which are not available to outsiders. Yet being set apart from other students can prove problematic in other respects. Garth's membership in a team effectively determined the scope and nature of his social life:

We kind of tend to stay within our group 'cause that's all we know. Like I don't have any friends outside of the hockey team.... That's a big thing, being part of, like, a family of 27 guys and you go out together in big groups.... Other guys don't like us, and we're intimidating being in such a big group, so it's really hard to meet people ... I haven't really met a lot of people over four years compared to what most people probably do.

Canadian athletes sometimes experienced their identity and distinctiveness *as* athletes as a social liability. Jane, a swimmer at an Ivy League school, doubts that she would have been accepted as a student there or granted as much student assistance as she received had she not been an athlete. She would certainly not have been able to afford to be there without that assistance. Her grades, she believed, were lower than they might otherwise have been because she was so exhausted most of the time: "I feel like a lot of the students—well not a lot but some of the students—look down on you and think you're stupid just because you are an athlete."

Keeping in touch with family and friends "back home" became an essential yet costly matter for most athletes or, more commonly, for their parents. Many mothers and fathers visited their sons and daughters in the US at least once and often more frequently. Trips home over Christmas or during the summer are not usually covered by scholarships or student aid, and athletes, who are encouraged by coaches to take summer courses to lighten their class loads during the playing season, often don't have the time to take a summer job, unless one is arranged on campus where athletes can also readily satisfy team requirements for off-season physical conditioning. While varsity athletes travel extensively by airplane and bus to away games and competitions across the US, they seldom have time to see much more of these places than the airport, hotel, and stadium. Several Canadian student athletes enrolled at universities and colleges in and around a major East Coast city felt that they had really not gotten to walk around it and to know it nearly as well as they would have liked to have done.

When an athlete's undergraduate years come to an end, advises a guide marketed to Canadian high school students and their parents,

> life in the real world begins. Some college athletes may catch the attention of professional sports scouts and be invited to attend a professional training camp. In the majority of cases, however, graduates must enter the work force after graduation. By combining athletics with a college degree, the individual has kept all of his options open. Many employers are eagerly willing to hire an individual who has successfully combined academics and the tough competitive athletics. (Lahey 1993, 157)

A few of the athletes interviewed for this study hoped to pursue professional sports careers or to extend their post-college amateur athletic careers for a few years more. Most of them were prepared to move on from sports and to discover whether former holders of athletic scholarships do, in fact, "have it made for life." A few had formed contacts with local boosters of campus athletics and hoped to land jobs through these ties in the United States. Several others planned to pursue graduate studies or professional degrees, either in Canada or in the States. A couple of athletes married Americans, while several others returned to Canada to long-term relationships that had started before and somehow continued throughout their college years.

A substantial proportion of them were not certain that, if given the opportunity to choose again, they would necessarily have done exactly the same thing and enrolled in this or that particular school. Yet almost to a man and a woman, they depicted their college years as having been "worth it," a time when they left home, became somewhat independent, and grew up. The years they spent as varsity athletes had not only coincided with but had actually constituted their particular coming of age. The interviews conducted with these young Canadians typically ended with affirmations that they had "no regrets" concerning their decision to move to the US for their university education. How could it be otherwise? For to move beyond the rhetoric of athletic and parental accomplishment that makes up this discourse might potentially throw into question not only the prestige that has been enjoyed but also the particular domestic lives, performances of astute parenting, and youthful athletic careers that have been constructed and lived around this premise for so many years.

DREAMING TOGETHER

Canadian athletes who receive athletic scholarships or equivalent forms of aid and consideration that enable them to attend colleges and universities in the United States become, in a sense, inadvertent transnationals. Only one of the athletes interviewed indicated that the possibility of using an athletic scholarship as a possible means to move permanently to the US had been a conscious part of her pursuit of the full ride from the beginning. Yet several of them had made local American contacts that might, they hoped, lead to jobs. All of these athletes would have still been able to afford a university education, even had they not received an athletic scholarship. Most of them had identified "fall back" options to enrol in Canadian universities and continue playing their sports if American scholarships had not been forthcoming. In many cases, parents declared that they were not prepared to provide any more in the way of financial assistance to underwrite the supplementary costs of a vastly more expensive American college education than they would otherwise have offered to subsidize the costs of post-secondary education in Canada. Yet some parents, nonetheless, discretely pay more than this would entail to permit a son or daughter to accept a partial scholarship or to complete a degree when scholarship funding has run out. Although Canadian athletes often manage to complete college more or less free of financial debt, it is not certain that the same can always be said of their parents. Parents who announce with pride that their daughter or son has won an athletic scholarship may be less forthcoming in explaining which part of the costs incurred by this option for post-secondary education will be financed by the college and which by mom and dad. In truth, the complete costs of taking up an athletic scholarship in the US may not become entirely apparent until, so to speak, all of the bills are submitted.

Why, then, and how has the pursuit of athletic scholarships that lead young athletes to the United States been so successful in capturing the attention and enlisting the involvement of countless boys and girls, parents and sport officials in Canada? The desire of American athletics directors and varsity coaches to recruit elite athletes—be they from Des Moines, Toronto, or Nairobi—to join their programs is easy enough to understand. Moreover, some college athletes—including Canadians—who compete in sports such as football, basketball, baseball, and hockey, do ultimately pursue longer or shorter careers as professional athletes, even though it is widely known that the overwhelming majority of varsity athletes in these sports will not do so. Canadian athletes who play one or another "non-professional" sport in American schools might improve their level of performance to Olympic qualifying standards, although in some sports moving outside of Canada may effectively serve to prevent one from being selected for Canadian national teams that compete at the world level.

When so few of the Canadians who accept American athletic scholarships end up with professional or elite amateur careers as competitive athletes beyond the one, two, three, or four years that they spend as varsity athletes, why do so many coaches and sport officials in Canada tailor their programs and focus their efforts upon encouraging athletically accomplished young Canadians to head off to the United States? Why do youths and parents become so caught up in the excitement that surrounds the annual pursuit of scholarships when anyone who lingers for a short while around even the outermost edges of Canadian sporting circles can scarcely avoid hearing *sotto voce* recitations about one or another athlete's discovery of the downsides of American athletic scholarships? Moving beyond the specificities of individual cases and circumstances, to account for the general features and outcomes of this fascination with American athletic scholarships obliges us to take note of the ways in which the prestige that steadfastly continues to be attributed to these awards reward not only the young men and women who are said to "win" them but also the adults who have helped them to do so.

For a Canadian teenager who has devoted much of her/his young life to sport, the acclaim that accompanies competitive success erupts when one becomes the object of open speculation and then actual negotiations leading to the awarding of an athletic scholarship by an American college or university.[11] Individuals accepting these awards report being thrilled by the prospect of being able to continue their sporting exploits by moving up to what is taken to be a higher and more celebrated level of competition. Many later acknowledge that their desire to keep playing sport after high school initially overshadowed their interest in the particular courses of study into which they would be entering. Although facing, along with the rest of their classmates, the uncertainties, excitement, and dislocation that come with the conclusion of one's high school years, those "heading south" to take up athletic scholarships assume that their college years will revolve in substantial measure around activities with which they have long been familiar. Although soon to be separated from family and friends, they look forward, as many of them put it, to being "paid" to play sports and getting their education for "free." Why would a young athlete second-guess the appropriateness of choosing to accept such an offer, given the pride and excitement so often exuded by their coaches and parents?

For coaches and local sport officials, the accomplishments registered by young athletes whom they mentored reflect well upon their sporting expertise and burnish the status of their organizations. For mothers and fathers who have not only underwritten the costs of many years of child and youth sport activities but also devoted thousands of hours to driving their son or daughter to sports practices and competitions and to watching them perform, an athletic scholarship may validate a distinctive form of child rearing that might otherwise be deemed somewhat obsessive. Ironically, the movement of some young Canadian athletes away from their homes and country offers not only a reassuring form of continuity in their own lives but also an impartial endorsement and sealing of family projects that children and parents may have been engaged in for a decade or more. The college years that young

Canadian athletes spend in the United States do, indeed, stretch the spatial bounds of family. Determining the eventual outcome of an athletic scholarship on the future life of a given award holder necessarily remains a matter for the future. In the meantime, young Canadian athletes, their parents, youth sport coaches, and American college athletics officials continue to play their respective parts in sustaining the premises and prestige of a distinctive sort of coming of age that continues to thrive as long as all involved in the field of community sport continue to honour the dream and overlook certain incongruent and, thus, less-spoken-of facets of the full ride.

NOTES

1 Some parts of this chapter previously appeared in Dyck (2006, 2010b, 2011) and are included here by permission of the journals in which these were originally published: *Anthropological Notebooks*; *Anthropology in Action*; and *Anthropologica.*

2 Canadian women are just as likely (and perhaps even more likely) to be recruited to attend universities in the US than are their male counterparts due to American gender equity guidelines.

3 In Canada, intercollegiate athletics have for the most part followed a rather different course of development than in the United States. The types and amounts of financial aid made available to student athletes in the US in the form of athletic scholarships (and differently named but similarly functioning awards) have until recently been eschewed by Canadian universities. A partial exception to this was Simon Fraser University, which for many years belonged to the National Association of Intercollegiate Athletics, an American sport association that allowed the granting of awards to athletes which is not permitted by the Canadian intercollegiate sport governing body, Canadian Interuniversity Sport (until 2001 this was known as the Canadian Interuniversity Athletics Union). Both Simon Fraser University and the University of British Columbia recently considered applying for membership in the American-based National Collegiate Athletic Association, a move that would separate them from other Canadian university sport programs. Simon Fraser's application for admission to NCAA provisional membership was adopted in principle in 2009, and SFU began to compete as an NCAA Division II school on September 1, 2011. Whether this will ultimately make the SFU athletics program a more prestigious destination for young Canadian athletes than other post-secondary intercollegiate athletic programs in Canada remains to be seen.

4 This is the acronym for the National Collegiate Athletics Association, the largest such body in the world and the one that governs intercollegiate athletics at many universities and colleges in the United States.

5 See Dyck (2006, 2010b, 2011) for references to and a review of parts of this literature. See also Adler and Adler (1991), Bailey and Littleton (1991), Bale (1991), Bok (2003), Bowen and Levin (2003), Byers and Hammer (1995), Duderstadt (2003), Funk (1991), Gerdy (2006), Sack (2008), Sack and Staurowsky (1998), Shulman and Bowen (2001), Smith (1988), Telander (1996), and Toma (2003).

6 See, for instance, Jonathan Mahler's article "Student–Athlete Equation Could Be a Win-Win" (2011) for an iteration of this stance.

7 The ethnographic research on which this chapter is based was undertaken as part of a larger project entitled "Coming of Age in an Era of Globalization: Achieving Cultural Distinction through Student Travel Abroad," directed by Vered Amit and Noel Dyck, and was funded by a standard research grant provided by the Social Sciences and Humanities Research Council of Canada. I would also like to acknowledge the assistance of a graduate student member of the research team, Meghan Gilgunn, who assisted with parts of the interviewing conducted with Canadian student athletes who received athletic scholarships from American colleges and universities. See also Gilgunn (2010).

8 Ethnographic encounters with various situated forms of prestige sometimes elicit a well-intended collegial suggestion that it would probably be well worth it to consider the operational workings of these arrangements in terms of Bourdieu's (1984) study of distinction and his notion of cultural capital. Although Bourdieu mentioned sport within this work (1984, 209–25), his insights into the oppositions between popular and bourgeois sports in France in the 1960s cannot be readily or usefully transposed upon the organization of child and youth sports in contemporary North America. Briefly, Bourdieu explained cultural distinctions in sport practices in terms of clearly delineated class oppositions; in contrast, child and youth sports in Canada tend to blur class distinctions, with middle-class youth athletes becoming increasingly focused upon pursuing athletic scholarships that have traditionally been identified as a means by which boys and girls of more modest means might be able to obtain a university education.

9 Adler and Adler (1991, 81) also discuss coaches' tactical shaming of varsity athletes, including acts such as threatening them with "benching," suspension, and non-renewal of scholarships. These and other forms of "status degradation" become part of what the Adlers identify as a "rite of passage" to reshape high school stars into more compliant college players.

10   NCAA regulations strictly regulate the number, duration, and nature of officially permitted and subsidized visits that each prospective athlete can make to universities and colleges prior to committing to attend a particular institution.

11   There are, of course, other paths to athletic acclaim than being awarded an American athletic scholarship. The member institutions of Canadian Interuniversity Sport (previously known as the Canadian Interuniversity Athletics Union) provide a broad range of post-secondary intercollegiate athletics programs for young Canadians. For boys, the prospect of being drafted and signed by a Canadian Hockey League (major junior, Tier 1) team by age 16 is a highly recognized accomplishment. Appearances by teenaged gymnasts and ice skaters, for instance, in national and international competitions tend to receive somewhat less attention at the neighbourhood level than do other more "mainstream" sports.

Chapter Eight

HOW THE GAME IS PLAYED

AS WE TRAVELLED TO an exhibition game in a neighbouring city, Barry and Ian, members of the under-13 North District all-star baseball team, glumly predicted that they would likely lose that afternoon by a wide margin. According to Barry, their hosts, the under-14 South District all-stars, had a week earlier routed another district's under-13 all-star team. Subsequently, that team had bounced back to defeat Barry and Ian's side. Arriving at the field, we could see that the host team was well into its pre-game preparations. After a few minutes of watching the South District squad flawlessly execute a set of fielding drills, a North District player asked his coach whether there would be a "mercy rule"[1] in effect that would end the game after five innings if one side was ahead by 10 or more runs. This prompted a frown from the coach, who shrugged and then surreptitiously looked back to the stands, sharing with the North District parents a look that comically conveyed impending doom.

Before the game commenced, the umpires spent several minutes with the coaches reviewing the rules that would be in effect that afternoon. These included specification of what would happen if a ball went under a fence, notification of an absolute prohibition on throwing bats, swearing, or objecting to umpires' calls, as well as advisement that the balk rule would be enforced. For the North District players, this had been their first season of competing under rules that permitted base runners to take a leadoff before the pitch to home plate. Accordingly, the team had been practising how to check and pick off base runners. Yet, since 13-year-olds' arms tend to be somewhat less proficient than their legs, games at this level sometimes feature intrepid base runners stealing bases more or less at will. This can extend games anywhere from 60 to 90 minutes longer than the hour and a half that is usual in the preceding level.

Hand-in-hand with leadoffs and attempted pickoffs came the enforcement of the balk rule that proscribes certain motions a pitcher might make to lure a base runner into moving before a pitch is thrown. In this game, the 14-year-old South District pitcher seemed fully conversant with this rule, even though he initially had only the occasional North District base runner to contend with. In contrast, the North District pitchers kept stumbling over the finer points of the balk rule, causing the umpire and their coach to make repeated trips to the pitcher's mound to clarify which delivery motions were permitted and which were not. Nevertheless, the visiting team's pitcher started with a reasonably accurate fastball that served to keep their opponents off the scoreboard in the first inning. In the next two innings he gamely tried to scatter a growing number of hits, but these inexorably led to a stream of runs, even though several of these constituted "unearned runs"[2] caused by fielding and throwing errors.[3] For his part, the South District starting pitcher unveiled an impressive curveball that set down opposing batters in order during the first two innings. In the third inning a few of the visiting team's batters began to make some contact with the ball and one of them even registered a hit. Yet by the end of the third inning the home side had put together an 8–0 lead. In the top of the fourth inning the visitors actually scored a run at approximately the mid-point of the scheduled seven-inning game.

It was in the bottom of the fourth inning that something unannounced and unnoticed by many, if not all, at the park happened. The South District base runners unobtrusively stopped taking leadoffs and stealing bases when the opposing catcher dropped the ball. This continued for another two innings. When I noticed what was happening, I pointed it out to the person sitting next to me. There was no indication that Terry, the North District coach, or any of his players were aware of this development.[4]

The South District coach opted to keep his starting pitcher in the game even as his effectiveness began to diminish. This led to more North District hits and several more runs. At one point, as the possibility that his team might not be entirely out of this game dawned on Terry, he seemed to get a bit on edge, verbally noting errors made by his players. This diverged from the otherwise consistently positive approach that he had exhibited in this and previous seasons when he only indirectly acknowledged mistakes by players.[5] With South District quietly choosing neither to steal bases nor to replace their pitcher, the score began to narrow, reaching 8–5. At the beginning of the next inning, when the host team sent out a new pitcher for the warm-up but then moved to continue the game with the same pitcher who had started the game, Terry approached the umpire to protest the move, insisting that the starting pitcher had in effect been replaced and, therefore, couldn't be brought back into the game. A couple of his own players tried to catch his attention and counsel him against lodging this protest, reasoning that the opposing starter, who was beginning to tire, would be easier to face than the kid who had just pitched the warm-up. Not to be deterred, Terry called for the opposing coach to join the conference. The other coach did so but restricted his comments to explaining that while his starting pitcher was a bit tired, the kid wanted to continue. After listening to a few further comments by Terry, the umpire simply overruled him and the game recommenced.

What Terry gave no indication of recognizing was the way in which the South District team was inconspicuously playing the game so as to ensure that it would not run up a lop-sided victory. Indeed, during the fifth inning, when the North District batters began to hammer out some hits and score some runs, the South District infielders suddenly seemed anchored to their bases until their pitcher delivered to home plate, thereby leaving a temporary but challenging fielding gap between, for instance, first and second base. Despite several North District hits leaking through this gap, the South District first and second basemen declined to move into it until the ball was pitched. This gap had not existed earlier in the game, and later, when North District came closer to evening the score, it was once again plugged. For two innings, however, the South District infielders had to move sharply just to get close to hit balls shooting through these spaces.

So the game proceeded until the top of the seventh inning when North District batters came in for what would prove to be their last plate appearances. South District now brought in the fastball-throwing pitcher who had tossed the disputed warm-up session a few innings earlier. He promptly retired the visiting side 1–2–3. The speed of his pitches overpowered the batters, reducing them to swinging wildly at balls that consistently found the outer edges of the strike zone. The game ended 17–12, with South District foregoing its last at bats, in accordance with the rules.

The undeclared moves by the home team to impose a multi-dimensional competitive handicap on its players and, thus, to limit the competition between them and the weaker visiting team was smoothly enacted. I heard none of the South District players mention these actions to their opponents. On the drive home Barry suggested that South District "might have gone a bit easy on us," but he explained this solely with respect to their pitcher being left in for six innings. He made no mention of the informal prohibition on base stealing or the temporary mooring of South District infielders to their bases that had allowed North District to get back into the game.

These subtle modifications on the part of the South District team allowed their younger opponents to avoid getting "skunked" and to score some runs. Thus, the game was rescued from the fate of ending prematurely in a demoralizing and humiliating blowout for the younger team. The more common approach within baseball or any competitive sport is to take full and timely benefit of an opponent's weaknesses. On this Sunday afternoon the home team coach and his players did just enough to craft a performance that kept alive a game for all concerned. Initially the South District parents had cheered their sons on with familiar forms of vocal support. As the afternoon proceeded, this characteristically partisan mode of baseball cheering subsided. On a couple of occasions, South District base runners even showed their appreciation of good catches and plays turned by their opponents. Later on, the father of one of the North District players reciprocated by applauding a particularly fine catch by the South District shortstop. What emerged was a game that left the coach and players of the defeated team not feeling destroyed. After all, they had ended up scoring 12 runs against a team of players a year older than them.

It was an intriguing performance by a team of 14-year-olds, a coach, and parents who seemed to have accepted that there was little to be gained by ruthlessly exploiting the competitive advantage that one team held over the other. Despite the attention paid before the game to sorting out the ground rules and conduct guidelines, not to mention the balk rule, nothing had been said about the "pond hockey rules" that the home team unilaterally introduced to limit competition without turning the game into an obvious and patronizing charade. What impressed me as much as anything was the manner in which the game was discreetly shaped by one side to draw out the individual and collective abilities possessed by members of the other squad. Out of this ensued a contest that established a certain degree of competitive balance between the two teams through a form of artfully handicapped but nonetheless keenly played baseball. That the South District players and coach possessed the magnanimity and self-discipline not only to do this but also to carry out their performance without feeling compelled to declare what they were doing made the afternoon an enjoyable one for all concerned.

Following the final "out," Terry offered a few congratulatory words to his players, noting that each of them had played for some part of the game and that they had made some fine plays both in the field and at the plate. They then headed towards the parking lot for the ride home. The South District players made for a shaded area down the first-base line, out of earshot, and sat while their coach spoke to them. They had, as I had seen it, responded impressively to the scaled-up athletic challenges and conditions that he had set for them within this exhibition match. They had also fashioned a socially congenial event out of a contest that would have yielded nothing like that had they simply played the game according to the rules that are normally supposed to govern sport.

What is the point of recounting certain aspects of what happened and what did not happen during this particular game? After all, it is not as though this was a typical youth baseball game (if, indeed, any such entity exists) that might be purported to stand for what normally transpires in community sport. Nor, I would hasten to add, is it presented here as an exemplary and definitive model of how community sport ideally *ought* to be conducted, whatever the sport, the nature of the contest, or the age of the players. What can, instead, be gained by looking closely into the regularities and irregularities, the expected and unexpected happenings that occur within this or any other community sport event is a fuller understanding of how the underlying properties of this field of endeavour connect with one another. In short, by taking account of the differing ways in which the activities, relationships, and purposes of community sports are pursued, we can better appreciate the possibilities that exist in how the game is played.

Working out what actually happens in community sports, how this is accomplished, and by whom is a more contingent and complicated matter than is allowed for in stereotypical depictions of child and youth sports. Those who are implacably skeptical or outright dismissive of the relative merits of child and youth sport often rely upon simplistic and sweeping claims about the "troubling" nature of these activities. Equally unconvincing are the saccharin and self-serving platitudes about sport traded in by sport bureaucrats and entrepreneurs who are angling to rebrand child and youth sports as a commodity that they are best positioned to take charge of. These insistently proclaimed but crudely drawn versions of community sports cannot begin to accommodate all that happens within these remarkably varied yet intricately constructed activities.

What was missing from the ballgame recounted above was the cast of apocryphal characters—including win-at-all-cost coaches, out-of-control parents, and egotistical child and youth athletes—that have become staple figures in discursive renderings of "what is wrong with community sports." Also absent were the sport consultants and bureaucrats who, according to the claims made in their marketing campaigns and policy statements, surely ought to have been there to ensure that the assembled children and adults would have been instructed how to play the game properly. Nevertheless, those who were actually present that afternoon somehow worked out on their own how to craft an event that transcended the rules of the game without falling victim to either the moral hazards or the piety of more commonly heard claims about what children's sport is all about. The winning coach, his players, the umpire, and all of the other individuals who came together that afternoon cumulatively pitched in to construct that game. It might just as easily have been played in another manner, for every sport performance represents, among other things, the outcome of the various choices made by the participants who show up on the day.

In this book I have noted instances of less positive and more vexed situations that also unfold within community sport. My reason for doing so has been to demonstrate that community sports involves rather more than either just a set of prosaic but healthy pastimes for children and youths or a deeply problematic form of adult-controlled practice that serves to colonize childhood. What I have attempted to reveal is the importance and intensity of athletic activities that bring together people of different ages to engage in a variety of intricately connected undertakings that they would not individually be able to accomplish. To appreciate the breadth and scope of these activities and the various individual and collective projects that they sustain it is necessary to look closely into the specificities that constitute community sports. In the process of doing this what also emerges is an appreciation of the types of challenges that face even the most modest of undertakings in this field. In view of these, what is truly remarkable is the persistence and passion with which a broad range of community-organized sports continues to be practised in every part of Canada. The notion that child and youth sports might be either too mundane a matter to warrant serious attention or too serious a concern to be left to children, parents, and community volunteers needs to be set aside.

Understanding community sports as a social field obliges us to take account of the respective positioning of and influences exerted by the diverse participants, groups, and institutions that engage in and, thereby, shape the activities that define this burgeoning sector. It is, as I have endeavoured to show, a large and complex field that both accommodates and relies upon the involvement of girls and boys of various ages as well as that of parents, coaches, sport organization personnel, and government officials (particularly at the municipal level). It features the ongoing interplay of a set of generally familiar but by no means static roles that can be enacted in differing ways with varying outcomes. Within the shifting dynamics of these relationships and undertakings are to be found motivations and manoeuvrings, expectations and experiences that are anything but child's play.

NOTES

1 A mercy rule brings a sporting contest to an early end when one team has an insurmountable lead over the other team. It is meant to spare the losing team the ignominy of having to endure an even more lopsided loss. The adoption of such a rule is usually restricted to child and youth sports.

2 An earned run in baseball is one for which the pitcher is deemed to be responsible, while an unearned run is attributed by the official scorer to have resulted from some action by a member of the defensive team other than the pitch that immediately preceded the scoring of that run. Although the official scoring of games at this level did not include the determining of unearned runs, many of the players at this age are, nonetheless, conversant with these matters and make a point of distinguishing between earned and unearned runs in their discussions with teammates and other players.

3 After striking out one batter, the pitcher could only look on in disbelief as his catcher dropped the ball and then failed to make the throw to first base quickly or accurately enough to get the out.

4 Sitting behind the North District team dugout, I heard no mention of this from its coach or players at any stage of the game, and neither did the person sitting next to me.

5 For instance, he would usually say, "Don't worry about missing that ball. It was a hard play to make, but at least you tried," and so on.

BIBLIOGRAPHY

Adler, Patricia A., and Peter Adler. 1991. *Backboards and Blackboards: College Athletes and Role Engulfment*. New York: Columbia University Press.

Adler, Patricia A., and Peter Adler. 1994. "Social Reproduction and the Corporate Other: The Institutionalization of Afterschool Activities." *Sociological Quarterly* 35 (2): 309–28. http://dx.doi.org/10.1111/j.1533-8525.1994.tb00412.x.

Alter, Joseph S. 1992. *The Wrestler's Body: Identity and Ideology in North India*. Berkeley: University of California Press.

Amit-Talai, Vered. 1995. "The Waltz of Sociability: Intimacy, Dislocation and Friendship in a Quebec High School." In *Youth Cultures: A Cross-Cultural Perspective*, ed. Vered Amit-Talai and Helena Wulff, 144–65. New York: Routledge.

Anderson, Sally. 2003. "Bodying Forth a Room for Everyone: Inclusive Recreational Badminton in Copenhagen." In *Sport, Dance and Embodied Identities*, ed. Noel Dyck and Eduardo P. Archetti, 23–53. Oxford: Berg.

Anderson, Sally. 2008. *Civil Sociality: Children, Sport, and Cultural Policy in Denmark*. Charlotte, NC: Information Age Publishing.

Andrews, David L., R. Pitter, D. Zwick, and D. Ambrose. 1997. "Soccer's Racial Frontier: Sport and the Suburbanization of Contemporary America." In *Entering the Field: New Perspectives on World Football*, ed. Gary Armstrong and Richard Giulianotti, 261–81. Oxford: Berg.

Andrusevich, Rob. 2003. "Hockey Dad Charged with Assaulting Daughter at Game." *Vancouver Sun*, March 18, A5.

Archetti, Eduardo P. 1997a. "The Moralities of Argentinian Football." In *The Ethnography of Moralities*, ed. Signe Howell, 98–123. London, New York: Routledge.

Archetti, Eduardo P. 1997b. "'And Give Joy to My Heart': Ideology and Emotions in the Argentinian Cult of Maradona." In *Entering the Field: New Perspectives on World Football*, ed. Gary Armstrong and Richard Giulianotti, 31–51. Oxford: Berg.

Archetti, Eduardo P. 1999. *Masculinities: Football, Polo and the Tango in Argentina*. New York: Berg.

Armstrong, Gary. 1998. *Football Hooligans: Knowing the Score*. Oxford: Berg.

Azoy, G. Whitney. 1982. *Buzkashi: Game and Power in Afghanistan*. Philadelphia: University of Pennsylvania Press.

Bailey, Wilford S., and Taylor D. Littleton. 1991. *Athletics and Academe: An Anatomy of Abuses and a Prescription for Reform*. New York: American Council on Education, and Macmillan Publishing Company.

Bale, John. 1991. *The Brawn Drain: Foreign Student-Athletes in American Universities*. Urbana: University of Illinois Press.

Ben-Ari, Eyal. 1997. *Body Projects in Japanese Daycare: Culture, Organization and Emotions in a Preschool*. Richmond, UK: Curzon.

Blanchard, Kendall. 1995. *The Anthropology of Sport: An Introduction*. Revised edition. Westport, CT: Bergin and Garvey.

Bloom, Michael R., Michael W. Grant, and Douglas Watt. 2005. *Strengthening Canada: The Socio-Economic Benefits of Sport Participation in Canada*. Ottawa: Conference Board of Canada.

Bok, Derek. 2003. *Universities in the Marketplace: The Commercialization of Higher Education*. Princeton, NJ: Princeton University Press.

Bourdieu, Pierre. 1984. *Distinctions: A Social Critique of the Judgement of Taste*. Cambridge: Cambridge University Press.

Bourdieu, Pierre. 1985. "The Social Space and the Genesis of Groups." *Theory and Society* 14 (6): 723–44. http://dx.doi.org/10.1007/BF00174048.

Bowen, William G., and Sarah A. Levin. 2003. *Reclaiming the Game of Life: College Sports and Educational Values*. Princeton, NJ: Princeton University Press.

Briggs, Jean L. 1998. *Inuit Morality Play: The Emotional Education of a Three-Year-Old*. St. John's, NL: Institute of Social and Economic Research, Memorial University of Newfoundland.

British Columbia. Sport Branch. 2004. *BC's Policy on Sport and Physical Activity*. Victoria, BC: Ministry of Small Business and Economic Development, Sport Branch.

Broch, Harald Beyer. 1990. *Growing Up Agreeably: Bonerate Childhood Observed*. Honolulu: University of Hawaii Press.

Broch, Harald Beyer. 2003. "Embodied Play and Gender Identities in Competitive Handball for Children in Norway." In *Sport, Dance and Embodied Identities*, ed. Noel Dyck and Eduardo P. Archetti, 75–93. New York: Berg.

Brownell, Susan. 1995. *Training the Body for China: Sports in the Moral Order of the People's Republic.* Chicago: University of Chicago Press.

Brownell, Susan. 2008. *Beijing's Games: What the Olympics Mean to China.* Lanham, MD: Rowman and Littlefield.

Carter, Thomas F. 2008. *The Quality of Home Runs: The Passion, Politics and Language of Cuban Baseball.* Durham, NC: Duke University Press.

Byers, Walter with Charles H. Hammer. 1995. *Unsportsmanlike Conduct: Exploiting College Athletes.* Ann Arbor: University of Michigan Press.

Chafetz, Janet Saltzman, and Joseph A. Kotarba. 1995. "Son Worshippers: The Role of Little League Mothers in Recreating Gender." *Studies in Symbolic Interaction* 18: 217–41.

Clark, Warren. 2008. *Kids' Sports.* Ottawa: Statistics Canada, Catalogue no.11–008-X.

Coakley, Jay. 2006. "The Good Father: Parental Expectations and Youth Sports." *Leisure Studies* 25 (2): 153–63. http://dx.doi.org/10.1080/02614360500467735.

Coleman, James S. 1987. "Families and Schools." *Educational Researcher* 16 (6): 32–8.

Csikszentmihalyi, Mihaly. 1993. "Contexts of Optimal Growth in Childhood." *Daedalus* 122 (1): 31–56.

Darrah, Charles N., James M. Freeman, and J.A. English-Lueck. 2007. *Busier Than Ever!: Why American Families Can't Slow Down.* Stanford, CA: Stanford University Press.

Doherty, Alison, and Katie Misener. 2008. "Community Sport Networks." In *Sport and Social Capital*, ed. Matthew Nicolson and Russell Hoye, 113–41. Boston: Elsevier.

Donnelly, Peter. 2000. "Young Athletes Need Child Law Protection." In *Taking Sport Seriously: Social Issues in Canadian Sport*, 2nd ed., ed. Peter Donnelly, 102–6. Toronto: Thompson Educational Publishing.

Duderstadt, James J. 2003. *Intercollegiate Athletics and the American University: A University President's Perspective.* Ann Arbor: University of Michigan Press.

Dukes, Richard L., and Jay Coakley. 2002. "Parental Commitment to Competitive Swimming." *Free Inquiry in Creative Sociology* 30 (2): 185–97.

Dyck, Noel. 1985. "Aboriginal Peoples and Nation-States: An Introduction to the Analytical Issues." In *Indigenous Peoples and the Nation-State: Fourth World Politics in Canada, Australia and Norway*, ed. Noel Dyck, 1–26. St. John's, NL: Institute of Social and Economic Research, Memorial University of Newfoundland.

Dyck, Noel. 1991. *What is the Indian "Problem"? Tutelage and Resistance in Canadian Indian Administration.* St. John's, NL: Institute of Social and Economic Research, Memorial University of Newfoundland.

Dyck, Noel. 1995. "Parents, Consociates and the Social Construction of Children's Athletics." *Anthropological Forum* 7 (2): 215–29. http://dx.doi.org/10.1080/00664 677.1995.9967455.

Dyck, Noel. 1997. *Differing Visions: Administering Indian Residential Schooling in Prince Albert, 1867–1995*. Halifax: Fernwood Publishing, and Prince Albert, Saskatchewan: The Prince Albert Grand Council.

Dyck, Noel. 2000a. "Home Field Advantage? Exploring the Social Construction of Children's Sports." In *Constructing the "Field": Ethnographic Fieldwork in the Contemporary World*, ed. Vered Amit, 32–53. London: Routledge.

Dyck, Noel, ed. 2000b. *Games, Sports, and Cultures*. Oxford: Berg.

Dyck, Noel. 2000c. "Introduction." In *Games, Sports and Cultures*, ed. Noel Dyck, 1–9. Oxford: Berg.

Dyck, Noel. 2000d. "Games, Bodies, Celebrations and Boundaries: Anthropological Perspectives on Sport." In *Games, Sports and Cultures*, ed. Noel Dyck, 13–42. Oxford: Berg.

Dyck, Noel. 2000e. "Parents, Kids and Coaches: Constructing Sport and Childhood in Canada." In *Games, Sports and Cultures*, ed. Noel Dyck, 137–61. Oxford: Berg.

Dyck, Noel. 2002. "'Have you been to Hayward Field?' Children's Sport and the Construction of Community in Suburban Canada." In *Realizing Community: Concepts, Social Relationships and Sentiments*, ed. Vered Amit, 105–23. London: Routledge.

Dyck, Noel. 2003. "Embodying Success: Identity and Performance in Children's Sport." In *Sport, Dance and Embodied Identities*, ed. Noel Dyck and Eduardo P. Archetti, 55–73. Oxford: Berg.

Dyck, Noel. 2006. "Athletic Scholarships and the Politics of Child Rearing in Canada." *Anthropological Notebooks* 12 (2): 65–78.

Dyck, Noel. 2007. "Playing Like Canadians: Improvising Nation and Identity through Sport." In *The Discipline of Leisure: Embodying Cultures of 'Recreation*, ed. Simon Coleman and Tamara Kohn, 109–25. New York: Berghahn.

Dyck, Noel, ed. 2008a. *Exploring Regimes of Discipline: The Dynamics of Restraint*. Oxford: Berghahn.

Dyck, Noel. 2008b. "Anthropological Perspectives on Discipline: An Introduction to the Issues." In *Exploring Regimes of Discipline: The Dynamics of Restraint*, ed. Noel Dyck, 1–22. Oxford: Berghahn.

Dyck, Noel. 2010a. "Remembering and the Ethnography of Children's Sports." In *The Ethnographic Self as Resource: Writing Memory into Ethnography*, ed. Peter Collins and Anselma Gallinat, 150–64. New York: Berghahn.

Dyck, Noel. 2010b. "Going South: Canadians' Engagement with American Athletic Scholarships." *Anthropology in Action* 17 (1): 41–54. http://dx.doi.org/10.3167/aia.2010.170105.

Dyck, Noel. 2010c. "Social Class, Competition, and Parental Jealousy in Children's Sports." In *The Handbook of Jealousy: Theory, Research, and Multidisciplinary Approaches*, ed. Sybil L. Hart and Maria Legerstee, 498–515. Malden, MA: Wiley-Blackwell. http://dx.doi.org/10.1002/9781444323542.ch21.

Dyck, Noel. 2011. "In Pursuit of the 'Full Ride': American Athletic Scholarships and Mobility, Sport and Childhood in Canada." *Anthropologica* 53 (1): 53–66.

Dyck, Noel, and Eduardo P. Archetti, eds. 2003. *Sport, Dance and Embodied Identities*. Oxford: Berg.

Dyck, Noel, and Grant Wildi. 1993. *Creating Community Sport for Kids: A Survey of Community Sport Clubs and Associations for Children and Youth in Coquitlam, Port Coquitlam, and Port Moody British Columbia, during the 1992–3 Season*. Burnaby, BC: Department of Sociology and Anthropology, Simon Fraser University.

Eastman, Benjamin, Michael Ralph, and Sean Brown, eds. 2008. *America's Game(s): A Critical Anthropology of Sport*. London: Routledge.

Federal-Provincial-Territorial Conference of Ministers Responsible for Sport and Recreation. 2002. The Canadian Sport Policy. Iqaluit, Nunavut: Ministers [Responsible for Sport, Fitness and Recreation].

Fine, Gary Alan. 1987. *With the Boys: Little League Baseball and Preadolescent Culture*. Chicago: University of Chicago Press.

Fine, Gary Alan, and Jay Mechling. 1991. "Minor Difficulties: Changing Children in the Late Twentieth Century." In *America at Century's End*, ed. Alan Wolfe, 58–78. Berkeley: University of California Press.

Foster, George M. 1972. "The Anatomy of Envy: A Study in Symbolic Behavior." *Current Anthropology* 13 (2): 165–86. http://dx.doi.org/10.1086/201267.

Frykman, Jonas, and Orvar Löfgren. 1987. *Culture Builders: A Historical Anthropology of Middle-Class Life*. New Brunswick, NJ: Rutgers University Press.

Funk, Gary D. 1991. *Major Violation: The Unbalanced Priorities of Athletics and Academics*. Campaign, IL: Leisure Press.

Fussell, Paul. 1983. *Class: A Guide through the American Status System*. New York: Summit Books.

Gerdy, John R. 2006. *Air Ball: American Education's Failed Experiment with Elite Athletics*. Jackson: University Press of Mississippi.

Gilgunn, Meghan. 2010. "'Obviously It's Worth It': The Value of Being a Canadian Student Athlete in the U.S.A." *Anthropology in Action* 17 (1): 55–65. http://dx.doi.org/10.3167/aia.2010.170106.

202 Bibliography

Grasmuck, Sherri. 2005. *Protecting Home: Class, Race, and Masculinity in Boy's Baseball.* New Brunswick, NJ: Rutgers University Press.

Green, Chris. 2009. *Every Boy's Dream: England's Football Future on the Line.* London: A&C Black Publishers.

Groupe Intersol Group. 2011. "Canadian Sport Policy Renewal National Gathering: Summary Report." Ottawa: GIG. Accessed 1 December 2011. http://sirc.ca/CSPRenewal/documents/Summary_National_Gathering.pdf.

Gubrium, Jaber F. 1988. "The Family as Project." *Sociological Review* 36 (2): 273–96. http://dx.doi.org/10.1111/j.1467-954X.1988.tb00838.x.

Guèvremont, Anne, Leanne Findlay, and Dafna Kohen. 2008. *Organized Extracurricular Activities of Canadian Children and Youth.* Ottawa: Statistics Canada, Catalogue no. 82–003-X.

Gulløv, Eva. 2003. "Creating a Natural Place for Children: An Ethnographic Study of Danish Kindergartens." In *Children's Places: Cross-Cultural Perspectives,* ed. Karen Fog Olwig and Eva Gulløv, 23–38. London: Routledge.

Hecht, Tobias. 1998. *At Home in the Street: Street Children in Northeast Brazil.* Cambridge: Cambridge University Press.

Heikkala, Juha. 1993. "Discipline and Excel: Techniques of the Self and Body and the Logic of Competing." *Sociology of Sport Journal* 10 (4): 397–412.

Howe, P. David. 2004. *Sport, Professionalism and Pain: Ethnographies of Injury and Risk.* London: Routledge. http://dx.doi.org/10.4324/9780203453261.

Hyman, Mark. 2009. *Until It Hurts: America's Obsession with Youth Sports and How It Harms Our Kids.* Boston: Beacon Press.

Ifedi, Fidelis. 2008. Sport Participation in Canada, 2005. Ottawa: Statistics Canada; Sport Canada, Catalogue no. 81–595–MIE2008060.

Jacobs, Jane. 1961. *The Death and Life of Great American Cities.* New York: Vintage Books.

James, Allison. 1998. "Imaging Children 'At Home,' 'In the Family' and 'At School': Movement between the Spatial and Temporal Markers of Childhood Identity in Britain." In *Migrants of Identity: Perceptions of Home in a World of Movement,* ed. Nigel Rapport and Andrew Dawson, 139–60. New York: Berg.

James, Allison. 2002. "The English Child: Toward a Cultural Politics of Childhood." In *British Subjects: An Anthropology of Britain,* ed. Nigel Rapport, 143–62. New York: Berg.

James, Allison, and Adrian L. James. 2004. *Constructing Childhood: Theory, Policy and Social Practice.* London: Palgrave Macmillan.

James, Allison, and Alan Prout. 1990. "Re-Presenting Childhood: Time and Transition in the Study of Childhood." In *Constructing and Reconstructing Childhood: Contemporary Issues in the Sociological Study of Childhood,* ed. Alan Prout and Allison James, 216–37. London: Falmer Press.

Klein, Alan M. 1991. *Sugarball: The American Game, the Dominican Dream*. New Haven, CT: Yale University Press.

Klein, Alan M. 1993. *Little Big Men: Bodybuilding Subculture and Gender Construction*. Albany: State University of New York Press.

Klein, Alan M. 1997. *Baseball on the Border: A Tale of the Two Laredos*. Princeton, NJ: Princeton University Press.

Klein, Alan M. 2006. *Growing the Game: The Globalization of Major League Baseball*. New Haven, CT: Yale University Press.

Knowles, Caroline. 1996. *Family Boundaries: The Invention of Normality and Dangerousness*. Peterborough, ON: Broadview Press.

Lahey, David, 1993. *Athletic Scholarships: Making Your Sports Pay*. Los Angeles: Warwick Publishing.

Lareau, Annette. 2003. *Unequal Childhoods: Class, Race, and Family Life*. Berkeley: University of California Press.

Lareau, Annette, and Elliot B. Weininger. 2008. "Time, Work, and Family Life: Reconceptualizing Gendered Time Patterns through the Case of Children's Organized Activities." *Sociological Forum* 23 (3): 419–54. http://dx.doi.org/10.1111/j.1573-7861.2008.00085.x.

Lee, Nick. 2001. *Childhood and Society: Growing Up in an Age of Uncertainty*. Buckingham: Open University Press.

Leite Lopes, Jose Sergio. 1997. "Successes and Contradictions in 'Multiracial' Brazilian Football." In *Entering the Field: New Perspectives on World Football*, ed. Gary Armstrong and Richard Giulianotti, 53–86. Oxford: Berg.

Lewin, Kurt. 1951. *Field Theory in Social Science*. Ed. Dorwin Cartwright. New York: Harper and Brothers.

Lithman, Yngve Georg. 2000. "Reflections on the Social and Cultural Dimensions of Children's Elite Sport in Sweden." In *Games, Sports and Cultures*, ed. Noel Dyck, 163–81. Oxford: Berg.

MacAloon, John J. 1981. *This Great Symbol: Pierre de Coubertin and the Origins of the Modern Olympic Games*. Chicago: University of Chicago Press.

MacClancy, Jeremy, ed. 1996. *Sport, Identity and Ethnicity*. Oxford: Berg.

MacGregor, Roy. 1995. *The Home Team: Fathers, Sons and Hockey*. Toronto: Viking.

McCormack, J.B., and Lawrence Chalip. 1988. "Sport as Socialization: A Critique of Methodological Premises." *Social Science Journal* 25 (1): 83–92. http://dx.doi.org/10.1016/0362-3319(88)90055-9.

Macintosh, Donald, and David Whitson. 1990. *The Game Planners: Transforming Canada's Sport System*. Montreal: McGill-Queen's University Press.

Mahler, Jonathan. 2011. "Student–Athlete Equation Could Be a Win-Win." *The New York Times*, 9 August, online edition. Accessed 9 August 2011. http://www.nytimes.com/2011/08/10/sports/time-for-colleges-to-add-education-back-into-the-student-athlete-equation.html.

Maki, Allan. 2010. "Hockey Dads (and Moms) Told to Chill." *Globe and Mail*, 20 October, R6.

Martin, John Levi. 2003. "What Is Field Theory?" *American Journal of Sociology* 109 (1): 1–49. http://dx.doi.org/10.1086/375201.

Messner, Michael A. 2009. *It's All for the Kids: Gender, Family, and Youth Sports.* Berkeley: University of California Press.

Miller, Daniel. 2001. *The Dialectics of Shopping.* Foreword by Anthony T. Carter. Chicago: University of Chicago Press.

Minister's Task Force on Federal Sport Policy. 1992. *Sport: The Way Ahead. An Overview of the Task Force Report.* Ottawa: Minister of State Fitness and Amateur Sport and Minister of Supply and Services Canada.

Moffatt, Michael. 1989. *Coming of Age in New Jersey: College and American Culture.* New Brunswick, NJ: Rutgers University Press.

Mulholland, Elizabeth. 2008. *What Sport Can Do: The True Sport Report.* Ottawa: Canadian Centre for Ethics in Sport.

Nathan, Rebekah. 2005. *My Freshman Year: What a Professor Learned by Becoming a Student.* Ithaca, NY: Cornell University Press.

Newman, Katherine S. 1988. *Falling from Grace: The Experience of Downward Mobility in the American Middle Class.* New York: Free Press.

Newman, Katherine S. 1991. "Uncertain Seas: Cultural Turmoil and the Domestic Economy." In *America at Century's End*, ed. Alan Wolfe, 112–30. Berkeley: University of California Press.

Olwig, Karen Fog, and Eva Gulløv. 2003. "Towards an Anthropology of Children and Place." In *Children's Places: Cross-Cultural Perspectives*, ed. Karen Fog Olwig and Eva Gulløv, 1–19. London: Routledge.

Ortner, Sherry B. 1991. "Reading America: Preliminary Notes on Class and Culture." In *Recapturing Anthropology: Working in the Present*, ed. Richard G. Fox, 163–89. Santa Fe, NM: School of American Research Press.

Paine, Robert. 1969. "In Search of Friendship: An Exploratory Analysis of 'Middle-Class' Culture." *Man* 4 (4): 505–24. http://dx.doi.org/10.2307/2798192.

Parent, Milena M., and Jean Harvey. 2009. "Towards a Management Model for Sport and Physical Activity Community-based Partnerships." *European Sport Management Quarterly* 9 (1): 23–45.

Percival, Lloyd. 1992. *The Hockey Handbook.* Revised edition. Toronto: McClelland and Stewart.

Persell, Caroline Hodges. 1991. "Schools under Pressure." In *America at Century's End*, ed. Alan Wolfe, 283–97. Berkeley: University of California Press.

Podlog, Leslie. 2002. "Perceptions of Success and Failure among University Athletes in Canada." *Journal of Sport Behavior* 25 (4): 368–93.

Rapport, Nigel. 2000. "The Narrative as Fieldwork Technique: Processual Ethnography for a World in Motion." In *Constructing the Field: Ethnographic Fieldwork in the Contemporary World*, ed. Vered Amit, 71–95. London: Routledge.

Rapport, Nigel, and Joanna Overing. 2000. *Social and Cultural Anthropology: The Key Concepts*. London: Routledge. http://dx.doi.org/10.4324/9780203451137.

Richards, Paul. 1997. "Soccer and Violence in War-Torn Africa: Soccer and Social Rehabilitation in Sierra Leone." In *Entering the Field: New Perspectives on World Football*, ed. Gary Armstrong and Richard Giulianotti, 141–57. New York: Berg.

Rose, Nicolas. 1989. *Governing the Soul: The Shaping of the Private Self*. London: Routledge.

Rosier, Katherine Brown, and William A. Corsaro. 1993. "Competent Parents, Complex Lives: Managing Parenthood in Poverty." *Journal of Contemporary Ethnography* 22 (2): 171–204. http://dx.doi.org/10.1177/089124193022002002.

Sack, Allen L. 2008. *Counterfeit Amateurs: An Athlete's Journey through the Sixties to the Age of Academic Capitalism*. University Park: Pennsylvania State University Press.

Sack, Allen L., and Ellen J. Staurowsky. 1998. *College Athletes for Hire: The Evolution and Legacy of the NCAA's Amateur Myth*. Westport, CT: Praeger.

Sansom, Basil. 1980. *The Camp at Wallaby Cross: Aboriginal Fringe Dwellers in Darwin*. Canberra: Australian Institute of Aboriginal Studies.

Shulman, James Lawrence, and William G. Bowen. 2001. *The Game of Life: College Sports and Educational Values*. Princeton, NJ: Princeton University Press.

Smith, Ronald A. 1988. *Sports and Freedom: The Rise of Big-Time College Athletics*. Oxford: Oxford University Press.

Sokolove, Michael. 2008. *Warrior Girls: Protecting Our Daughters against the Injury Epidemic in Women's Sports*. New York: Simon and Schuster.

Sport Information Resource Centre. 2011. "Towards a Renewed Canadian Sport Policy Discussion Paper." Ottawa: SIRC. Accessed 1 December 2011. http://sirc.ca/CSPRenewal/documents/2011/Discussion_Paper.pdf.

Sport Information Resource Centre. 2012. "Canadian Sport Policy 2.0 – Draft – February 14, 2012." Ottawa: SIRC. Accessed 28 February 2012. http://sirc.ca/CSPRenewal/documents/CSP20DRAFTEN.pdf.

Statistics Canada. 2001. "National Longitudinal Survey of Children and Youth: Participation in Activities, Cycle 3." *The Daily*, Wednesday, May 30, 2001, 1–5. Ottawa: Statistics Canada.

Stephens, Sharon. 1995. "Children and the Politics of Culture in 'Late Capitalism'." In *Children and the Politics of Culture,* ed. Sharon Stephens, 3–48. Princeton, NJ: Princeton University Press.

Stinson, Dan. 2004. "High-stepping Senior." *Vancouver Sun,* 23, April, G5.

Telander, Rick. 1996. *The Hundred Yard Lie: The Corruption of College Football and What We Can Do to Stop It.* Urbana: University of Illinois Press.

Thibault, Lucie, Trevor Slack, and Bob Hinings. 1991. "Professionalism, Structures, and Systems: The Impact of Professional Staff on Voluntary Sport Organizations." *International Review for the Sociology of Sport* 26 (2): 83–97. http://dx.doi.org/10.1177/101269029102600202.

Thompson, Shona M. 1999. *Mother's Taxi: Sport and Women's Labor.* Albany: State University of New York Press.

Thorne, Barrie. 1993. *Gender Play: Girls and Boys in School.* New Brunswick, NJ: Rutgers University Press.

Toma, J. Douglas. 2003. *Football U.: Spectator Sports at the American University.* Ann Arbor: University of Michigan Press.

Trotter, Kate. 2001. "13 and Too Busy for Sports: City Study." *Tri-City News* (BC), 23 October.

Trussell, Dawn E. 2009. "Organized Youth Sport, Parenthood Ideologies and Gender Relations: Parents' and Children's Experiences and the Construction of 'Team Family.'" Ph.D. diss., University of Waterloo, Ontario.

Walker, Tom. 2009. "The Role of the 'Builder' in Community Sport in Canada." MA thesis, Simon Fraser University.

Ward, Steven. 1996. "Filling the World with Self-Esteem: A Social History of Truth-Making." *Canadian Journal of Sociology* 21 (1): 1–23. http://dx.doi.org/10.2307/3341430.

Weiss, Melford S. 2000. "Culture, Context and Content Analysis: An Exploration of Elite Women Gymnasts in the High School World." In *Games, Sports and Cultures,* ed. Noel Dyck, 183–98. Oxford: Berg.

Wolfe, Alan. 1991. "Change from the Bottom Up." In *America at Century's End,* ed. Alan Wolfe, 1–13. Berkeley: University of California Press.

Woodhead, Martin. 1990. "Psychology and the Cultural Construction of Children's Needs." In *Constructing and Reconstructing Childhood: Contemporary Issues in the Social Study of Childhood,* ed. Allison James and Alan Prout, 60–77. London: Falmer Press.

Wulff, Helena. 1988. *Twenty Girls: Growing Up, Ethnicity and Excitement in a South London Microculture.* Stockholm: Department of Social Anthropology, University of Stockholm.

INDEX